LENIN FOR TODAY

John Molyneux

About the author

John Molyneux is a socialist writer and activist, formerly a lecturer a Portsmouth University and now living in Dublin. His publications include *Marxism and the Party* (1978), *What is the Real Marxist Tradition?* (1985), *Rembrandt and Revolution* (2001), *Anarchism: A Marxist Criticism* (2011) and *The Point is to Change It: An Introduction to Marxist Philosophy* (2012). He is a member of the Socialist Workers Party in Ireland and editor of the *Irish Marxist Review*.

Acknowledgements

The fundamental intellectual debt that requires acknowledgement is to Tony Cliff, author of *State Capitalism in Russia* and *Lenin: a Political Biography*, and founder of the International Socialist Tendency. Duncan Hallas and Chris Harman were also major influences.

I would like to thank Sally Campbell, Lina Nicolli, Martin Empson, Sameh Naguib and Huw Williams for reading the manuscript and for their many helpful comments, though naturally all responsibility for any errors of fact or judgement remain mine. I also thank Peter Robinson, Carol Williams, Ben Windsor and the Bookmarks team for their work in bringing the book to publication.

Lenin for Today

John Molyneux

Bookmarks Publications

Lenin for Today by John Molyneux

Published 2017
© Bookmarks Publications
c/o 1 Bloomsbury Street, London WC1B 3QE
Designed and typeset by Peter Robinson
Cover design by Ben Windsor
Printed by Melita Press

ISBN 978-1-910885-61-1 (pbk)
978-1-910885-62-8 (Kindle)
978-1-910885-63-5 (ePub)
978-1-910885-64-2 (PDF)

Contents

Preface

WALKING with my partner through the streets of Athens in the summer of 2016 we saw a large piece of graffiti which read, "Fuck May '68, Fight Now!" Now May '68 meant a lot to me. My visit to Paris at the time of the student revolt and the workers' general strike confirmed my decision to become a revolutionary socialist and Marxist and led directly to my joining the International Socialists a month or so later. Nevertheless, the spirit of the graffiti appealed to me and I hope that some of that spirit informs this book.

There is a vast literature on Lenin. Some of it, rather a lot, is in my view rubbish. Much of it is very useful. And there are, again in my view, two great books about him. These are Georg Lukács's *Lenin: a Study on the Unity of his Thought*, written in 1924 shortly after Lenin's death, and Tony Cliff's four-volume political biography written in the 1970s. The Lukács is a superb condensation of Lenin's theoretical "system" demonstrating with great élan, as its title suggests, the dialectical unity of his thought, while justifying his claim that Lenin is "the only theoretician equal to Marx yet produced by the struggle for the liberation of the proletariat". The Cliff study is a detailed examination of the entirety of Lenin's political life (Cliff has minimal interest in the personal). It is less well written, much less artistically composed than the Lukács but more thorough and much closer to Lenin as a practicing revolutionary and leader of a revolutionary party, doubtless because that is what Cliff was when he wrote it.

So why add to this body of work? I am not going to outdo Lukács in his command of the dialectic or his theoretical brilliance, nor will I match Cliff's scope, detail and intense understanding of the historical context and Lenin's response to it. In truth I am also not going to match the likes of Lars Lih in his formidable scholarship. Nor am I proposing any radically new "interpretation" of Lenin. Broadly, with differences here and there, I accept the interpretation made by Lukács in 1924 (as opposed to his 1967 Postscript), by Trotsky in his historical defence of Leninism against Stalinism, by Cliff in the studies mentioned above, and by Paul Le Blanc in his *Lenin and the Revolutionary Party*.

I reject, root and branch, the interpretation developed during the Cold War by establishment academics which became what Lars Lih calls "the textbook interpretation". I also reject the Stalinist hagiographical version of Lenin as an omniscient and infallible born leader—this will be less apparent here because this version has very much faded from the scene. (The interested reader will find plenty of corrections to it in the Cliff study). I welcome Lars Lih's meticulous dismantling of "the textbook" view in *Lenin Rediscovered*. However, I think he underestimates the way in which Lenin's position on the party developed and changed through experience and in response to changing circumstances and I disagree strongly with Lih's tendency to play down the difference between Lenin and Kautsky, between Bolshevism and German Social Democracy.[1]

Rather, what this book tries to offer is an argument: a sustained case for the relevance of Lenin's main political principles for the world today. I should explain what I do and do not mean by this. Lukács, in his 1967 Postscript to his *Lenin*, refers to "the twenties as a past period...which is now entirely closed",[2] meaning forget all that stuff about proletarian revolution and smashing the state, what remains relevant about Lenin is that he represents "a new human type" and "a new form of exemplary attitude to reality".[3] Similarly, Slavoj Žižek writes of making a "Leninist gesture today".[4] This is not my intention. I am well aware and much in awe of Lenin's unique personal characteristics, but I am arguing for something much more mundane and also more important: namely, that the core of his politics, the central ideas articulated in his main works and in his political practice as a Bolshevik and in the Communist International—commitment to working class revolution, total opposition to imperialism, the need to destroy the capitalist state, the necessity of a revolutionary party and the need to fight all forms of oppression—remain central to socialist practice today. This is why the book begins with an argument about the present state of the world—why we need a revolution and why that revolution will be a workers' revolution—rather than with Lenin in 1893 or in 1917 for that matter.

Of course this is an argument that runs "against the stream"—not just the mainstream of bourgeois politics, the capitalist media and the academic consensus, but also against the predominant "stream" on the left. The current "zeitgeist" on the left is many different versions of left reformism ranging from Syriza in 2015, which generated immense enthusiasm on the European left, to Podemos, the Corbyn phenomenon and Sanders's "political revolution" which, of course, was only ever a metaphorical revolution. These various movements are all very positive developments and deserving of support against the right but whether or not they can win—that is, not just win an election but also significantly transform society—is a different matter. If they can and do, then the case made here will clearly prove mistaken and irrelevant. But, unfortunately, I believe this is extremely unlikely for reasons spelt out in detail in this book and that therefore it is necessary, while working with and supporting these progressive movements, to prepare on a different, more revolutionary basis.

Again it is necessary to stress, and I shall return to this point later, this does not mean any attempt to mechanically copy Lenin or reproduce the specific organisational form of the Bolshevik Party. Times have changed and circumstances are different and mechanical repetition, which anyway would be quite contrary to the spirit of Lenin, would produce only parody—what Tony Cliff used to call "toy bolshevism". Moreover, to be a Marxist and a revolutionary today involves addressing a multitude of issues that arose after Lenin's death and about which he said little or nothing. I discuss this in the final chapter. But, in my view, this does not change the fact that there were a number of absolutely crucial questions about which Lenin was right a hundred years ago and remains right today, in the sense that Marx was right about the accumulation of capital in 1867 and Darwin was right about evolution in 1859 and they remain right today.

Finally, on a personal note, I first encountered Lenin back in the heady days of 1968 and then, in more depth, while working on my first book *Marxism and the Party* in the early seventies. At that time my view of Lenin was particularly shaped by the influence of Tony Cliff, who edited *Marxism and the Party*, and the wave of great industrial struggles in Britain in those years. In many ways, my attitude to Lenin has remained essentially unchanged since then, but it is also the case that the last seven years working politically in Ireland have shifted and I hope deepened my understanding of him. They certainly affected the form and content of this book.

For this reason (and for others) I dedicate it to Mary Smith and all my comrades in Ireland. I should also thank Sameh Naguib, the Egyptian revolutionary, who persuaded me to write it—needless to say he bears no responsibility for its content.

Introduction: We need a revolution

THE present state of the world is morally indefensible. It is morally indefensible that 358 billionaires own as much wealth as the bottom 50 percent of the world's population; that the world spends US$1,766 billion a year on arms when more than a billion people live on less than a dollar a day; that there is terrible poverty and inequality even within the handful of richest countries in the world such as the United States, Britain and Ireland. It is indefensible that refugees fleeing from inhuman conditions, especially wars, largely created by the Western powers, are treated as scroungers and a threat by those same Western powers. It is morally indefensible that in the USA, 150 years after the abolition of slavery and 50 years after the death of Malcolm X, black people are regularly and systematically murdered by cops with more or less complete impunity. Such a list of the morally indefensible characteristics of the world we live in could be continued indefinitely.

Unfortunately, there is nothing new about this. The world order has been morally indefensible ever since the material prerequisites for a much better society were developed about 150 years ago. The slaughter of 30,000 Communards on the streets of Paris in 1871 was indefensible. The "late Victorian holocausts" in which tens of millions starved to death in India, China and elsewhere were indefensible.[5] The First World War was indefensible and so on, again indefinitely.

But what distinguishes the present situation is not just its moral iniquity, but that the world order is becoming increasingly unstable and unsustainable. The instability consists of a) increasing inequality, b) the increasing likelihood of economic crisis and c) increasing geo-political rivalry leading to war. The unsustainability consists of all these things together plus climate change as the key component of a wider environmental crisis.

That global and national economic inequality is increasing, and has been increasing for several decades, is clear and widely perceived by ordinary people. It has been empirically proved beyond all reasonable doubt by Thomas Piketty in his famous study *Capital in the 21st Century* and by many other scholars. Particularly striking is the growing gap between the super-rich, the 1 percent, and the rest of us. We also know from the careful work done by Richard Wilkinson and Kate Pickett in *The Spirit Level* that inequality is seriously bad for society as a whole—that it increases ill health, violence, crime, drug addiction and many other social evils. Moreover this rising inequality is a major driver of protest and revolt. Danny Dorling observes:

> In the UK members of the general public are surer that the gap between rich and poor is unwarranted than ever before recorded, and they are becoming more sure of this with every year that passes. In 2010, 75 percent of the people who responded to the annual British Attitudes Survey said that the income gap was too large. By 2012 this figure had risen to 82 percent.
>
> Around the world, a majority of the global protests that have occurred since 2006 have centred on issues of economic justice. In 2006 there were just 59 large protests recorded worldwide. In just the first half of 2013 there were 112 protests of similar size.[6]

The growth of inequality has been exacerbated by the Great Recession of 2008-2009 as governments and ruling classes have sought to make ordinary people pay for the crisis. Capitalism has always alternated between booms and slumps but the recession of 2008 was the most serious since the depression of the 1930s and the recovery from it was both very slow and very weak. In Europe as a whole, there has been virtually no recovery at all. Moreover there is a serious possibility of another economic collapse in the next year or so and economic growth in China—the most successful large economy of recent times—is slowing, with the distinct possibility looming that it too may crash.

Major recessions have major social and political consequences. For a start they massively increase unemployment, with all the direct misery that entails[7] and this in turn feeds into a multitude of other ills, such as child poverty and homelessness. Recessions and economic crises do not, by themselves, usually generate immediate revolt. For example neither in the United States nor in Britain was the Wall Street Crash of 1929 and the subsequent depression met with large-scale resistance or rebellion and the same was true internationally in 2008-2009. But as they grind on, extended recessions do create mass bitterness and resentment which result in the radicalisation of people over a period of time, provided political forces exist to articulate and express this bitterness. They also create the possibility that the bitterness will be harnessed by the far right by turning it against scapegoats (Jews, immigrants and Muslims for example).

The Great Depression of the 1930s saw both these things happen and, despite titanic struggles such as the great strike wave and unionisation drive in the United States in 1934-1935 and the French general strike and the Spanish Revolution of 1936, it was predominantly the far right that proved victorious. The period since 2008-2009 has also seen and continues to see both processes at work with, basically, radicalisation taking place in Greece, Spain, Portugal, Ireland and Scotland and movements of the far right and fascism also growing in places: the Front National in France, Jobbik in Hungary, Golden Dawn in Greece, Ukip in Britain and so on. In the United States we have seen both the Sanders phenomenon and the victory of Trump, which in turn has been greeted by mass protest and resistance. In short, serious recessions lead to political polarisation.

If the world economy experiences another large-scale recession in the next couple of years before there has been any substantial recovery, both the economic and the political effects will be enormous. In particular, it will be a spectacular demonstration of the failure and bankruptcy of neoliberal capitalism and will have huge ideological repercussions. One of the main political features of the last 30 years, and especially the last eight years, has been the steady erosion of support for the so-called "mainstream" parties of the centre in much of Europe. Another recession will accelerate this process and generate all sorts of political turmoil and crises including the intensification of various forms of nationalism and separatism.[8]

Recession will also intensify what is already a well established trend in the late 20th and early 21st centuries: the proliferation of international tensions and rivalries leading to wars and the possibility of wars. When "communism" collapsed in 1989-1991, George Bush Snr announced the arrival of a "New World Order"—an era of peace and stability presided over by a hegemonic United States—and Francis Fukuyama famously proclaimed "the end of history", by which he meant the end of any serious challenge to western "liberal" capitalist democracy. Nothing of the kind happened, of course. Instead the last quarter of a century has seen a rapid succession of conflicts and wars, concentrated particularly in the Middle East, but by no means confined to it (the Balkans War of the 1990s, the Afghan War from 2001 to the present, the war in the Ukraine, various wars in Africa, etc).

Underlying this development has been the opposite of the uncontested US power that American strategists dreamed of, namely the continued relative decline in the economic and military dominance of the world's number one superpower. This statement should not be misunderstood; the emphasis is on the word relative: the United States remains the world's most powerful economy and, overwhelmingly, its leading military force.[9] But its ability to impose its will on the rest of the world is considerably less than it was. At root this comes down to the fact that US share of world GDP stood at 19.31 percent in 2013[10] as compared to 27.3 percent in 1950 and 22.1 percent in 1973.[11] Its most striking military expression has been the abject failure of the United States to achieve its aims in Afghanistan and Iraq and its more or less forced troop withdrawals from these theatres of war. This does not all lead to a less dangerous or more peaceful world. On the contrary it leads to a situation where the United States, reluctant to "put boots on the ground", seeks to maintain its hegemony via relations with various regional powers (such as Saudi Arabia, Turkey, Iran and Israel) and these regional powers bid for favoured status while simultaneously falling out with each other. Horrors like the war in Syria, the rise of Isis, the disaster in Libya and the Saudi bombing of Yemen are the result.

At the same time, we see the return, especially over the Ukraine, of the spectre of the Cold War, supposedly long laid to rest. Even more importantly in the long run, we see the growth of tension between the United States and China in the South China Sea, which is symptomatic of emerging rivalry between the world's two largest economies. In terms of real policy rather than media rhetoric (overwhelmingly focused on the threat of Muslim "extremists"), the United States under Obama has already undertaken its "Asian pivot", making China the real object of its long-term strategic concerns.[12] While the US share of world GDP has been declining, that of China has been rising (from 4.5 percent in 1950 to 15.4 percent in 2014).[13] China displaced first Germany and then Japan in the pecking order of the world economy to come within striking distance of the United States. What this could mean in military terms is shown by a 2014 report from the UK Ministry of Defence which outlines projected defence expenditure of major powers for the year 2045 as follows:[14]

Rank	Country	Spending in PPP (US$ bn)
1	United States	1,335
2	China	1,270
3	India	654

Obviously such a projection for 30 years ahead is guesswork, but it is a guess that will haunt the minds of the strategists in the Pentagon. And one thing we can be fairly sure of is that fear of such parity will drive the policies of the American ruling class for decades to come. An era of peace and stability is not on the agenda.

Framing and overarching everything else is the environmental crisis. This is both already happening and looming in the sense that it is certain to get worse. It is both multifaceted—ranging from the mass extinction of species (on a scale not seen since the Cretaceous-Paleogene extinction event which disposed of the dinosaurs along with three quarters of the plant and animal species on earth 66 million years ago)[15] to the pollution of rivers and cities (witness China and innumerable local communities from Alexandria to Ballyfermot and Ballyogan),[16] to fracking—and dominated by one cataclysmic issue: climate change. Climate change dominates for the simple reason that it threatens the whole future of humanity.

This last point needs clarification. The problem is not that at some unspecifiable time in the future all seven billion humans will suddenly be wiped out; it is that from where we are now, year in and year out, decade after decade, global warming and the extreme weather that comes with it (heat waves, droughts, fires, storms, floods, etc) will make life more and more difficult and, in parts of the world, impossible for millions upon millions of people. And let us be clear, some of this is going to happen whatever is done because of the warming that has already been built into the system. Even if fossil fuels were abandoned forthwith and carbon emissions were thrown dramatically into reverse, there would be immense problems to be dealt with and there is not the slightest sign of this happening.

In short, this is a society—a global society—headed for catastrophe. It is a world in which productive power and the wealth actually produced far exceeds anything that has ever existed in human history. Angus Maddison, the foremost expert on this question, uses a measure, international Geary-Kharmis dollars, to compare World GDP over the centuries. On this basis he estimates that world GDP in 1000 AD stood at approximately GK\$117 billion, by 1500 it was GK\$248 billion, by 1870 it was GK\$1.1 trillion and by 2001 it had reached GK\$37 trillion.[17] Yet we are manifestly headed, on a number of fronts, for disaster on an immense scale.

As I write these words I am aware that I run the risk of sounding like the man with the billboard saying "The End of the World is nigh!" I write them because I think the evidence, only a tiny fraction of which I have referred to here, is both compelling and indeed widely known. So I will say only that prophets of doom are not always wrong. In the years running up to 1914, the international socialist movement, which at that time had the allegiance of millions of workers across Europe, warned repeatedly of the impending catastrophe of imperialist world war; and they were right. When Trotsky, in exile on the Princes Islands in Turkey, tried to warn the German left of the terrible danger posed by Hitler and wrote in December 1931, 'should fascism come to power, it will ride over your skulls and spines like a terrific tank"[18] and called urgently for a united front against the Nazis, he was right. The real problem is what conclusion we should draw, what should we try to do about it.

Each of the "issues" I have outlined has a small army of concerned citizens trying to do something about it. There are those who say, with good cause, that inequality is the central issue and they produce endless data and reports designed to highlight the question in its many facets (child poverty, food poverty, fuel poverty, poverty in the global south and so on). They seek to alert the public to this iniquity and to persuade the powerful to do something about it. The "public" is powerless to do anything except give to charity and the powerful take no notice. The recession produces legions of "economists" and "pundits" who say solving the economic crisis and restoring growth is the central question. Some of them argue that the way to do that is to reduce inequality and put more money in the pockets of working people while increasing government spending, so as to kick start the economy. These people are generally ignored.

Others say that the solution is that "we" should all learn to live within our means and accept cutbacks and austerity in order to get the economy going again. They are generally listened to, but this makes inequality worse and doesn't solve the problem. At the same time more economic growth, should it be achieved, simply accelerates the process of climate change. The prevalence of war produces both perennial peace campaigners and mass anti-war movements. They are generally ignored; Tony Blair ignored the biggest demonstration in British history in 2003 to go to war in Iraq. Around the world people, both serious scientists and ordinary people in their millions, are rightly raising the alarm about the environment and climate change. In theory, or rather in words, they are being listened to, but in practice they are being ignored.

Of course from the point of view of the individual and their limited energies, focusing on one issue can seem to make sense, especially when the big picture simply seems too big to tackle. Unfortunately, it is clear that all of these issues intersect and interact and none of them can be tackled or solved separately. For example, the problem of inequality is not just a matter of those who suffer from it but also of those who benefit from it—and they are precisely the people who dominate the political system, run the state, control the media and own and manage ExxonMobil and BP. They are also those who make the decisions about war and peace. *If* we didn't live in such an unequal world *and* there was no economic crisis demanding the restoration of growth *and* there was no great power rivalry, it *might* be possible to persuade the US, Chinese, Indian, Russian and EU governments to wage serious war on climate change and thus stop it or slow it down in time. But that is not the world we live in.

It is also clear that the problems have a common source and it can be summed up in one word—profit. It is production for profit that enables a tiny number of people to become billionaires while requiring that the incomes of the majority are held down, thus generating extreme inequality. It is production for profit that produces recessions when capitalists find they can't make enough profits and lay off workers. It is the competitive struggle for profit that lies behind wars to control oil supplies in the Middle East and the growing rivalry in the South China Sea. And it is profit—in the form of the immense amounts of capital invested in and derived from fossil fuels—that drives the carbon emissions that are changing the climate.

But is a society not based on production for profit—that is, a non-capitalist society—possible and how could it be brought about? Daunted by these questions, and they can seem very daunting ("It is easier to imagine the end of the world, than to imagine the end of capitalism")[19], many people who understand that there is a general, global problem say that the problem is neoliberalism or neoliberal capitalism. Now, of course, there is a lot of truth in this in that there is no doubt that the doctrine of neoliberalism (the supremacy of the free market) is the hegemonic ideology of our time and that some form or other of neoliberal capitalism is the predominant form of capitalism today and has been since at least the 1980s and the days of Thatcher and Reagan. But one of the implications of focusing attacks on neoliberalism, and one of the reasons why many on the left do this, is that it leaves open the possibility that if we could just displace this ideology or get rid of this form of capitalism (and get back to the decent, regulated capitalism of, say, the 1950s and 1960s) things would be alright or at least a lot better. Sadly, this is wishful thinking.

First, though it is true that inequality in the 1950s and 1960s in Europe and North America was not as extreme as it is now, it was still very great indeed and international inequality, with mass malnutrition in South Asia and much of Africa, was utterly monstrous. Second, regulated (or Keynesian) capitalism in no way overcomes or prevents the international economic competition and rivalry that leads to wars, as a glance at the history of the 20th century demonstrates. Third, and for the same reason, it would not weaken the compulsion to grow that wreaks such environmental havoc. A Keynesian capitalism would not address the environmental crisis any more than the state capitalisms of Russia and China have done. Fourth, it needs to be understood that the dominance of neoliberalism was established precisely because of the international crisis of Keynesian regulated capitalism in 1973-1974. This crisis was rooted in the declining rate of return on investment that had been slowly developing during the long post-war boom. Ruling classes internationally turned to neoliberalism as a means of restoring the rate of profit because, to repeat, it is profit that drives production under capitalism. In other words, daunting or not, it is capitalism not just neoliberalism that has to be dealt with.

And the obvious way to deal with capitalism is to elect an anti-capitalist government or series of governments in a succession of countries.

Or so it might seem. The main reason this seems obvious is that we are all told, practically from birth and on an almost daily basis, that governments run countries and that if you don't like the way things are you should change the government. This message is not only taught in school, it is reinforced continually by media coverage of the statements and doings of presidents, prime ministers and other leading politicians, by reporting of parliamentary proceedings and by the whole paraphernalia and fanfare surrounding elections.

Unfortunately, it doesn't work. It doesn't work because the premise on which this method of change is based is false. Governments do not run "countries", in particular they do not run economies. Rather economies run governments. This is an oversimplification of course— governments do make a certain amount of difference—but *fundamentally* it is true. And if we are talking about getting rid of capitalism, we are talking about fundamentals. Elected governments do not own or control the vast bulk of wealth or productive power in society. That remains in the hands of corporations and private companies whose CEOs and senior managers are not elected but appointed. These people use this immense economic power to persuade, pressure and bully governments into doing what they want; to set the parameters within which governments operate (parameters which definitely do not include anti-capitalism or anything remotely resembling it); and to sabotage and wreck the national economy if the "anti-capitalist" government shows any signs of stubbornness.

But couldn't the government use its power to pass laws stopping the corporations and private capitalists engaging in this sabotage or even better take the capitalists' economic power away from them by nationalising the banks and main industries? Well it could, but how would it enforce these laws? This is a key question because there is no chance that the rich, the owners and shareholders and senior managers of corporate capital, would simply acquiesce to having their wealth taken off them. On the contrary, they would fight back with all the resources at their disposal and they would be a lot of resources—both national and international.

The main means governments have for enforcing their decisions and laws are the apparatuses of the state: the civil service, the police, the courts, the secret services and, ultimately, the armed forces. These are the institutions on which the government relies when it faces defiance from some section of the population—strikers who defy industrial rela-tions legislation, squatters who illegally occupy empty buildings, demonstrators who hold illegal marches or get out of hand, rioters who set fire to things and terrorists who plant bombs. But in a confrontation of the kind we are talking about—between the elected government and the economically dominant class—whose side would these state institu-tions be on?

Both reason and experience demonstrate clearly that they would side with the rich. These are hierarchical institutions built on the prin-ciple of obedience to superiors. These superiors—police chiefs, the judges, the generals and so on—are overwhelmingly drawn from the same class background as the financiers, bankers and industrialists. They have family ties, went to the same private schools and elite univer-sities and belong to the same clubs and social circles. They share, by and large, the same political ideology, at least in so far as it would include hostility to radical or anti-capitalist change. Even when a small minor-ity, by way of exception, come from a different (lower) class background it will have been an absolute condition of their promotion to senior posts that they prove their willingness to play by the established rules of the game.[20]

Moreover, many even in the lower ranks in these institutions, most obviously the police but it applies to the others as well, will have been accustomed in their daily work to dealing in an authoritarian fashion with ordinary people while deferring to the rich and powerful. This practice cannot fail to colour their attitudes and political ideology—witness what is often described as the "canteen culture" in the police[21] or observe the US police in action on YouTube.

What is important to remember here is that an alternative state apparatus will not come into being simultaneously with the election of a radical government. The state apparatus of capitalist society has been fashioned over many decades and, in the main countries, over centuries as an instrument of rule by the very people it would be required to keep in line. This is not going to happen. On the contrary it will work with the rich to undermine and disrupt any temporary "upstart" radical government hell bent on destroying society as we know it.

The historical record on this also leaves no room for doubt. From the Peterloo Massacre in 1819, to the July insurrection in Paris in 1848, to the Paris Commune in 1871, to Bloody Sunday in St Petersburg in

1905, to the murder of Rosa Luxemburg and Karl Liebknecht and the suppression of the Spartacist Revolt in 1919, all the way through to the Pinochet coup against Allende in 1973, the crushing of Solidarność by the Polish military in 1980, the police war on the Great Miners Strike in 1984-1985 and the military coup to defeat the Egyptian Revolution in 2013, history is littered with examples of the forces of the state being used to suppress the people and any sort of revolt from below. There is not a single instance of them assisting in the process of transforming society in an anti-capitalist direction.

In the first six months of 2015 we saw with the victory of Syriza in Greece, the most serious attempt in many decades in Europe to use parliamentary elections to install a government of the radical left pledged to at least begin the process of anti-capitalist transformation. Within six months, the Syriza project had foundered on the rocks and was in the process of disintegrating. The rocks on which it foundered were "the institutions" of the Troika (the Commission of the European Union [EU], the European Central Bank and the International Monetary Fund [IMF]).

For six months Alexis Tsipras and the Syriza leadership declared that they regarded these institutions as their "partners" and committed themselves to reaching a "fair" deal with them in order to secure a bail out for the Greek banks. The Troika responded with total intransigence and extreme economic blackmail, including securing the closure of the Greek banks. The working people of Greece responded with a resounding *"Oxi"* (No!) when asked in a referendum whether they wanted to accept the Troika's terms. But within days the Syriza government capitulated and abandoned not only all its anti-capitalist aspirations and its own election programme, but even its most basic commitment to end austerity.

This capitulation has been attributed, by a number of leading Greek left wingers, to the Syriza leadership's Left Europeanism—its mistaken belief that the EU is in some way a progressive project, a "family" of European peoples, rather than a project of European capital, of the bankers and big business designed to enforce their interests against the interests of the mass of people in Greece *and* the rest of Europe. This undoubtedly is a mistaken belief and it clearly played an important role in the capitulation, but it was not the root of the problem. Left Europeanism is a transfer to the level of the EU institutions of a deeper illusion; the illusion that it is possible to move in an anti-capitalist direction in partnership with the institutions of the national capitalist state.

This is not going to happen. To move in an anti-capitalist direction, to even make a serious beginning in this direction—and that is what the whole condition of the world is demanding we do—requires a *revolution*. This means not a military campaign by a small armed minority (á la Che Guevara in the mountains or the IRA in Northern Ireland), but a mass uprising by the working class and its allies which takes control of society, both its politics *and* its economy.

This is not at all the end of this argument, just its starting point. It raises a multitude of other political and strategic questions—is such a revolution possible? Who would make it and how?—many of which will be pursued in this book. In particular, it is necessary to understand that the large mass of working class people, without whom this revolution is impossible, will not be converted to the need for revolution by this or any other book. They will have to come to it through their own experiences and their own struggles and that probably includes going through the experience in practice of a left government. As we shall see later, Lenin has much to say on this question. But an understanding that we need a revolution is a precondition of taking the Russian Revolution and Lenin seriously for the 21st century.

Of course the Russian Revolution is a major historical event and Lenin a major historical figure. However, my concern in this work is not to investigate them for their own sake, but to make an argument about their relevance for us today.

In saying this, one further point needs to be emphasised. Everything I have written about the crisis facing humanity indicates that this is a global crisis requiring a global solution—an international revolution. Unfortunately, the different conditions applying in different parts of the world make it unlikely that there will be a simultaneous revolution across many countries. But to survive in today's globalised world, any revolution beginning in one country will need to spread to others and will need to have an international perspective. This again directs our attention to the relevance of 1917 and Lenin.

1

The relevance of Lenin

LENIN is relevant in the 21st century because the Russian Revolution is relevant. The Russian Revolution is relevant because the revolution of the 21st century will be a workers' revolution and the Russian Revolution was a workers' revolution. These are big claims that require justification.

Workers' revolution today

When I say that the revolution of the 21st century will be a workers' revolution this is not rhetoric. It has a very precise meaning. It means that the revolution that is necessary for human kind to have a future that is other than utterly disastrous will be made by the working class, the working class internationally, and will bring the working class to power internationally.

The working class here signifies that class of people who live exclusively or almost exclusively by the sale of their labour power. It includes, therefore, both blue collar and white collar workers, teachers and nurses as well as factory workers and firefighters, administrative staff along with office cleaners, shop workers and bus drivers. It does not include salaried employees whose job is exclusively or mainly to manage the work of others, such as head teachers or shop managers, or whose job makes them employers of workers, for example a solicitor. Defined in this way, the working class constitutes 70 percent or more of the population in advanced capitalist countries such as the United States, Germany or Ireland.

The last 60 years, ever since the post-war boom set in, has seen the production at regular intervals of studies and theories announcing the incorporation, demise or disappearance of Marx's proletariat: that is, of a working class capable of overthrowing capitalism.

First came the embourgeoisement thesis that affluent workers were becoming middle class due to their acquisition of consumer goods and thus adopting "a middle class orientation".[22] This was empirically "refuted" by John Goldthorpe and David Lockwood in their study of affluent workers in Luton, but they nevertheless insisted that these workers were "privatised" and "atomised" and so not potentially a force for social change.[23] In fact all the very considerable body of "left" sociologists (sometimes referred to as "Marxists") in the 1960s (Bottomore, Dahrendorf, Rex, etc) were agreed in rejecting the revolutionary role of the working class. The same was true of most of the leading spokespersons internationally of what was thought of as the New Left—the likes of Herbert Marcuse, Paul Baran and Paul Sweezy, Frantz Fanon, Regis Debray and Rudi Dutschke. The two leading political influences on the activist movements of the 1960s—Maoism and Guevarism—were founded on the explicit decision to opt for the peasantry as opposed to the proletariat as the agent of revolution.[24]

In 1978 the leading Marxist historian, Eric Hobsbawm, delivered a lecture, "The Forward March of Labour Halted?", in which he maintained that the working class had lost its central role in society and that left parties should no longer relate only to this class but aim to appeal also to the middle class. In 1980 the French theorist, André Gorz published his *Adieu le Proletariat*. More recently Michael Hardt and Antonio Negri proposed "the multitude", rather than the working class, as the agent of social change.[25] And Guy Standing opted for "the precariat" as "the new dangerous class.[26]

Some of these theories were based on an identification of the working class with one of its historical manifestations—the industrial proletariat of the so-called "Fordist" era of capitalism; they viewed the working class as consisting of factory workers, dockers, miners, steel workers and so on. When these industries declined, as they did in Europe, this was seen as tantamount to the disappearance of the class. Others contrasted the actual working class they saw before them in 1964, 1984, 2004 or whenever, with an idealised view of the working class in the past which was imagined to be permeated with socialist or even revolutionary consciousness as if the Petrograd working class in October 1917 or the Turin working class in 1919 were somehow the norm in "the good old days". But what all of them missed was the extraordinary international spread and growth of the working class that was taking place during this period as a result of the growth of capitalism in large parts of what was known as the Third World.

When Marx wrote in the *Communist Manifesto* that "the proletarian movement is the self-conscious, independent movement of the immense majority, in the interest of the immense majority", this was empirically true of only a small part of northwestern Europe—Britain and maybe the Netherlands and Belgium—and even then at a stretch. Urbanisation is not equivalent to proletarianisation because many who live in cities are not workers and some workers do not live in cities but nevertheless figures for urbanisation give us something to go on. Urban studies analysts Paul Bairoch and Gary Goertz have calculated that in 1850 the proportion of the population living in cities of 5,000 or more was as follows: United Kingdom 39.6 percent, Netherlands 35.6 percent and Belgium 33.5 percent. For France the figure was 19.5 percent and Germany approximately 15 percent. For Russia it stood at 7.2 percent and the United States only 5.3 percent.[27]

At that time the small peasantry constituted by far the most numerous social class in France, Germany, Spain and Italy and even more so the whole of eastern Europe. And when Marx issued the fundamental slogan of the international socialist and communist movement, "Workers of the world, unite!", it was a proclamation that was empirically speaking meaningless in most of the globe. In 1848 there was virtually nothing approximating to a modern working class in Asia and Africa, where 75 percent of the world population then lived.[28]

By 1917 and the Russian Revolution, the proletariat had grown massively in Europe, especially Britain, France, Germany and Italy and also in the United States, but in Eastern Europe and Russia itself it remained a small minority and in global terms still a really tiny minority. In the course of the last century, and especially the last 25 years, this has changed fundamentally. The agencies who gather global statistics do not operate with Marxist or socialist categories so it is not possible to give exact figures for the size of the world proletariat or working class; instead we have to make do with approximations such as figures for waged employees and urbanisation. But this lack of precision does not matter because it is the broad picture that counts and the broad picture is both dramatic and compelling.

In 1993 the figure for waged or salaried employees was 985 million out of a world population of approximately 5.526 billion, or about

18 percent. By 2013 the number of waged/salaried employees had grown to 1.575 billion out of a total of 7.086 billion, or just over 22 percent. And significantly, this figure constituted just over 50 percent of the world's total labour force of about 3 billion. Of course, not all these waged employees were workers (a minority would be managers) but most of them were and this meant that, for the first time in history, Marx's proletariat really did constitute something like a majority of society globally.

Even more important than the absolute figures is the trend. In the 20 years from 1993 to 2013 the number of waged or salaried employees grew by 589,814,000 (a staggering 60 percent of the 1993 figure). An average of 29 million people joined the waged labour force each year. Moreover, the growth of waged labour was concentrated in the developing countries. In the developed countries, the salaried/waged employee figure rose slowly from 345 million (1993) to 410 million (2013). In developing countries the growth was explosive, rising from 640 million (1993) to 1,165 million (2013). The waged labour force in the developing world is bigger than the global waged labour force 20 years ago. There were an estimated 445 million waged or salaried employees in East Asia in 2013, more than in all the developed countries combined!

When it comes to assessing the growth of the international working class the most important individual country is obviously China. This presents us with a problem in that Chinese statistics are notoriously unreliable. Nevertheless the figures from the Chinese National Bureau of Statistics present a remarkable picture. They state that in China in 2013 there were about 769 million people in employment of whom 382.4 million were in urban employment, with about 61.4 million self-employed. Rural employment accounted for 387.3 million, with about 32 million self-employed. In 2011 in China 225.4 million people worked in industry, 273 million in services and 266 million in agriculture. The Chinese Marxist economist Minqi Li[29] has written:

> Nonagricultural employment, as a share of China's total employment, increased from 31 percent in 1980 to 50 percent in 2000, and increased further to 60 percent in 2008. According to a report prepared by the Chinese Academy of Social Sciences in 2002, about 80 percent of the nonagricultural labor force consisted of proletarianized wage workers,

such as industrial workers, service workers, clerical workers, and the unemployed. Since the overwhelming majority of nonagricultural workers are wage workers who have to sell their labor power to make a living, the rapid growth of nonagricultural employment suggests massive formations of the proletarianised working class in China.[30]

Regardless of the exact accuracy of these figures and estimates, what is undeniable is that the Chinese working class is now by far the largest national proletariat that has ever existed and is 50 to a 100 times larger than the entire international proletariat in Marx's day.

In addition to the size of the global proletariat, another important factor, because it is indicative of its immense potential social and political power, is its increasing concentration in great cities. The World Bank's list of countries by degree of urbanisation shows over 30 countries that are more than 80 percent urban including Argentina (92 percent), Australia (89 percent), Belgium (98 percent), Brazil (85 percent), Chile (89 percent), Netherlands (90 percent), Qatar (96 percent), Saudi Arabia (83 percent), UK (82 percent), US (81 percent) and Uruguay (95 percent).[31] As with the spread of wage labour, it is in the developing countries that the process of urbanisation is most rapid and many that were predominantly rural until very recently are now substantially urban, for example Algeria (70 percent), Bolivia (68 percent), Mongolia (71 percent), Peru (78 percent) and Turkey (73 percent).[32] The World Atlas lists 69 cities with a population over 5 million and 26 over 10 million.[33]

And again China, because of its huge population and massive economic growth, is the most important example. For centuries China has had by far the largest peasant population in the world and in the second half of the 20th century it was above all the size of the Chinese peasantry that prevented the proletariat being a global majority. The last 25 years have seen a vast and intense migration from the countryside to the towns, especially of young women.[34] In 2010 China became a predominantly urban society and it now has more than 60 cities of over a million including such giants as Shanghai with about 24 million and Beijing with over 21 million inhabitants. Perhaps the whole development is best expressed in the example of Guangdong (formerly Canton) which has become a vast urban sprawl and the most populous province in China with a population at the 2010 census of 104 million. It is estimated that Guangdong now contains 60,000 factories "which every day produce some $300 million worth of goods and account for about 30 percent of China's exports and one-third of the world's production of shoes, textiles and toys".[35]

If we take seriously the necessity for global revolution, and the crisis facing humanity compels us to take it seriously, then we have to talk about a social force that can defeat the immense economic and political power of global capital; that can take on and defeat the great corporations, the IMF, the World Bank, the US state and military, the EU and its economic and state forces, the immense Chinese state apparatus, the Russian state, the Saudi state and that's just listing a few of the major players. There is only one social force remotely capable of doing this: the 1.5 billion-strong international working class—in Marx's words "the independent movement of the immense majority, in the interest of the immense majority".

If the perspective is to change just one country or perhaps a number of countries, separately (perhaps one after another), then talk of the international working class is superfluous. If the perspective is to do this by winning elections, which are essentially national, and carrying through legislative reform in parliament, it may be possible to conjure up various kinds of social coalition that would yield electoral victory. But experience, both from the past century and a half and recent years shows that this is not possible.

Faced with *either* an elected left government *or* a revolutionary government in any one country, the ruling classes internationally will go into action to defend capitalism and crush the possibility of real change. This is how they responded to the Arab Spring and to Syriza in Greece. It is how they will always respond. Only a social force that exists internationally and a movement with an international perspective will be able to overcome this ruling class counteroffensive. This doesn't mean the utopian notion of a simultaneous global uprising. It means a revolution, beginning probably in one country but with the aim of spreading as a rolling movement to other countries within a space of months or years and thus building international momentum. To repeat, *only* the working class has the potential economic, social and political power in all the world's key centres to achieve this.

There are, of course, a number of well known objections to the proposition that the working class is or will become the agent of revolutionary change. They can be summarised as follows: a) the concept of "working class" is too restrictive or exclusive; b) those designated as working class, or many of them, are privileged in relation to the really oppressed and downtrodden; c) changes in capitalist production and the advent of neoliberalism has rendered the working class too weak to overthrow capitalism; and d) working class consciousness shows no signs of being anti-capitalist or revolutionary. I will respond briefly to these objections.

The objection that the term "working class" is exclusionary or divisive is one commonly put by newly radicalising or politically naïve people ("Why don't we all just get together?"), but it has also been put by Hardt and Negri who prefer the concept of "the multitude":

> The concept of the working class has come to be used as an exclusive concept...to refer only to industrial workers, separating them from workers in agriculture, services and other sectors...[or] to all waged workers, separating them from the poor, unpaid domestic labourers, and all others who do not receive a wage. The multitude, in contrast is an open inclusive concept.[36]

This is completely wrongheaded. First, the concept of the working class proposed here and by Marxists generally does not at all refer only to industrial workers, nor is this the common usage. Numerous surveys in Britain show that about 60 percent of people identify themselves as working class, which is far in excess of the number of industrial workers. Bus drivers, refuse collectors, office cleaners, hospital workers, supermarket cashiers are just a few examples of groups who are not "industrial" workers but are more or less universally regarded as workers. Trade unions in all countries organise white collar and service workers and these play a massive role in the trade union movement. Second, identifying the working class or proletariat as the key revolutionary force does not at all involve "excluding" other oppressed groups from the struggle or the revolution. On the contrary history shows that when the working class takes mass action and especially revolutionary action, this greatly facilitates the inclusion in the struggle of all sorts of oppressed groups and helps to win over middle class groups, like small shopkeepers, to the side of the working class.

It is, however, essential to make a *distinction* between the working class and small business people (petty bourgeois in Marxist terms) because while the latter can and should be won to the side of the working class, they cannot be the anchor or driving force of the struggle. The fact that they are in reality small exploiters means that if they lead or dominate the movement it will tend to move in a reactionary direction. It is also necessary to make a *strategic* distinction between different sections of the exploited and oppressed not on the basis of their degree of suffering but on the basis of their social weight: that is, their potential economic and political power. The unfortunate fact, but it is a fact, is that workers in employment and especially in certain key industries have more power than the unemployed because of their role in the economy and in making profits for the bosses and because their workplaces form them into collectives.

The idea that either the working class as a whole, or major sections of it, are not or are no longer potentially revolutionary because of their material privileges compared to more impoverished layers is a very old argument indeed. It has been put at various times in relation to the peasantry (by the Narodniks in Russia, Che Guevara, Frantz Fanon and others), in terms of the existence of a "labour aristocracy" (by Lenin), in relation to the unemployed (by Negri and Italian autonomists), in relation to the so-called "precariat",[37] and most recently in terms of white collar and public sector workers being a "salaried bourgeoisie" (by Slavoj Žižek).[38]

Of course it has always been the case that levels of pay and general living standards differed in different sections of the working class, with skilled workers generally paid more than the unskilled, white collar more than blue collar, those with full-time jobs more than those on part time, employed workers more than the unemployed, workers in the advanced countries much more than workers or peasants in the global south and so on. But suggesting that these obvious facts undermine the revolutionary potential of the working class makes two basic mistakes. It misses the fact that even (relatively) well paid workers remain exploited by capital in that surplus value is extracted from their labour and that therefore they stand in a permanently antagonistic relationship to capital.[39]

It also equates revolutionary potential with degree of impoverishment or suffering. This has been disproved by history both in that extremes of poverty, famine and oppression have existed throughout the history of class divided society and in that during revolutionary upheavals and mass struggles it is frequently the better paid workers who play a leading role, for example the skilled metal and engineering workers in the revolutionary wave that swept Europe at the end of the First World War. Moreover, counterposing sections such as precarious workers, the unemployed, black people (say in the United States), "youth", etc, to the working class as a whole as the "new" revolutionary subject is a disastrous strategy nationally and internationally. All of these sections constitute quite small minorities in their societies who are being set up against both the hugely powerful ruling class *and* the majority of "ordinary" people—a recipe for defeat.

The claim that developments in capitalism in its neoliberal or globalised phase have fundamentally weakened the working class and undermined its potential to overthrow capitalism have most resonance in Britain and other European countries where a high level of strikes and industrial militancy in the 1960s and 1970s gave way to a very low level of workplace-based struggle from the 1980s onwards. But regardless of the merits of this argument (which I do not accept) in relation to Britain,[40] it is plainly false when viewed on a world scale given the rise in numbers and urban concentration I have outlined above. Recent years have seen huge general strikes in countries such as Brazil and India as well as mass mobilizations and strikes in Greece, Spain, Portugal and Egypt and continual bubbling of strikes and protests in China. All that is needed here is a little imagination. Imagine a wave of factory occupations in Guangdong's 60,000 factories or a general strike by even a significant proportion of China's 3-400 million urban workers. This would constitute a mass movement with the power to defeat capitalism the like of which has never been seen in history.

This leaves the argument based on the existing political consciousness of the working class. "The working class shows no inclination to fulfil the revolutionary role assigned to it by Marx", as it can somewhat cynically be put. And if we are speaking about the current political attitudes of the mass of working class people this is clearly true. In so far as it is possible to assess this on an international scale, one would have to say that the prevailing consciousness is a combination of reformism and nationalism, with a significant surge of left reformism in certain places (Greece, Spain, Ireland, for example, and perhaps in Britain), and a mixture or oscillation between left and right nationalism (Sinn Féin in Ireland, the SNP in Scotland, Catalan nationalism in the Spanish state versus Ukip, the Front National in France, the BJP in India, etc). Certainly revolutionary socialism on any significant scale is generally notable for its absence.

This absence is clearly a major problem, but it is also something we should expect. The designation of the working class as the revolutionary class is based on the potential of the class not its existing consciousness.[41] In normal times, as Marx pointed out as far back as 1845,

> The ideas of the ruling class are in every epoch the ruling ideas, ie the class which is the ruling material force of society, is at the same time its ruling intellectual force. The class which has the means of material production at its disposal, has control at the same time over the means of mental production, so that thereby, generally speaking, the ideas of those who lack the means of mental production are subject to it.[42]

And in the days of Fox News, Disney, Rupert Murdoch and the X Factor, this may be truer than ever. Revolutions do not occur because the mass of the working class has first been converted to revolutionary ideas. Revolutions occur when mass struggles break out over concrete and immediate demands and these struggles overflow the bounds of normal politics—they bring the masses onto the stage of history and in the process these masses get a sense of their collective power. In other words, large-scale revolutionary consciousness does not precede the outbreak of revolution but rather follows it and develops out of the process of revolutionary struggles.

When it comes to the development of mass revolutionary consciousness in the working class, at the present time there is a specific problem which has to do with more than just the dominance of the right wing media or "bourgeois hegemony" in general and which is, perhaps, most acute where that consciousness is most needed (for example in China). This is that the language and names most closely associated with revolution—Marx, Lenin, 1917, class struggle, soviets, communism, even socialism are also closely associated in the minds of millions with a deeply discredited history: the history of the Soviet Union and of Stalinism and of its Chinese variant ("Maoism").

This book is, in part, an attempt to address this issue, and I will return to it with some suggestions in the last chapter, but, ultimately, it is a problem that will be solved only by life not by books. In my opinion, it will be climate change that will be the decisive game changer in this regard because the necessity of revolution for human survival will trump the fear of replacing one tyranny with something worse.

In that whole immense upheaval towards which capitalism is dragging the world it will be working class people in their hundreds of millions worldwide that will come to the fore. That is why to prepare for this we have to turn to the experience of the last great workers' revolution and the ideas of its main political leader, Lenin.

The working class and the Russian Revolution

What distinguishes the Russian Revolution of 1917 from all other successful revolutions (the English Revolution of 1649, the French Revolution of 1789, the Chinese Revolution of 1949, the Cuban Revolution of 1959, the Algerian Revolution of 1962, the Portuguese Revolution of 1974, etc) and numerous failed attempts at revolution (the German Revolution of 1919-1923, the Spanish Revolution of 1936, the Hungarian Revolution of 1956, the Egyptian Revolution of 2011 and many others) is that in it and through it the working class actually came to power in society, at least for a few years. Historically, the closest parallel to it is the Paris Commune of 1871 when the working class took control of Paris, but that was only one city and lasted just 74 days.

The working class character of the Russian Revolution has, of course, always been contested. It was contested at the time by the large majority of anti-Tsarist figures who came to the fore after the fall of Tsarism in February 1917, namely the liberal democrats of the bourgeois Cadet Party, the populist Socialist Revolutionaries (SRs), the Trudoviks (Kerensky and others) and the Mensheviks. All of these groups agreed that the Revolution should not go beyond establishing a capitalist constitutional democracy along the lines of Britain or France. The Mensheviks, including veteran socialists such as Plekhanov (the founder of Russian Marxism), Martov and Dan, argued this on "Marxist" grounds, maintaining that because Russia had not yet had a full scale industrial revolution and remained largely a peasant country where the proletariat still constituted a small minority of the population, it had to go through the stage of a bourgeois democratic revolution—like France in 1789-1793—led by the bourgeoisie before there could be any thought of the proletariat struggling for power. It has been contested subsequently by a majority of "mainstream" historians on the grounds that the October Revolution was not a working class revolution but a coup imposed on the working class from above by Lenin and the Bolsheviks.

However, the evidence that the Revolution was driven by the struggle of the urban working class, above all in Petrograd and Moscow, is overwhelming. This can be shown on the basis of well known and incontestable facts. The first of these facts is the spontaneous character of the February Revolution. This has never been seriously disputed. On 18 February 1917 workers in one section of the giant Putilov works in Petrograd staged a sit-down strike for a 50 percent wage claim. On 21 February they were sacked, the strike spread and the whole factory was closed. On 23 February (International Women's Day) food shortages led to crowds of women coming out into the streets calling for bread. The report from the Okhrana, the Russian secret police, provides a very clear description of what happened:

> On 23 February at 9 am, the workers of the plants and factories of the Vyborg district went on strike in protest against the shortage of black bread in bakeries and groceries; the strike spread to some plants located in the Petrograd, Rozhdestvenskii and Liteinyi districts, and in the course of the day 50 industrial enterprises ceased working, with 87,534 men going on strike.
>
> At about 1 pm, the workmen of the Vyborg district, walking out in crowds into the streets and shouting "Give us bread," started at the same time to become disorderly in various places, taking with them on the way their comrades who were at work and stopping tramcars; the demonstrators took away from the tram drivers the keys to the electric motors, which forced 15 tramway trains to quit the lines and retire to the Petrograd tramway yard.
>
> The strikers, who were resolutely chased by police and troops summoned [for this purpose], were dispersed in one place but quickly gathered in other places, showing themselves to be exceptionally stubborn; in the Vyborg district order was restored only toward 7 pm.[43]

Over the next couple of days the strikes continued to grow until there was a Petrograd-wide general strike and on the streets the soldiers, sent to restore order, started to side with the people. At this point the strikes spread to Moscow. By the end of the month the regime had completely lost control of the capital and had virtually no forces at its disposal. On 2 March 1917 the Tsar abdicated.

None of this was planned or directed from above. The Cadets and other bourgeois parties were actually against the revolution. The main revolutionary leaders (Lenin, Trotsky, Zinoviev, Kamenev, Lunacharsky, etc) were out of the country and as for the Bolsheviks in Russia, they at first judged the situation not favourable and warned against coming out in the streets. The workers ignored them. As the Menshevik sympathiser Sukhanov records in his memoirs, "Not one party was preparing for the great upheaval".[44] Of course, as Gramsci has observed, "'pure' spontaneity does not exist in history...it is simply the case that the elements of 'conscious leadership' cannot be checked".[45] And Trotsky, in *The History of the Russian Revolution*, devotes his eighth chapter to arguing that on the ground the February Revolution was led by "conscious and tempered workers educated for the most part by the party of Lenin".[46] Be that as it may, it is indisputable that the February Revolution was initiated and carried through primarily by the working class of Petrograd with the assistance of the soldiers and the support of the workers of Moscow.

As the Revolution developed in the course of 1917, so its working class character deepened. Even before the Tsar abdicated on 27 February in the midst of the strikes, street fights and mutinies, the Petrograd working class took up from where it had left off in the 1905 Revolution by re-forming the Petrograd Soviet of Workers' Deputies.[47] By 28 February it had issued the first copy of its paper *Izvestiia* (News of the Soviet) and on 1 March it was joined by the establishment of the Moscow Soviet. Thereafter soviets (workers' councils) spread across Russia. By 17 March there were soviets in 49 cities and by June in 519.[48] Also on 1 March, the Petrograd Soviet issued its famous Order No 1 which called for company committees to be elected throughout the armed forces and stated, "The orders of the Military Commission of the State Duma [the Provisional Parliament] shall be executed only in such cases as do not conflict with the orders and resolutions of the Soviet of Workers' and Soldiers' Deputies."[49] This document, which within days was being read to military units right along the front, set the stage for the situation of "dual power" between the Provisional Government established by the State Duma and the Soviets, which lasted from the end of February until 25 October.

Dual power—two rival authorities contending for power in society— was created by the workers' revolution of February because when the workers and soldiers of Petrograd and elsewhere elected deputies to the

Soviets they mainly chose the most well known opponents of the old regime who at that time tended to be the more moderate socialists—Mensheviks, Trudoviks, independents and, above all, the populist (peasant-based) SRs. Despite the fact that the working class and the Soviets were clearly master of the situation in Petrograd, these representatives, convinced of the bourgeois democratic nature of the Revolution, handed power to the bourgeoisie in the form of Prince Lvov, the Cadets and so on.

The election of these deputies and their policy (which was initially accepted by the revolutionary masses) reflected the consciousness of the majority of the workers and soldiers at this stage. One the one hand, they had risen against the hated Tsarist regime and especially its hated war and they wanted bread, peace and land, but they did not believe they had to take power into their own hands to achieve these things. The story of the nine months from February to October is the story of the working class resolving this contradiction.

Lenin said more than once that "the masses are to the left of the party"[50] and on a number of occasions in 1917 this was demonstratively true as far as the workers of Petrograd were concerned. On 1 March the Executive Committee of the Petrograd Soviet discussed the handover of power to the bourgeois Provisional Government and the proposal was accepted without opposition, including by the Bolshevik representatives on the Committee. However, the Soviet's Vyborg District Committee, which represented the main proletarian and factory area of the city, did oppose this and issued leaflets calling for the transfer of power to the Soviet.[51] This was before Lenin's return to Russia or his *April Theses* arguing for no confidence in the Provisional Government and "All power to the Soviets".

When Lenin arrived back from exile at the Finland Station on 3 April and spoke immediately in favour of a second revolution and the establishment of workers' power, he found himself completely isolated among the Bolshevik leadership who were still wedded to the old Bolshevik formula that the Revolution should not go beyond the limits of bourgeois democracy. Yet within three weeks, his position was accepted by considerable majorities first at the Party's Petrograd City Conference and then at its All-Russian Conference.

How did this happen? Was it because the Bolsheviks were in the habit of doing what their leader told them? This was not how it was at all—at both conferences many of the most experienced members spoke against him. The reason Lenin won the votes and won over the Party was because what he was arguing for dovetailed with what was wanted by the new worker members who were joining the Party in droves. And those new worker-Bolsheviks reflected the mood among the Petrograd masses who, in the so-called April Days, were taking to the streets in armed demonstrations against the declaration by the Foreign Minister, Miliukov, in favour of continuing the War. At this point the Petrograd workers were actually to the left of Lenin who urged caution because he feared, rightly, that armed demonstrations could easily lead to premature confrontation with the government before the majority of the working class had been won over nationwide.

This pattern repeated itself with increasing intensity in June and again in July. The Bolsheviks planned a major demonstration in Petrograd for 10 June, but the Executive of the Petrograd Soviet issued an order banning it. As in April, Lenin and the Bolshevik leadership wished to avoid premature confrontation (bearing in mind that these demonstrations were armed and therefore close to insurrection) but it was only with difficulty that they persuaded the rank-and-file workers to back down. Then, eight days later, the Soviet leadership called a demonstration of its own hoping to reinforce its position. Virtually the entire Petrograd working class of 400,000 turned out, but overwhelmingly they marched under anti-Provisional Government and pro-Bolshevik banners.

On 4 July, hundreds of thousands of workers and soldiers, especially soldiers, took to the streets of the capital with guns in their hands. They were enraged by government plans to transfer regiments to the front and many of them were bent on overthrowing the government there and then, which would not have been difficult. But once again Lenin and the Bolshevik leadership acted to restrain the Petrograd masses and prevent any attempt at insurrection. This was because Lenin was convinced that although it would be possible to seize power in Petrograd, it was still premature as far as the situation in the country as a whole was concerned and that if insurrection conquered in Petrograd, it would be isolated and crushed by the counter-revolution, like the Paris Commune in 1871.

This swift and dramatic radicalisation of the Russian working class along with the soldiers and sailors is the main feature of the spring, summer and autumn of 1917 and the driving force of the Revolution. It was concentrated in Petrograd and Moscow, the two main cities, but not confined to them, and it had many manifestations. These ranged from the Kronstadt Soviet declaring itself the sole governing power in the Kronstadt Naval Base as early as 17 May; to the regular monster meetings in the Modern Circus, addressed particularly by Trotsky[52] but also by other speakers such as Lunacharsky (discussing ancient Greek drama); to the ever-growing struggles in the factories for the eight-hour day and for workers' control. They also included the fact that the first Conference of Factory and Shop Committees on 30 May had a Bolshevik majority from the start and that the Petrograd, Moscow and other Soviets began to produce Bolshevik majorities in early September.

Another important consequence of this radicalisation and of the role of the working class in the revolution was the rapid collapse in support for the Mensheviks, who denied the leading role of the working class. This can be seen not only in the Soviets and on the streets, but even in the elections to the Constituent Assembly which were held after the October Revolution. The Mensheviks won only 16 seats compared to the Bolsheviks' 175.[53] We shall return to the question of these election results shortly.

In the face of this overwhelming historical evidence of working class revolutionary self-activity in 1917, the principal response from those who deny the working class character of the Russian Revolution retrospectively has been to turn to an argument about the culmination of the Revolution, the October insurrection. This insurrection, they have argued, was not the working class taking power but a putsch or coup executed from above by Lenin and the Bolsheviks to seize power for themselves.

What gives this view a certain plausibility is the extraordinarily swift and bloodless victory of the insurrection on the night of 24-25 October. Unlike the "classic" examples of Paris in 1848 and 1871 (or May 1968) or the February Revolution, there were no street barricades, riots or street fighting, nor were there monster demonstrations or a general strike. There was simply a kind of police operation in which a few thousand Red Guards, acting under the direction of the Military Revolutionary Committee of the Petrograd Soviet (whose President was Leon Trotsky) occupied key buildings and arrested the Provisional Government. Moreover, unlike the February Revolution, October was clearly planned in advance; the decision in favour of insurrection being taken, after Lenin's intense prompting, at a meeting of the Bolshevik Party Central Committee on 10 October. There were only 12 people present (11 out of 21 Central Committee members plus one candidate member) and the vote for insurrection was ten to two, with Zinoviev and Kamenev opposed. The action began on the evening of 24 October and was effectively all over by the next day.[54]

I say this interpretation has a certain plausibility, but it is nevertheless superficial and false. Perhaps the first point to make is simply to ask what would happen if a few thousand revolutionaries tried to take power in London, Paris or Moscow today by seizing the Houses of Parliament and Buckingham Palace, or the Elysée Palace or the Kremlin? Or to put it another way what happened when a couple of thousand revolutionaries seized the GPO and other sites in Dublin in 1916?

The answer to the second question we know: the forces of the state, in that case the British state, simply bombarded the GPO and the centre of Dublin until the rebels, facing certain defeat, were obliged to surrender. The answer to the first question is pretty obvious: if the police were not able to cope with the situation the army would be sent in, backed by whatever special forces were deemed necessary, and the revolt would be crushed in hours or days. The obviousness of this answer is why no would-be revolutionary group or party has attempted such an action in Europe in the last 70 years and why no serious revolutionaries even contemplate it.

The reason why this didn't happen in October 1917 is that by the time we get to 24 October the insurrection is already nine tenths accomplished. Overthrowing a capitalist state, or indeed an imperial state, has never been a matter of defeating it in open battle. In the ordinary run of things workers do not have guns and a single machine gun regiment can destroy and scatter an unarmed crowd of hundreds of thousands in minutes. Even armed workers cannot overcome artillery, tanks and planes in a set piece confrontation. Consequently the working class, as opposed to another regular army or guerrilla force, can only defeat the state by virtue of the fact that the armed forces of the state are composed at their base of workers (and, in the Russian case, also peasants). It is, therefore, possible for the revolution to disintegrate the state by winning over the rank-and-file of the armed forces. For this to occur there needs, of course, to be mass discontent within the armed forces and they need to be confronted and influenced by a serious mass movement so that every soldier feels that if he opens fire he will be shooting his brothers, sisters, cousins and child-hood friends and knows also that there is a real social force to which he can "go over" if he defies his officers or turns his guns on them.

This is something that has occurred or started to occur again and again in the history of revolutions. It was how the Paris Commune began on the Butte of Montmartre on 18 March 1871; how the German Revolution began with the Kiel Mutiny in November 1918; and how the Portuguese Revolution developed in 1974-1975. It is what brought the fall of the Shah of Iran in 1979 and it was the fear of this happening which prevented Egypt's generals using the army to save Hosni Mubarak in February 2011. Russia in 1917 was the extreme case of this process.

The basic difference between the first Russian Revolution of 1905, "the great dress rehearsal", and the February Revolution of 1917 was that in 1905 the army remained loyal to the Tsar whereas in February it broke decisively from Tsarism. This is evident in the fact that after a few days' street fighting the Tsarist regime had no forces with which to defend itself and in the fact, already noted, that by 28 February the Petrograd Soviet was already effectively master of the city. By October, the Russian soldiers and sailors, under the influence and pressure of the workers in the factories, had broken not just with Tsarism but also with the capitalists and, crucially, with those "socialists" and "revolutionar-ies" who wanted to compromise with the capitalists.

The ground for this development was laid by the disastrous First World War and the immense losses suffered by the Russian army. It was accentuated and driven by the realisation that the bourgeois liberals (the Cadets), Kerensky and the SRs, and the Mensheviks were all intent on continuing the catastrophic war. This fact made overthrowing the Provisional Government a life or death issue for the likes of the Kronstadt sailors and the Petrograd garrison: would they or would they not be sent to the front? To this was added the rapidly worsening eco-nomic crisis and the growing revolt of the peasants in the countryside. The latter was particularly significant because the majority of the army were peasants in uniform.

Then, at the end of August, came the attempted counter-revolution-ary coup by the Tsarist General Kornilov whose intentions were clearly to crush the Soviets and drown the Revolution in blood. This coup attempt was defeated by the large-scale mobilisation of workers and soldiers for defence and by the dispatch of agitators to win over

Kornilov's troops (both of which were organised primarily by the Bolsheviks).[55] As a result, the counter-revolutionary army evaporated before it could reach the capital.

It was this episode that produced, within days, Bolshevik majorities in most of the main Soviets and convinced the majority of workers, soldiers and sailors—not only in Petrograd but also in the other main cities, in the Baltic fleet and on the Western front—that only decisive revolutionary action would prevent all the gains of the Revolution being destroyed. This conviction was given added urgency by evidence that Kerensky was initially implicated in the attempted coup and by the widespread belief in Petrograd that the bourgeoisie, and therefore the Provisional Government, were preparing to surrender Petrograd to the Germans in order to secure the crushing of the Soviet and the Revolution that they couldn't achieve themselves.[56]

In response, on 13 October the Petrograd Soviet established a Military Revolutionary Committee, under the direction of Leon Trotsky, in order, in conjunction with the Petrograd garrison, to secure the defence of the revolutionary city. When Kerensky attempted to order the Petrograd garrison out of the city, the Military Revolutionary Committee secured agreement from a conference of the Petrograd garrison on 21 October that it would henceforth act only on the orders of the Military Revolutionary Committee and the Soviet and not the Provisional Government or its Military Headquarters. The garrison conference passed a resolution, drafted by Trotsky, which stated:

> The time for words has passed. The All-Russian Congress of Soviets must take power in its hands and guarantee to the people peace, land and bread... The Petrograd garrison solemnly promises to put at the disposal of the All-Russian Congress of Soviets all its forces, to the last man, to fight for these demands. Rely on us, authorised representatives of the soldiers, workers and peasants. We are at our posts, ready to conquer or die.[57]

Commenting on this episode seven years later Trotsky observed:

> From the moment when we, as the Petrograd Soviet, invalidated Kerensky's order transferring two-thirds of the garrison to the front, we had actually entered a state of armed insurrection... Yet the outcome of the insurrection of October 25 was at least three-quarters settled, if not

more, the moment that we opposed the transfer of the Petrograd garrison; created the Revolutionary Military Committee (October 16); appointed our own commissars in all army divisions and institutions; and thereby completely isolated not only the general staff of the Petrograd zone, but also the government. As a matter of fact, we had here an armed insurrection—an armed though bloodless insurrection of the Petrograd regiments against the Provisional Government— under the leadership of the Revolutionary Military Committee and under the slogan of preparing the defense of the Second Soviet Congress, which would decide the ultimate fate of the state power.[58]

Trotsky and the Military Revolutionary Committee were also able to win over in those days the garrison at the Peter and Paul Fortress on the banks of the Neva and even a number of Cossack regiments.

This is how it came about that the seizure of power on 25 October was so easy and went so smoothly. The Provisional Government fell without a struggle because there was no one left to defend it. In other words, the swift and bloodless nature of the insurrection which can be used to sustain the notion of a Bolshevik coup was in fact testimony to the opposite, to its profound support in the working class and among workers and peasants in uniform.

Saying that by the eve of the insurrection it was nine tenths already achieved does not mean that the final tenth, the actual "seizure of power" on 25 October, was not important. On the contrary, as Lenin insisted at the time, it was vitally important and without it the whole window of opportunity, the "moment of revolution", could have been let slip, as it was six years later in October 1923 in Germany. Moreover, it is clear that although it was carried out in the name of the Soviet and organised through the Soviet's Military Revolutionary Committee, the political driving force behind the insurrection was the Bolshevik Party of Lenin. Consequently in making the claim that October was specifically a workers' revolution much depends on the character of the Bolshevik Party and its relationship to the working class. If, as is often said, the Bolsheviks were a small unrepresentative group standing above or outside of the proletariat or basically, as Robert Conquest calls them, "a group of armed intellectuals" then, indeed, the October insurrection can be seen as a hijacking or usurpation of the workers' Revolution. But the facts show conclusively that this was not the case.

Ever since 1905, the Bolshevik Party had been overwhelmingly proletarian in composition. David Lane has produced the following breakdown of Bolshevik membership for 1905: workers, 61.9 percent; peasants, 4.8 percent; white collar, 27.4 percent; others 5.9 percent.[59] Of all the donations to *Pravda*, the Bolshevik paper, in the first quarter of 1914, 87 percent came from workers' collections and 13 percent from non-workers.[60] And already on the eve of the February Revolution, Bolshevik membership stood at 23,600, again with workers making up 60 percent.[61] Of course, out of an overall population of about 160 million, this is a tiny figure and could be dismissed as an insignificant minority. However, relative to the urban population of only 24 million and specifically to the industrial working class, which was its main social base, this is not unimpressive, especially when one bears in mind that it was an anti-war party operating in the midst of a war and under conditions of illegality. In the course of 1917, the party grew rapidly. By the end of April, it had grown to 79,204, and in August it was estimated to be about 250,000; by October it was even larger. This growth was overwhelmingly among the working class and the sailors. The Menshevik Sukhanov notes, "this party was growing swiftly and irresistibly. And it was growing almost exclusively amongst the proletariat".[62] And Trotsky remarks, "The intelligentsia hardly came into the Bolshevik Party at all".[63]

Leonard Schapiro, no friend of Bolshevism, records that, "A sample of replies from organisations in twenty five towns shows that the percentage of organised Bolsheviks among the factory workers in the towns at this date (August 1917) varied from 1 percent to 12 percent—the average for the twenty five towns being 5.4 percent".[64] Given the relatively high level of activism involved in being a Bolshevik militant and that this was activity on both economic and political questions and concentrated in the factories themselves, this is a very high density. It meant there was a highly organic relationship between the party and the working class, a relationship of strong interaction and mutual influence. In such conditions, it would not be possible for the party to stage an insurrection against the wishes of the workers without suffering a catastrophic haemorrhage of membership.[65]

Finally there is the eyewitness testimony of two opponents of Bolshevism who were excellently placed to observe the situation. Sukhanov writes:

[W]as the Petersburg proletariat in sympathy or not with the organisers of the October insurrection? Was it with the Bolsheviks or were the Bolsheviks acting independently of it? Was it on the side of the over-turn, was it neutral, or was it hostile?

Here there can be no two replies. Yes, the Bolsheviks acted with the full backing of the Petersburg workers and soldiers. And they brought about an insurrection, throwing into it as many (very few!) forces as were required for its successful consummation.[66]

Similarly Lenin's old antagonist, Martov, wrote, "Understand, please, what we have before us after all is a victorious uprising of the proletariat—almost the entire proletariat supports Lenin and expects its social liberation from the uprising."[67]

Lenin and the working class

If the Russian Revolution was a workers' revolution and the Bolsheviks were a workers' party, what of Lenin himself? Lenin came from a middle class background, though his grandfather was a serf, and was a highly educated intellectual, but what was his political relationship to the working class? The question has to be posed because it is highly controversial.

The dominant view among mainstream academics and, importantly, in the mass media[68] is, and has been for many decades, that Lenin's relationship to the mass of working class people was elitist and manipu-lative. According to this view, which I would call "the Machiavellian interpretation"[69] of Lenin, he was, more or less from the outset, a would-be dictator, ruthless in his pursuit of power for its own sake, whose attitude to ordinary people, to workers and indeed to other Social Democrats and even other Bolsheviks, as well to all matters of democ-racy and political freedom, was purely instrumental. If this view of Lenin is correct, then it is possible to argue that even if the revolution-ary events of 1917 as a whole were driven by working class struggle and even if the Bolshevik Party was, in its large majority, a workers' party deeply embedded in the Russian factory proletariat, and even if the large majority of workers supported the October insurrection, none-theless they were all just being used by Lenin or by Lenin and his closest associates, who were of a similar "totalitarian" mindset.

The Machiavellian interpretation walks on two legs. The first leg is a pretty sustained character assassination presenting itself as a "knowing" interpretation of Lenin's actions throughout his life. Thus, if in 1903 the Russian Social Democratic and Labour Party split into Bolshevik and Menshevik factions over who should be allowed to be a member, this was not just about two different concepts of organisation, but really about Lenin making a grab for power. Robert Daniels writes, "The issue in essence was Lenin—his ideas for tight organisation, his plans for shaking up the party leadership, his personality as a revolutionary leader, and his drive to dominate the movement".[70] If in 1903 Lenin argued that the editorial board of the newspaper *Iskra* ("The Spark") should consist of Plekhanov, Martov and himself rather than those three plus Zasulich, Potresov and Axelrod, this was because Lenin wanted to increase his personal control, not because he thought Zasulich, Potresov and Axelrod were useless editors.

Similarly, if in 1908-1909 he wrote *Materialism and Empirio-Criticism* against the philosophical views of Bogdanov and the Machists, this was really because he could not tolerate opposition or dissent, not because he disagreed with these philosophical views and thought them harmful to the cause.

The second leg is theoretical. It focuses on Lenin's book of 1902, *What is to be Done?*, and in particular on two arguments in that book: namely, that the working class is able, by its own efforts, to develop only "trade union consciousness", and that socialist consciousness had to be introduced into the working class "from the outside".

These two legs interact and reinforce each other. The arguments from *What is to be Done?* are presented as a kind of "smoking gun" revealing the otherwise concealed manipulative essence of Lenin's thought and justifying the Machiavellian interpretation of his character and conduct as a whole. At the same time the overall Machiavellian interpretation of his political life serves to justify the most incriminating interpretation of *What is to be Done?* and its elevation to the status of a, or even the, key text of Leninism. Because of this interaction I propose to make some observations about the overall context and meaning of the Machiavellian interpretation, followed by an examination of the specifics of *What is to be Done?* and then return to the question of Lenin's actual relation to the working class.

Lenin's will to power?

The idea that throughout his political career Lenin was primarily driven by desire for personal and/or absolute power derives much of its credibility and force from the widely accepted notion that lust for power is what motivates all politicians and all political struggle. This in turn has roots in the Nietzschean view that the will-to-power underlies the whole of human history or even the whole history of the world and in the Christian doctrine of original sin and a fundamentally selfish human nature. This is not the place for a discussion of these metaphysical theories which if valid would rule out any possibility of socialism or a free and equal society,[71] but it is worth noting that their pervasiveness within the culture, their status as "common sense", encourages and permits some sloppy scholarship.

For example Marc Ferro, who was Co-Director of Annales, writes of October:

> Taking power by violence, even though it might have been seized peacefully, was probably Lenin's notion of exorcising the violent streak when he tried to convince his colleagues to prepare for an armed rising, in the face of Kamenev's and Trotsky's arguments that the regime would in any event disintegrate. This notion reflected, in all probability, the very basis of Lenin's thought.[72]

Not only is this statement internally incoherent but it also includes a clear factual error in that Trotsky was in favour of the rising and did not argue that "the regime would in any event disintegrate". Even more importantly its two central claims, namely that "taking power by violence" was "Lenin's notion of exercising the violent streak" [in Lenin or in the people?] and that this "reflected, in all probability, the very basis of Lenin's thought" are both presented without any evidence or reference to back them at all. This doesn't matter because "everybody knows" that something like this motivated Lenin. Similarly Ferro writes:

> [U]p to the taking of power, the Bolsheviks left the constituent assembly on their agenda. To his intimates, however, Lenin confided that when soviet power had been established, to convoke a constituent assembly would be to step back: the assembly was "a liberal joke". He added that "Events may carry us into power, and when we have got it, we will not let it go".[73]

This is an important and damning claim. It is said that Lenin confided this to his intimates. If so how does Ferro know? You would expect there to be a quote, a witness, a reference—some evidence presented. There is none. It is simply asserted as fact. Picking on Ferro here is unfair. There is a vast body of literature on Lenin in this mode. Fifty or seventy years after the events "scholars" write as if they had access to Lenin's inner thoughts and motives and these are invariably presented as cynical, power-driven inner thoughts and motives. This is encouraged and goes largely unchallenged (within the mainstream) because such a view of Lenin corresponds to the instincts and interests of very powerful forces in our society.[74]

In reality, however, the Machiavellian interpretation of Lenin's character is highly implausible and conflicts with many of the main, and indisputable, facts of his life. In 1887 when he was 17 his elder brother was executed for attempting to assassinate the Tsar, so the young Lenin was aware from the outset of the likely consequences of revolutionary activity in Tsarist Russia. He responded by joining a Narodnik cell getting himself arrested and expelled from university. This did not deter him. He joined another cell where he encountered Marx's *Capital* and around 1889 became a Marxist and started reading Plekhanov, the "father of Russian Marxism". In 1893 he moved to St Petersburg, took part in a Marxist workers' circle and joined up with Plekhanov's Emancipation of Labour Group, the penalty for which was always going to be arrest and being sent to Siberia, as actually happened in December 1895. Are we really asked to believe that this youthful heroism and self-sacrifice was all undertaken as part of a long term strategy for the acquisition of personal power? If that was the goal would it not have been simpler to join the Tsarist bureaucracy or, a little bit later, Russia's main bourgeois party, the Cadets?

Then there is Lenin's response to the defeat of the 1905 Revolution and the period of dark reaction that followed it. This reaction, which really took hold from the Stolypin coup of June 1907 onwards, was intense. The level of strikes fell from involving 2,863,000 workers in 1905 to only 47,000 in 1910 and membership of the Bolsheviks collapsed dramatically falling from about 7,000 in St Petersburg in 1907 to only 300 to 400 in December 1908 and in Moscow from 5,320 in May 1906 to 150 in late 1908.[75] Now, if ever, was the moment for an ambitious opportunist to jump ship; to abandon the failed disintegrating movement and make peace with established society, as so many other intellectuals did at that time.[76] But Lenin's response was quite the opposite; it was to cling ever more fiercely to the revolution and the party.

Then there was the outbreak of the First World War. From 1912 to 1914 the movement and the party in Russia were recovering and gaining ground but the start of the War in August 1914 cut right across this. It was accompanied by a huge upsurge of patriotism and war fever, both in Russia and throughout Europe. This put all Socialist parties and leaders under pressure and the large majority of them capitulated. From Germany to Britain, Austria to France more or less every socialist MP or would-be government minister, who had been anti-war until July 1914, turned into supporters of their "own" governments and supporters of the war. The German Social Democratic Party had 112 MPs. They voted 111 to 1 in favour of war credits: the one against was Karl Liebknecht. Let us look at the handful who, across Europe, stood with Liebknecht at this time: Rosa Luxemburg, Leon Trotsky, John MacLean, James Connolly. And look at what happened to them—jail and death. So where did Lenin stand? Actually he took the hardest, most uncompromising anti-war stand of anyone, including his fellow Bolsheviks, arguing for turning the imperialist war into a civil war and taking the ultra-unpopular position of "revolutionary defeatism".[77]

Of course our penetrating psychologists could argue that aged 23 the young Lenin was possessed of such foresight that he knew that 24 or so years later his tiny Marxist circle would turn into a mass party that would propel both itself and himself as its leader into power. And that in the dark and isolated days of 1908 and 1914 Lenin knew that the tide was shortly to turn and he was destined to emerge as Russia's ruler. Except that there is evidence that even in January 1917 Lenin was unsure that he would survive to see "the decisive battles of this forthcoming revolution".[78] Also we must remember that up until the February Revolution Lenin's perspective was that the coming Russian Revolution would be a bourgeois democratic revolution and that therefore the prospect of him or his party becoming absolute rulers of Russia was remote in the extreme.

Socialism from the outside?

Let's now turn to the theoretical argument for the Machiavellian interpretation of Lenin. As we have already noted this centres, indeed rests almost entirely, on two passages from *What is to be Done?* Lenin wrote this book in 1901 and it was published in 1902. It had two main aims: to persuade the numerous scattered Russian social democratic (social-ist) organisations and groups to come together in a single national party, the Russian Social Democratic Party, around a core of profes-sional revolutionaries and an all-Russian newspaper, and to combat the trend in the Russian socialist movement known as "economism". The "economists" argued that the main task of social democrats in Russia was to concentrate on assisting the economic struggles of the workers, without raising political demands such as "Down with the Autocracy!" Lenin took the opposite view, insisting that it was essential that social-ists raise political demands within the workers' movement and especially the demand for the downfall of autocracy. He maintained that leaving the struggle against Tsarism and in favour of political democracy to the bourgeois liberals would wreck the Russian Revolution, because he believed the liberals were far too cautious and cowardly to carry through the anti-Tsarist revolution. That would be possible only under the leadership of the working class and therefore it was crucial that the working class should take up political questions.

In the process of making his case against economism Lenin wrote in relation to the strikes in Russia in the 1890s:

Taken by themselves, these strikes were simply trade union struggles, not yet Social Democratic struggles. They marked the awakening antag-onisms between workers and employers; but the workers, were not, and could not be, conscious of the irreconcilable antagonism of their inter-ests to the whole of the modern political and social system, ie, theirs was not yet Social-Democratic consciousness. In this sense, the strikes of the nineties, despite the enormous progress they represented as compared with the "revolts", remained a purely spontaneous movement.

Then he added the observation that:

We have said that *there could not have been* Social-Democratic con-sciousness among the workers. It would have to be brought to them from without. The history of all countries shows that the working class, exclu-sively by its own effort, is able to develop only trade union consciousness, ie, the conviction that it is necessary to combine in unions, fight the employers, and strive to compel the government to pass necessary labour legislation, etc. The theory of socialism, however, grew out of the philosophic, historical, and economic theories elaborated by educated representatives of the propertied classes, by intellectuals. By their social status the founders of modern scientific socialism, Marx and Engels, themselves belonged to the bourgeois intelligentsia. In the very same way, in Russia, the theoretical doctrine of Social-Democracy arose altogether independently of the spontaneous growth of the working-class movement; it arose as a natural and inevitable outcome of the development of thought among the revolutionary socialist intelligentsia.[79]

This argument, and this passage, have been seized on by numerous, generally anti-Marxist, writers as representing Lenin's real or fundamental attitude to the working class and presented also as a core or defining doctrine of Bolshevism and Leninism. They suggest it shows that Lenin had a sceptical and condescending view of the political capacities of the working class, and believed that left to their own devices working class people would not become revolutionary. Consequently it would be necessary for middle class intellectuals, like him, to impose revolutionary consciousness and goals on the working class by means of an authoritarian centralised party.

Thus Adam Ulam, a leading representative of this approach, writes:

Although the argument is directed at German revisionism and its alleged Russian followers, there is this basic agreement between Lenin and Eduard Bernstein; the forces of history are not making the workers a revolutionary class; the spontaneous organisation of the workers leads them not to revolution but to the struggle for economic and professional improvement... Bernstein believes in the workers party following the inclinations of the workers and bowing to the inherent labourism of the industrialized worker, whereas Lenin believes in forcible conversion of the worker to revolutionary Marxism...

Who is to divert the growing working class movement in Russia from its natural course? A handful of revolutionaries—some of them in Tsarist jails—operating through a newspaper published abroad. But the statement contains the essence of Leninism, the perception that the natural development of material forces and the natural response of people to them will, in time, lead far away from Marx's expectations about the effects of industrialisation on the worker. You "improve" and advance this psychology in the revolutionary direction by means of a party.[80]

Ulam's commentary contains an obvious absurdity: the idea that Lenin in 1901 was advocating "the forcible conversion of the worker to revolutionary Marxism" when this was manifestly impossible and when Lenin was clearly talking only about the need for Social Democrats to make propaganda for socialism among the workers. Unfortunately this kind of claim is common in the anti-Lenin literature.

In fact Lenin's specific formulation here is "one-sided and therefore erroneous"[81] as Trotsky was to put it many years later. It was mistaken in terms of its account of the historical development of Marxism in that while the "theory of socialism [was] elaborated by educated representatives of the propertied classes, by intellectuals" this did not occur "independently of the spontaneous growth of the working-class movement" but was profoundly influenced by it. There would have been no Marxism without the communist workers Marx met in Paris, or the Silesian weavers' revolt or the mass Chartist movement in Britain.[82] And this influence of the working class struggle on the development of Marxist theory was to continue through the 1848 Revolutions, the struggle for the 10-hour day, the Paris Commune and beyond.[83] And the claim that "the working class, exclusively by its own effort, is able to develop only trade union consciousness" was disproved in practice in both the 1905 Revolution and in 1917. But the fact that this formulation is a mistaken one does not at all justify the construction and weight put on it by so many anti-Leninists.

First, there is no basis for the claim, so often made, that *What is to be Done?* was the basic document of Bolshevism or Leninism. Rather it was a polemical work written to combat "economism" and was produced before Bolshevism (still less "Leninism") came into existence and before anyone realised it might come into existence. It was supported and regarded as uncontroversial at the time by those who became the leaders of Menshevism. The "socialism from without" formula was inserted into this polemic in response to those who opposed political propaganda and demands in the name of spontaneity.

Lenin, himself, made this very clear, in the Preface he wrote in 1907 when *What is to be Done?* and other texts from the period were republished:

> The basic mistake made by those who now criticise *What Is To Be Done?* is to treat the pamphlet apart from its connection with the concrete

historical situation of a definite, and now long past, period in the development of our Party...

   What Is To Be Done? is a *summary* of *Iskra* tactics and *Iskra* organisational policy in 1901 and 1902. Precisely a "*summary*", no more and no less.

   Nor...did I have any intention of elevating my own formulations, as given in *What Is To Be Done?*, to "programmatic" level, constituting special principles. On the contrary, the expression I used—and it has since been frequently quoted—was that the Economists had gone to one extreme. *What Is To Be Done?*, I said, straightens out what had been twisted by the Economists... The meaning of these words is clear enough: *What Is To Be Done?* is a controversial correction of Economist distortions and it would be wrong to regard the pamphlet in any other light.[84]

Second, it is clear that under the impact of the great spontaneous revolutionary struggles that broke out in the 1905 Revolution, which included the formation of the Petersburg Soviet, a major advance on trade unionism, Lenin changed the position. In the Preface to his important brochure *Two Tactics of Social Democracy in the Democratic Revolution* he writes, "At such a time the working class feels an instinctive urge for open revolutionary action".[85] Later in that text he quotes Franz Mehring in relation to 1848 on "how the elementary instinct of the working class movement is able to correct the conceptions of the greatest minds [Marx and Engels]"[86] and in November 1905 he writes: "The working class is instinctively, spontaneously Social-Democratic".[87] And after 1905 Lenin never repeated the clumsy "socialism from the outside" formula.

Third, regardless of how exactly he formulated it, it is absolutely clear that Lenin believed that under the influence of Social Democratic agitation and propaganda, the working class was able to reach and *would* reach full socialist consciousness:

   Both our old acquaintance, Comrade Martynov, and the new *Iskra* are guilty of the sin peculiar to the intelligentsia—lack of faith in the strength of the proletariat; in its ability to organise, in general, and to create a party organisation, in particular; in its ability to conduct the political struggle. *Rabocheye Dyelo* believed that the proletariat was still incapable, and would be incapable for a long time to come, of conducting the political struggle that goes beyond the limits of the economic struggle against the employers and the government. The new *Iskra* believes that the proletariat is still incapable, and will be incapable for a long time to come, of independent revolutionary action.[88]

Lars Lih, in his major study, *Lenin Rediscovered*, argues, and demonstrates with much evidence, that of all the socialist writers in Russia at the time, Lenin was the most consistently enthusiastic and optimistic about the potential politicisation of the working class. In contrast many of Lenin's critics who appear to condemn him for his negative appraisal, in 1901, of working class consciousness, actually share the view that workers will never become socialist unless it is imposed on them from above just as capitalist governments and the capitalist media generally think that "ordinary" people are only interested in "bread-and-butter" issues and that any sign of them becoming politicised must be the result of malicious "outside" influences.

Having been obliged to answer the deluge of anti-Lenin denigration we can now turn to Lenin's actual relationship to the working class.

An organic relation

Lenin moved away from the populism (Narodism) of his executed older brother and, under the influence of *The Communist Manifesto* and *Capital* and the writings of George Plekhanov, became a Marxist in about 1892. This break with the Narodniks centred on three connected issues: a) recognition of the fact of the development of capitalism in Russia and abandonment of the idea that Russia could avoid or prevent this development; b) rejection of individual terrorism as a method of political struggle; c) recognition of the working class (and not the peasantry or the undifferentiated "people") as the leading revolutionary class. These issues were completely interconnected because it was precisely the development of capitalism that was producing a modern working class or proletariat that would become the gravedigger of capitalism and it was the shift from the peasantry to the proletariat as the principal revolutionary class that entailed the rejection of individual terrorism.

While he was in prison in 1895-1896 the young Lenin wrote the *Draft of a Programme* for an as yet non-existent Russian Social Democratic party. Compared to his later writings the formulations are clumsy, but the draft focuses overwhelmingly on the development and role of the working class. Here are some extracts:

> Big factories are developing in Russia with ever growing rapidity, ruin-ing the small handicraftsmen and peasants, turning them into propertyless workers...the big factories are creating a special class of workers which is enabled to wage a struggle against capital... This strug-gle of the working class against the capitalist class is a struggle against all classes who live by the labour of others, and against all exploitation. It can only end in the passage of political power into the hands of the working class... The movement of the Russian working class is, according to its character and aims, part of the international (Social-Democratic) movement of the working class of all countries...The emancipation of the workers must be the act of the working class itself.[89]

From this point on Lenin's conviction that Marxism is the theory of the proletariat and its revolution and that the Social Democratic Party, later the Bolshevik Party and later still the Communist Party, is, or has to be, the party of the proletariat remains unshakeable.

The central strategic debate in the Russian revolutionary movement at the end of the 19th and beginning of the 20th centuries was on the class character and dynamics of the coming revolution. More or less everyone in the movement accepted that Russia was heading for revolu-tion. The Populists and their heirs, the Socialist Revolutionaries (SRs), argued in vague terms that it would simply be a "people's revolution", which meant in reality a peasant-based revolution, since the peasants were the overwhelming majority, lead by intellectuals. The Mensheviks, believing themselves to be "orthodox" Marxists, argued that it would be a bourgeois revolution led by the bourgeoisie—more or less a repeat of the French Revolution of 1789.

Lenin accepted (until 1917) that the revolution would not ulti-mately go beyond the limits of bourgeois democracy, but he insisted that the proletariat would lead the revolution. The liberal bourgeoisie (the Cadets, etc), he said, were far too conservative, timid and depend-ent on European investment, and too afraid of the working class to be capable of any revolutionary initiative. For Tsarism to be overthrown, the proletariat would have to establish its hegemony in the revolution and that meant leading all of Russia's toilers, above all the peasants, in the struggle for land and freedom. This in turn meant the working class organising an insurrection and setting up a Provisional Revolutionary Government to sweep away the autocracy and every remnant of feudal privilege. Whereas the Menshevik position meant that the working class should moderate its demands and its struggle so as not to scare away the liberal bourgeoisie (and thus abort the revolution), Lenin's position involved struggling to raise the proletarian struggle to the highest possible level.[90]

Thus Lenin's specific analysis of the nature of the Russian Revolution confirmed and reinforced his general Marxist commitment to the working class. Not only was the proletariat the revolutionary and socialist class in general world historical terms, but it was the class called on to lead the overthrow of Tsarism in Russia in the immediate present.

As a consequence of this, right through *all* Lenin's writings, not just in major programmatic or theoretical texts but in the most minor documents as well, he refers constantly to the "revolutionary proletariat", "the proletariat, the advanced class", the "class-conscious proletarians", "the Social Democrats who are the Party of the proletariat", etc. Almost always, Lenin speaks and writes in the name of "the proletariat"—both international and Russian—and not, for example, of "the left" or "the radical left" or as a "radical intellectual". This is not in an egotistical or substitutionist way—in so far as he refers to himself at all it is usually as only a "publicist". He is not speaking of the proletariat as "his followers" in the way union leaders often speak of the workers as "my members" but with a combination of admiration and confidence about what they have achieved and what he is convinced they will achieve and in a spirit of total identification.

To appreciate the extent and force of this, it is necessary to read Lenin extensively, his minor texts as well as the famous books, but here are a few extracts from different periods that can perhaps give the reader a flavour (emphasis added throughout).

From 1901:

> The Editorial Board of *Iskra* joins whole-heartedly in celebrating the twenty-fifth anniversary of the revolutionary activity of G V Plekhanov. May this celebration serve to strengthen the positions of revolutionary Marxism, which alone can guide *the world struggle of the proletariat* for emancipation.[91]

From 1907:

When the Social-Democrats, from an analysis of Russia's economic realities, deduced the leading role, *the hegemony of the proletariat in our revolution*, this seemed to be a bookish infatuation of theoreticians. The revolution [of 1905] confirmed our theory... *The proletariat actually took the lead in the revolution all the time.* The Social-Democrats actually proved to be *the ideological vanguard of the proletariat.*[92]

From 1912:

Events [mass strikes in response to the shooting of strikers in the Lena goldfield] show that the tradition of the revolutionary mass strike lives on among the workers and *that the workers at once took up and revived this tradition.* The Russian revolution was the first to develop on a large scale this *proletarian* method of agitation, of rousing and uniting the masses and of drawing them into the struggle. Now *the proletariat* is applying this method once again and with an even firmer hand. No power on earth could achieve what *the revolutionary vanguard of the proletariat* is achieving by this method.[93]

From 1915:

The only class in Russia that they did not succeed in infecting with chauvinism is the proletariat. Only the most ignorant strata of the workers were involved in the few excesses that occurred at the beginning of the war. The part played by workers in the Moscow anti-German riots was greatly exaggerated. In general, and on the whole, the working class of Russia proved to be immune to chauvinism. This is to be explained by the revolutionary situation in the country and by the general conditions of life of the Russian proletariat.[94]

It might, of course, be thought that these were mere words, a rhetorical device, or the "abstract" theorising of an intellectual with no relationship with real, living, workers. After all, Plekhanov, the theoretical founder of Russian Marxism, was also committed in theory to the proletariat and famously stated at the foundation of the Second International in 1889, "The Russian Revolution will triumph as a workers' revolution, or it will not triumph at all." Yet Plekhanov was unable to relate to real workers and rebuffed them when they approached him with requests. This was not the case with Lenin.

The first relationship of Russian Marxists with workers was through Marxist study circles. These involved a tiny minority of "advanced" workers who were keen to educate themselves. However, in 1894-1895, the year before his arrest, and as strikes started to mount in Russia, Lenin threw himself enthusiastically into factory agitation. He wrote a detailed *Explanation of the Law on Fines Imposed on Factory Workers* and leaflets for the workers of the Thornton Works and other factories in St Petersburg.[95] The leaflets were written on the basis of personally interviewing and questioning individual workers in great detail about their working conditions. In her memoirs, Lenin's wife, Nadezhda Krupskaya, offered a vivid account of how this information was painstakingly collected and made the following observation about the significance of this episode:

> This St Petersburg period of Vladimir Ilyich's work was of great importance, although the work itself was not noteworthy and hardly noticeable. He had described it so himself. It did not show. It was a matter not of heroic deeds but of establishing close contact with the masses, getting closer to them, learning to be the vehicle of their finest aspirations, learning how to win their confidence, and rally them behind us. But it was during this period of his St Petersburg work that Vladimir Ilyich was moulded as a leader of the working masses.[96]

Thus, Lenin at this time first established an organic relationship with Russian workers, a dialectical relationship of learning and teaching. In *My Life,* Trotsky recounts a similar experience a year or so later in Nikolayev in Southern Russia and then again, on a much more dramatic scale, in his speeches and meetings at the Modern Circus, Kronstadt and elsewhere in 1917.[97] For Gramsci, it was his engagement with the workers of Turin via the journal *L'Ordine Nuovo* in 1919-1920:

> At that time no initiative was taken that was not tested in reality...if the opinions of the workers were not taken fully into account. For this reason, our initiatives appeared as the interpretation of a felt need, never as the cold application of intellectual schema.[98]

Moreover, Lenin maintains this organic relationship, and in particular the ability to learn from the working class, through years of exile because of his intense hands-on involvement (theoretical, journalistic and organisational) with the Bolshevik Party and its implantation in the class. Two examples illustrate this very clearly.

The first is the question of the Soviet in 1905. Many of the "professional revolutionaries", including the Bolshevik Petersburg Committee with whom Lenin had built the party in the period 1903-1904, responded in a very suspicious and sectarian way to the emergence of the Petersburg Soviet in 1905. They saw in this new institution a potential rival to the influence of the party and tried to demand that the Soviet adopt the party's programme or even formally affiliate to it. Trotsky comments, "The Petersburg soviet as a whole, including the contingent of Bolshevik workingmen as well, ignored this ultimatum without batting an eyelash".[99] Lenin, acknowledging the fact that he was only an "onlooker" giving advice from afar, took up the debate:

> It seems to me that Comrade Radin is wrong in raising the question...the Soviet of Workers' Deputies or the Party? I think that it is wrong to put the question in this way and that the decision must *certainly* be: *both* the Soviet of Workers' Deputies *and* the Party. The only question—and a highly important one—is how to divide, and how to combine, the tasks of the Soviet and those of the Russian Social-Democratic Labour Party...
>
> I think it would be inadvisable for the Soviet to adhere wholly to any one party...
>
> I may be wrong, but I believe (on the strength of the incomplete and only "paper" information at my disposal) that politically the Soviet of Workers' Deputies should be regarded as the embryo of a *provisional revolutionary government*. I think the Soviet should proclaim itself the provisional revolutionary government of the whole of Russia as early as possible, or should *set up* a provisional revolutionary government (which would amount to the same thing, only in another form).[100]

Obviously history proved Lenin's instinct, even from afar, to be correct on this matter. As Trotsky noted, he "knew how to eavesdrop thoroughly on the Petersburg masses who called the Soviet 'the proletarian Government'".[101]

The second is a story Lenin recounts in his booklet *Can the Bolsheviks Retain State Power?* regarding the July Days in 1917. Even slightly edited it is a lengthy quote but worth it because it is very revealing of Lenin's outlook:

> After the July days...I was obliged to go underground. Of course, it was the workers who sheltered people like us. In a small working-class house

in a remote working-class suburb of Petrograd, dinner is being served. The hostess puts bread on the table. The host says: "Look what fine bread. "They" dare not give us bad bread now. And we had almost given up even thinking that we'd ever get good bread in Petrograd again."

I was amazed at this class appraisal of the July days. My thoughts had been revolving around the political significance of those events, weighing the role they played in the general course of events, analysing the situation that caused this zigzag in history and the situation it would create, and how we ought to change our slogans and alter our Party apparatus to adapt it to the changed situation. As for bread, I, who had not known want, did not give it a thought. I took bread for granted, as a by-product of the writer's work, as it were. The mind approaches the foundation of everything, the class struggle for bread, through political analysis that follows an extremely complicated and devious path.

This member of the oppressed class, however, even though one of the well-paid and quite intelligent workers, takes the bull by the horns with that astonishing simplicity and straightforwardness, with that firm determination and amazing clarity of outlook from which we intellectuals are as remote as the stars in the sky...

"What a painful thing is this "exceptionally complicated situation" created by the revolution," that's how the bourgeois intellectual thinks and feels.

"We squeezed "them" a bit; "they" won't dare to lord it over us as they did before. We'll squeeze again—and chuck them out altogether," that's how the worker thinks and feels.[102]

Another episode from 1917 that reveals Lenin's relationship to the working class from a different angle occurred at the end of September. At this time, Lenin was engaged in a ferocious battle with the Bolshevik Party Central Committee to convince them to organise the insurrection to take power. He bombards them with letter after letter making ever more urgent demands that they "seize the time". The theme of these texts, repeated again and again, is that the Revolution has reached a decisive turning point and that "procrastination is like unto death". On 29 September 1917 Lenin writes:

The crisis has matured. The whole future of the Russian Revolution is at stake. The honour of the Bolshevik Party is in question. The future of the international workers' revolution for socialism is at stake...

To refrain from seizing power now, to "wait"...is to *doom the revolution to failure.* [Emphasis in original]

Then, in the face of the other Bolshevik leaders' failure to act and in fear that they are going to let the moment go, Lenin tenders his resignation from the Central Committee:

I am compelled to *tender my resignation from the Central Committee,* which I hereby do, reserving for myself freedom to campaign among the *rank and file* of the Party and at the Party Congress.

For it is my profound conviction that if we "wait" for the Congress of Soviets and let the present moment pass, we shall *ruin* the revolution.[103]

Thus at the most crucial moment Lenin threatens to resign from the leadership of the party he has devoted his entire political life to building in order to campaign among the party rank and file—the workers and sailors. Discussing this incident Trotsky comments:

By announcing his resignation, an act which could not possibly be with him the fruit of momentary irritation, Lenin obviously wanted to make it possible to free himself in case of need from the internal discipline of the Central Committee. He could be quite sure that as in April a direct appeal to the lower ranks would assure him the victory.[104]

As Trotsky says, this "required a mighty confidence in the proletariat".[105]

Finally, on this subject, I want to cite two examples from after Lenin was in power. The first is from his famous pamphlet, *Left-Wing Communism—an Infantile Disorder,* written in 1920. Lenin is explaining why, in his view, it is essential for revolutionaries to participate in bourgeois parliamentary elections and he quotes a letter from Willie Gallacher of the Clydeside Shop Stewards movement, who opposes this idea. Lenin fulsomely praises the letter for expressing "excellently the temper and point of view of the young Communists, or of rank-and-file workers" and being "full of a noble and working-class hatred for the bourgeois class politicians" without which "it would be hopeless to expect the victory of the proletarian revolution in Great Britain, or in any other country for that matter".[106] He then proceeds respectfully but systematically to demonstrate the flaws and omissions in Gallacher's position.

The point is this: here is Lenin, who at this time stands at the helm of the Soviet state in the middle of an absolutely desperate civil war, taking the time and trouble to engage in detailed debate with a shop steward from Glasgow in the interest of advancing the workers' revolution in Britain (and it should be said winning him over).[107] It is hard to imagine any other revolutionary "leader" or leading socialist politician or theorist in such a position who would have done this.

The second is from near the very end of his life in December 1922. Responding to the oppressive behaviour of Stalin and Ordzhonikidze towards Georgian Communists over the question of Georgian autonomy, Lenin wrote:

> I suppose I have been very remiss *with respect to the workers of Russia* for not having intervened energetically and decisively enough in the notorious question of autonomisation, which, it appears, is officially called the question of the Soviet socialist republics.[108]

The subject at issue here, the right of oppressed nations to self-determination, was and is very important (and we shall return to it), but what stands out here is Lenin's point of reference in recognising his mistake. In very poor health, barely able to work at all, Lenin is worrying desperately about the direction the Revolution is taking, above all its increasing bureaucratisation, and is becoming steadily more alarmed about the role Stalin is playing in this. In extremis, it is in terms of his duty to the workers that he feels and expresses guilt—not to Marxism or Communism or the Revolution or the Party (though he was undoubtedly loyal to all of them) but to "the workers".

What these examples all illustrate and what the totality of Lenin's writing and political activity demonstrates is a deep theoretical and practical commitment to the working class struggle for its emancipation and an adoption of what Lukács called "the standpoint of the proletariat" not just as a theoretical abstraction but also as an organic and profoundly internalised world outlook.

Why this matters

I have not laboured this point in order to historically vindicate Lenin. While this would be a valid and justifiable endeavour, my purpose is different: it is to demonstrate his contemporary relevance. The Russian

Revolution is relevant and Lenin is relevant because the international revolution of the 21st century will be a workers' revolution and because there is real continuity in the history and experience of workers' struggles and working class revolutions.

Despite Marx's famous aphorism from the *Eighteenth Brumaire* that "all great world-historic facts and personages appear, so to speak, twice...the first time as tragedy, the second time as farce", the fact is that history, obviously, never repeats itself in any exact or mechanical way. What does happen, however, is the recurrence of certain broad patterns in the development and dynamic of workers' revolutions and the recurrence of certain fundamental issues. This is what makes learning from history, from experience, a meaningful endeavour.

One such pattern that we have seen on a number of occasions runs roughly as follows:

Revolution, as in the eruption of mass revolt on the streets, breaks out more or less spontaneously and advances rapidly and spectacularly. In a short space of time, it achieves the overthrow of the principal figurehead of the old regime (the Tsar, emperor, dictator, etc) who resigns/abdicates/flees in the face of the revolt from below and at the behest of the ruling class. For a moment there is widespread euphoria as virtually the whole society, apart from the old ruling clique, seems united in celebrating the victory of the revolution and proclaiming the start of new era. Before long, however, the cracks in this "national" revolutionary unity start to appear as fundamental divergences in class interests and political perspectives begin to appear. Although the hated figurehead has gone, many aspects of the old order are still intact, but with the difference that they now confront what the Irish call "a risen people", first and foremost a working class that has lost its fear and is rapidly radicalising. There then follows a "revolutionary period", which can last from months to several years, in which the bourgeoisie and its political representatives struggle to restore "order" and "stability", if necessary by counter-revolutionary violence, while the working class tries to push the revolution through to a conclusion—the real establishment of a new order of society.

The 1848 Revolution in France, the Russian Revolution of 1917, the German Revolution of 1918-1923, the Portuguese Revolution of 1974-1975, the Tunisian Revolution of 2010-2012, and the Egyptian Revolution of 2011-2013, all correspond to this basic pattern. Other revolutions or near revolutions exhibit some features of this scenario, but with major variations. For example, the Italian "biennio rosso" of 1919-1920, the May Events in France in 1968, the Polish Solidarność revolt of 1979. Sometimes, as in Chile in 1970 and Spain in 1936, it is an election victory by the left, rather than a spontaneous revolt from below, that opens up the revolutionary period, but then a similar dynamic can set it.

Within the revolutionary period a number of issues arise again and again. First and foremost there is the question of the state: how will the state apparatuses (the police, army, judges, civil service, etc) respond to the revolutionary people and how should revolutionaries respond to the state? This has been, and will in the future be, an inescapable problem in any revolution, any serious attempt to change society. Linked to this is the question of whether what is proposed is to operate with the currently existing form of government and parliament—but with different social and economic priorities and different policies—or to establish a new form of democracy or rule. And if the latter, what should it be and how can it be developed? Then there is the problem posed by enormously enthused, but very inexperienced, workers and revolutionaries who believe that the hallmark of a revolution is an absolute refusal to compromise and are determined simply to march forward, regardless of realities. This was particularly a difficulty in Russian in July 1917, in Germany in 1919 and 1921, in Italy during and immediately after the "biennio rosso" and in Egypt in 2012. And this in turn is bound up with the question of whether and how to use the electoral system.

Then there are a host of strategic questions regarding the relationship between the working class and other social forces. In Russia this meant above all the relationship between the workers and the peasants. This is not a major issue in many highly urbanised western societies but played a certain role in the Egyptian Revolution and would clearly be hugely significant today in China or India or many other countries of great revolutionary importance. Relations with the "petty bourgeoisie" and other "middle" or intermediate layers (such as students) would also be important as would dealing with problems of minority national, ethnic and religious groups or overcoming gender, racial or sectarian divisions within the working class and "the people".

This list of questions can be considerably extended: What is the international dynamic of the revolution and how is the revolution in one country to be related to the struggle in all other countries? What is the role of strikes, both economic and political, and trade unions in the revolutionary process? In every past mass revolution without exception a conflict has emerged between those who wanted to push the struggle through to, in Marx's words, "the revolutionary reconstitution of society at large" and those who, judging that to be impossible or too risky, seek a compromise with the existing order. This will undoubtedly occur in any future revolution. How is that to be dealt with? And a question of long debate and controversy: How should revolutionaries organise to achieve their goals?

Any workers' revolution today or in the future will obviously throw up a host of new and, at present, unforeseen problems but it is very hard to see how it would not involve most or many of the issues outlined above and the point of this book is to show that on all of them Lenin has much to say that is extremely useful.

2

Imperialism, war and revolution

In his *Lenin*, Georg Lukács writes, "Lenin's concept of party organisation presupposes the fact—the actuality—of the revolution." He quotes Lenin: "Anybody who accepts or rejects the Bolshevik party organisation independently of whether or not we live at a time of proletarian revolution has completely misunderstood it".[109]

For Lenin, the actuality of the revolution in Russia, when Bolshevism first developed in the early years of the 20th century, was given by the crisis ridden and anachronistic nature of the Tsarist regime. Russia was standing on the brink of its 1789, its bourgeois democratic revolution—indeed, it was already over-ripe for it. This much was common ground among Russian Marxists, Mensheviks and Bolsheviks alike.

They disagreed profoundly on the nature and dynamics of the coming revolution,[110] but they agreed it was on its way, as indeed it was. After 1914 the actuality of the revolution, not only in Russia but internationally, is given by the dreadful fact of the First World War with its millions of casualties and the analysis of imperialism that accompanies it. Lenin saw the War as a double catastrophe: a catastrophe for the international working class whose members would be induced to slaughter one another on an historically unprecedented scale, and a catastrophe for the international socialist movement whose principal leaders and main parties abandoned their pre-war opposition to war and supported their "own" nations—that is, their own ruling classes—in the War.

For Lenin, this was a watershed moment. He was utterly shocked and dismayed by what he saw as the dreadful betrayal of socialist internationalism by parties (above all the German Social Democratic Party (SPD), the leading party of the Second International) and theorists (above all Karl Kautsky, the so-called "Pope of Marxism") whom he had previously respected. From the outset, Lenin denounced the War as imperialist and came out in total opposition to it, along with a small minority of other internationalists (Rosa Luxemburg and Karl Liebknecht in Germany, Trotsky, John MacLean in Scotland, James Connolly in Ireland, etc). Of all of these Lenin was the most "extreme" and intransigent in his opposition, insisting that in an imperialist war, revolutionary socialists must stand for the defeat of their "own" government and issuing the call to "Turn the imperialist war into a civil war!"

> "In all the advanced countries the war has placed on the order of the day the slogan of socialist revolution... The conversion of the present imperialist war into a civil war is the only correct proletarian slogan".[111]

At the same time, Lenin broke decisively with the reformist Second International and started to call for the building of a new, Third International:

> The Second International is dead, overcome by opportunism. Down with opportunism, and long live the Third International... The Second International did its share of useful preparatory work in preliminarily organising the proletarian masses during the long, "peaceful" period of the most brutal capitalist slavery and most rapid capitalist progress in the last third of the nineteenth and the beginning of the twentieth centuries. To the Third International falls the task of organising the proletarian forces for a revolutionary onslaught against the capitalist governments, for civil war against the bourgeoisie of all countries for the capture of political power, for the triumph of socialism.[112]

However, Lenin responded to this crisis not only politically but also theoretically. He engaged in an intense process of study in which he re-examined the philosophical, economic and political foundations of his Marxism. He reread Hegel, deepening and revitalising his understanding of dialectics.[113] He researched intensely into the economic roots of imperialism and he revisited the Marxist theory of the state. In this chapter, I shall focus on his analysis of imperialism, which was summarised, principally, in his famous booklet, *Imperialism, the Highest Stage of Capitalism*, written in the spring of 1916. The first purpose of this work was to prove:

> [T]hat the war of 1914-18 was imperialistic (that is an annexationist, predatory, plunderous war) on the part of both sides; it was a war for

the division of the world, for the partition and repartition of colonies, "spheres of influence" of finance capital, etc.[114]

The second purpose of the book was to present an analysis of the current phase of international capitalism, called "imperialism" by Lenin and other Marxists, which would show that system was "in decay", "parasitical" and in its "highest" or "last" stage of development prior to the proletarian revolution and the transition to socialism. Moreover, this was a stage of which imperialist wars, both wars of conquest in the colonies and wars between the imperial powers themselves, were a fundamental and inevitable feature.

There were two other features of Lenin's theory of imperialism which are not really developed in this particular pamphlet, because it "was written with an eye to the Tsarist censor",[115] but which were and remain of major importance. These were a) an explanation of the split in the international socialist movement between reformism and revolution which, having simmered for nearly two decades, broke into the open with the outbreak of war in 1914; and b) the way in which the imperialist stage of capitalism inevitably generates resistance to imperialism and leads to wars of national liberation.

Overall Lenin's theory of imperialism depicted capitalism as in its "final stages", in an epoch of war and revolution. He was convinced it demonstrated that the outbreak of revolution was imminent. In a lecture on the Russian Revolution of 1905, delivered in Zurich in January 1917, he said:

> We must not be deceived by the present grave-like stillness in Europe. Europe is pregnant with revolution. The monstrous horrors of the imperialist war, the suffering caused by the high cost of living everywhere engender a revolutionary mood...
>
> [In] Europe, the coming years, precisely because of this predatory war, will lead to popular uprisings under the leadership of the proletariat against the power of finance capital, against the big banks, against the capitalists; and these upheavals cannot end otherwise than with the expropriation of the bourgeoisie, with the victory of socialism.[116]

Lenin's theory

Imperialism, in the sense of the conquest of numerous territories by a strong central power (city state, ruling dynasty, imperial family, etc,), has a very long history. One thinks of the Persian Empire, the Roman Empire, the Mongol Empire, the Holy Roman Empire, the Ottoman Empire and numerous other examples. It is also the case that in the 16th, 17th and 18th centuries a number of European countries (Spain, Portugal, the Netherlands, England, and France) established large colonial empires and fought many wars over them. However, the actual term "imperialism" only seems to gain currency in the latter part of the 19th century with the assumption of the title of Empress of India by Queen Victoria in 1877 and the intense 'scramble for Africa'. Lenin then uses this term as the name for what he argues is a new and specific stage of capitalism as a global economic system.[117] This was not an innovation. In 1902 the British economist J A Hobson had published *Imperialism: a Study* and in the years before the First World War the term was widely used on the international left.

A major Marxist theoretical debate also developed, beginning with the Austrian Marxist Rudolf Hilferding's *Finance Capital* in 1910, followed by Rosa Luxemburg's *The Accumulation of Capital* in 1913, an intervention by Karl Kautsky in 1914, and a reply in 1915 by Luxemburg to her critics. Then in 1915 Bukharin produced his *Imperialism and World Economy*, which was in Lenin's hands as he wrote *Imperialism, the Highest Stage of Capitalism*. Lenin's work was unusual in that it was simultaneously an intervention in, and summing up of, this highly theoretical debate and a popular presentation (it carried the subtitle, *A Popular Outline*) of his view. What is beyond doubt, however, is that Lenin's work proved more influential than all the others put together.[118] Lenin's theory runs as follows:

The first characteristic of imperialism, marking it out as a new and distinct phase of capitalism is the concentration of production and the development of monopolies. This, Lenin argues, is a fulfilment of what Marx had seen as a fundamental law of capitalism—the concentration and centralisation of capital—and he presents a large amount of empirical evidence of this occurring, particularly in Germany, the United States and Britain. This evidence suggests, he says, that "the time when the new capitalism definitely superseded the old [pre-monopoly, free market capitalism] can be established with some precision: it was the beginning of the twentieth century".[119]

Lenin then says that it is only possible to grasp the real significance of monopolies if the new role of the banks is considered. Just as there has been a dramatic rise in the concentration of production so there has been a qualitative transformation in the role of the banks from "humble middlemen into powerful monopolies having at their disposal almost the whole of the money capital of all the capitalists and small businessmen and also the larger part of the means of production and of the sources of raw materials of a given country and in a number of countries".[120] Again Lenin cites a lot of evidence, mainly from Germany, to illustrate this claim. With this rise in the size and power of the banks comes the rise of what Lenin, following Hilferding, calls finance capital. "Finance capital is capital controlled by banks and employed by industrialists".[121] Typical of imperialism, says Lenin, is the economic domination and rule of the major capitalist countries by tiny financial oligarchies. "The supremacy of finance capital over all other forms of capital means the predominance of the rentier and of the financial oligarchy; it means the singling out of a small number of financially powerful states from among all the rest."[122]

The rise of monopoly and finance capital brings with it another important shift which is characteristic of capitalism in its imperialist stage, the rise of export capital:

> Typical of the old capitalism, when free competition held undivided sway, was the export of *goods*. Typical of the latest stage of capitalism, when monopolies rule, is the export of *capital*...
>
> On the threshold of the twentieth century we see the formation of a new type of monopoly: firstly, monopolist capital combines in all capitalistically developed countries; secondly, the monopolist position of a few very rich countries, in which the accumulation of capital has reached gigantic proportions. An enormous "super abundance of capital" has arisen in the advanced countries.[123]

This surplus capital is used, Lenin argues, not to raise living standards in a given country as this would mean a decline in profits:

> [B]ut for the purpose of exporting capital abroad to the backward countries [where] profits are usually high, for capital is scarce, the price of land is relatively cheap, wages are low, raw materials are cheap... The necessity for exporting capital arises from the fact that in a few countries capitalism has become "overripe" and (owing to the backward stage of agriculture and the impoverished state of the masses) capital cannot find a field for "profitable investment".[124]

In this way finance capital "spreads its net over all countries of the world"[125] and leads to a struggle for "the division of the world among capitalist combines".[126] As concrete illustrations of this process Lenin gives the examples of the electrical industry—where agreement was reached between two great trusts, the American GEC and the German AEG, in which GEC "got" the United States and Canada and AEG "got" Germany, Austria, Russia, Holland, Denmark, Switzerland, Turkey and the Balkans—and the oil industry where Rockefeller's Standard Oil defeated a combine including Anglo-Dutch Shell and the Deutsche Bank and forced the Deutsche Bank to agree "not to attempt anything which might injure American interests".[127]

This growth in the export of capital and the carving up of the world among capitalist combines leads, in turn, to the territorial division of the world among the great powers. "In the most flourishing period of free competition in Great Britain, ie between 1840 and 1860", Lenin notes, "the leading British bourgeois politicians were *opposed* to colonial policy". But by the end of the 19th century "the British heroes of the hour were Cecil Rhodes and Joseph Chamberlain, who openly advocated imperialism":[128]

> The principal feature of the latest stage of capitalism is the domination of monopolist associations of big employers. These monopolies are most firmly established when *all* the sources of raw materials are captured by one group, and we have seen with what zeal the international capitalist associations exert every effort to deprive their rivals of all opportunity of competing, to buy up, for example, ironfields, oilfields, etc. Colonial possession alone gives the monopolies complete guarantee against all contingencies in the struggle against competitors, including the case of the adversary wanting to be protected by a law establishing a state monopoly. The more capitalism is developed, the more strongly the shortage of raw materials is felt, the more intense the competition and the hunt for sources of raw materials throughout the whole world, the more desperate the struggle for the acquisition of colonies.[129]

The result of this is that by 1914 practically the entire planet had been divided up between six "great" imperialist powers (Great Britain, Russia, France, Germany, the United States and Japan), which between them oppress and "enslave" (Lenin's expression) a colonial population of over 1.6 billion people. Moreover, this division occurs, and under capitalism can only occur, "in proportion to strength" and it is very unequal and not mechanically proportional to economic development. Thus in 1914 the "older capitalist powers" (Britain and France) possess by far the largest empires, whereas the newly emergent imperial power, Germany, has almost no colonies despite having overtaken Britain and France in terms of growth of productive forces. It was, Lenin is arguing, precisely this uneven development that set the scene for the First World War.

The whole world has been divided up. There is no scope for further colonial expansion by the great imperial powers except at the expense of their rivals and that means war:

> The question is: what means other than war could there be *under capitalism* to overcome the disparity between the development of productive forces and the accumulation of capital on the one side, and the division of colonies and spheres of influence for finance capital on the other?[130]

The War, with its terrible slaughter of millions of soldiers and civilians, was, therefore, neither an accident nor a "foolish" mistake by antiquated aristocrats but a necessary consequence of capitalism in its imperialist stage. And if this particular war were to be resolved through the defeat of either side the resulting peace would only be a temporary breathing space, an interval before the next imperialist war to bring about a re-division of the world on the basis of a new distribution of economic and military power.

Lenin was particularly keen to contrast his conception of imperialism with that advanced by Karl Kautsky, the principal theorist of the Second International, which had, in August 1914, collapsed into support for the War.[131] Kautsky argued a) that imperialism was not a stage of capitalism or even a necessary consequence of capitalism but merely a policy "preferred" by finance capital or sections of finance capital and b) that it was perfectly possible that after the War the strongest cartels and states would form an international agreement renouncing war and the arms race, thus bringing about a phase of "ultra-imperialism":

> There can be no doubt that the construction of railways, the exploitation of mines, the increased production of raw materials and foodstuffs in the agrarian countries has become a life-necessity for capitalism. The capitalist class is as little likely to commit suicide as to renounce it...

Rule over the agrarian zones and the reduction of their populations to slaves with no rights is too closely bound up with this tendency for any of the bourgeois parties to sincerely oppose these things... This side of imperialism can only be overcome by socialism.

But imperialism has another side. The tendency towards the occupation and subjugation of the agrarian zones has produced sharp contradictions between the industrialized capitalist States, with the result that the arms race which was previously only a race for land armaments has now also become naval arms race, and that the long prophesied World War has now become a fact. Is this side of imperialism, too, a necessity for the continued existence of capitalism, one that can only be overcome with capitalism itself?

There is no economic necessity for continuing the arms race after the World War, even from the standpoint of the capitalist class itself, with the exception of at most certain armaments interests. On the contrary, the capitalist economy is seriously threatened precisely by the contradictions between its States. Every far-sighted capitalist today must call on his fellows: capitalists of all countries, unite!...

[T]he result of the World War between the great imperialist powers may be a federation of the strongest, who renounce their arms race.

Hence from the purely economic standpoint it is not impossible that capitalism may still live through another phase, the translation of cartelization into foreign policy: a phase of ultra-imperialism.[132]

The purpose of Kautsky's argument, his separation of imperialism into two sides—one necessary, the other optional—was to hold out the possibility of a reformist solution to the War and of a "peaceful" capitalism that would permit a return to the "peaceful" (parliamentary) methods of struggle practised by German Social Democracy and most of the Second International. In contrast, Lenin wanted to assert that the only way out of the hell of imperialist war was by proletarian revolution. Lenin charged Kautsky with trying to console and in reality deceive the masses with the idea that imperialism is "not so bad" because it is quite close to "ultra-imperialism" that can deliver permanent peace. It is worth quoting Lenin's reply at length:

Indeed, it is enough to compare well-known and indisputable facts to become convinced of the utter falsity of the prospects which Kautsky tries to conjure up... Let us consider India, Indo-China and China. It is known that these three colonial and semi-colonial countries, with a population of six to seven hundred million, are subjected to the exploitation of the finance capital of several imperialist powers: Great Britain, France, Japan, the USA, etc. Let us assume that these imperialist countries form alliances against one another in order to protect or enlarge their possessions...these alliances will be "inter-imperialist", or "ultra-imperialist" alliances. Let us assume that *all* the imperialist countries conclude an alliance for the "peaceful" division of these parts of Asia; this alliance would be an alliance of "internationally united finance capital". There are actual examples of alliances of this kind in the history of the twentieth century the attitude of the powers to China, for instance. We ask, is it "conceivable", assuming that the capitalist system remains intact—and this is precisely the assumption that Kautsky does make—that such alliances would be more than temporary, that they would eliminate friction, conflicts and struggle in every possible form?

The question has only to be presented clearly for any other than a negative answer to be impossible. This is because the only conceivable basis under capitalism for the division of spheres of influence, interests, colonies, etc, is a calculation of the *strength* of those participating, their general economic, financial, military strength, etc. And the strength of these participants in the division does not change to an equal degree, for the *even* development of different undertakings, trusts, branches of industry, or countries is impossible under capitalism. Half a century ago Germany was a miserable, insignificant country, if her capitalist strength is compared with that of the Britain of that time; Japan compared with Russia in the same way. Is it "conceivable" that in ten or twenty years' time the relative strength of the imperialist powers will have remained unchanged? It is out of the question.

Therefore, in the realities of the capitalist system, and not in the banal philistine fantasies of English parsons, or of the German "Marxist", Kautsky, "inter-imperialist" or "ultra-imperialist" alliances, no matter what form they may assume, whether of one imperialist coalition against another, or of a general alliance embracing *all* the imperialist powers, are *inevitably nothing* more than a "truce" in periods between wars.[133]

Tragically, this dispute was put to the test of history in that capitalism did survive and the peace did prove to be only a truce before another even more destructive and terrible world war. As Chris Harman has written, "The Second World War was the great and barbaric confirmation of the classic theory of imperialism".[134]

Another important element in Lenin's theory was his contention that there was a material link between imperialism and the rise of opportunism (reformism) in the Second International. This argument was developed particularly in his article "Imperialism and the split in socialism" written in October 1916. Citing the example of the reformism dominant in the English labour movement of the mid-to-late 19th century, he asks, "why does England's [industrial and colonial] monopoly explain the (temporary) victory of opportunism in England?"

> Because monopoly yields *superprofits*, ie, a surplus of profits over and above the capitalist profits that are normal and customary all over the world. The capitalists *can* devote a part (and not a small one, at that!) of these superprofits to bribe *their own* workers, to create something like an alliance...between the workers of the given nation and their capitalists *against* the other countries.[135]

What, in the mid-19th century, applied only to England, now in the full imperialist stage of capitalism applies generally, albeit only to a thin upper strata not to the whole of the working class:

> The bourgeoisie of an imperialist "Great" Power *can economically* bribe the upper strata of "its" workers by spending on this a hundred million or so francs a year, for its *super*profits most likely amount to about a thousand million. And how this little sop is divided among the labour ministers, "labour representatives" (remember Engels's splendid analysis of the term), labour members of War Industries Committees, labour officials, workers belonging to the narrow craft unions, office employees, etc, etc, is a secondary question.[136]

In this way Lenin depicted the Social Democratic and reformist leaders not as fellow socialists with different, albeit erroneous, views but as objectively agents of the bourgeoisie within the working class movement. I shall discuss later in this chapter the strengths and weaknesses of this analysis of reformism.

A further key feature of Lenin's theory was his insistence that imperialism would generate anti-imperialist struggles in its colonies and that it was the duty of revolutionary socialists actively to support those struggles. The Bolshevik Party had always included the right of nations to self-determination in its programme and Lenin had always defended this principle with great vigour.[137] He regarded it as a fundamental democratic demand which should be supported as part of Russian Social Democracy's general struggle for democracy and also as a means of uniting the proletariat in the oppressor nation with the proletariat in the oppressed nation. But up to 1914 Lenin's focus in this matter was primarily on Russia and the oppressed nations within the Russian empire (and also to an extent on the national question in the Austro-Hungarian Empire).[138] But with the War and the development of his general theory of imperialism Lenin's focus widened to the struggle of the colonial peoples as a whole.[139]

This marked a major departure from the previous thinking of the Second International and, indeed, the socialist movement as a whole. Whereas previously there was occasional consideration of the struggles in the colonies and there were scattered observations on the question in Marx and Engels, the socialist movement had never before regarded national liberation movements in the colonies as of central strategic significance. With Lenin this changed, especially with the foundation of the Communist International. At the Second Comintern Congress in 1920 "the national and colonial question" was placed centre stage with the Congress theses being drafted and presented by Lenin himself:

> First, what is the cardinal idea underlying our theses? It is the distinction between oppressed and oppressor nations. Unlike the Second International and bourgeois democracy, we emphasise this distinction...
>
> The characteristic feature of imperialism consists in the whole world, as we now see, being divided into a large number of oppressed nations and an insignificant number of oppressor nations, the latter possessing colossal wealth and powerful armed forces. The vast majority of the world's population, over a thousand million, perhaps even 1,250 million people, if we take the total population of the world as 1,750 million, in other words, about 70 percent of the world's population, belong to the oppressed nations, which are either in a state of direct colonial dependence or are semi-colonies, as, for example, Persia, Turkey and China, or else, conquered by some big imperialist power, have become greatly dependent on that power by virtue of peace treaties. This idea of distinction, of dividing the nations into oppressor and oppressed, runs through the theses.[140]

Lenin now proposes a revolutionary alliance between the proletariat of the advanced capitalist countries, the Soviet Union and the oppressed peoples of what today might be called the third world or the global south:

4) From these fundamental premises it follows that the Communist International's entire policy on the national and the colonial questions should rest primarily on a closer union of the proletarians and the working masses of all nations and countries for a joint revolutionary struggle to overthrow the landowners and the bourgeoisie. This union alone will guarantee victory over capitalism, without which the abolition of national oppression and inequality is impossible.

5) The world political situation has now placed the dictatorship of the proletariat on the order of the day. World political developments are of necessity concentrated on a single focus—the struggle of the world bourgeoisie against the Soviet Russian Republic, around which are inevitably grouped, on the one hand, the Soviet movements of the advanced workers in all countries, and, on the other, all the national liberation movements in the colonies and among the oppressed nationalities, who are learning from bitter experience that their only salvation lies in the Soviet system's victory over world imperialism.[141]

Lenin is careful to warn of:

[T]he need for a determined struggle against attempts to give a communist colouring to bourgeois-democratic liberation trends in the backward countries... The Communist International must enter into a temporary alliance with bourgeois democracy in the colonial and backward countries, but should not merge with it, and should under all circumstances uphold the independence of the proletarian movement even if it is in its most embryonic form.[142]

But the main emphasis is on the necessity of anti-imperialism. Support "in deed, not merely in word for every colonial liberation movement" is made obligatory, a condition of membership, for every party wishing to join the Third International. And in September of 1920 the Comintern launched an important initiative with the First Congress of the Peoples of the East in Baku[143] with the slogan "Workers of the world and oppressed peoples unite!"

What has been achieved therefore under the rubric of "Lenin's theory of imperialism" is a most remarkable synthesis of 1) an indictment of the First World War and a clarion call to rise up against it; 2) an analysis of the economic roots of the War, which is at the same time an analysis of the current stage of capitalism as a global system; 3) an analysis of the crisis of the international socialist movement and a call for its renewal on a revolutionary internationalist basis; and 4) a strategic vision of world revolution uniting the majority of the world's population under proletarian and communist leadership.

The question is how much of this synthesis is still relevant today?

The legacy of the war

So terrible and traumatic was the mass slaughter of the First World War, leaving such a deep imprint on the collective social memory, that a century later the causation and nature of the War remain a live political issue. This was most evident on the centenary of its outbreak in 2014 when there was extensive public debate. The question came up again with the anniversary of the Battle of the Somme and will doubtless resurface in 2018 with Armistice Day and then again with the Treaty of Versailles. On this matter it is clear that Lenin's diagnosis of the War as imperialist—in his words, "an annexationist, predatory, plunderous war, on both sides", has been completely vindicated.

I do not mean by this that it has been generally accepted by "mainstream" historians or media commentators, of course not. I mean that other interpretations simply do not withstand scrutiny. In Britain, and to some extent internationally, the dominant narrative remains that of the victors: it was Germany's fault. In February 2014 the BBC asked ten leading British historians to answer the question, "Who started World War I?"[144] Of the ten, six answered unequivocally Germany or Austria-Hungary and Germany. One answered Austria-Hungary and Germany plus Russia, three also apportioned some blame to Britain, France, Russia and Serbia and one held Serbia mainly responsible. Thus Professor Gary Sheffield stated:

> The war was started by the leaders of Germany and Austria-Hungary. Vienna seized the opportunity presented by the assassination of the archduke [Franz Ferdinand] to attempt to destroy its Balkan rival Serbia. This was done in the full knowledge that Serbia's protector

Russia was unlikely to stand by and this might lead to a general European war.

Germany gave Austria unconditional support in its actions, again fully aware of the likely consequences. Germany sought to break up the French-Russian alliance and was fully prepared to take the risk that this would bring about a major war. Some in the German elite welcomed the prospect of beginning an expansionist war of conquest. The response of Russia, France and later Britain, were reactive and responsive.

I quote Professor Sheffield, but most of the other historians said more or less the same. However, this position has two major weaknesses. The first is its focus on how the war actually started in contrast to the wider historical context in which the war was prepared. The second is that establishing the culpability of Austria-Hungary and Germany is not at all the same as establishing the innocence of Russia, France and Britain.

The question of "who fired the first shot?" or "who started it?", the traditional question posed in relation to a playground scrap, is completely inadequate in determining responsibility for wars. For example, the Algerian War of Independence was undoubtedly "started" by the Algerian National Liberation Front (FLN) on 1 November 1954 with a series of attacks on French targets, if we leave out of account the inconvenient fact that Algeria had been subject to brutal French colonial rule since 1830. Similarly the Irish War of Independence was "begun" by Irish Volunteers who refused to accept the further prolongation of centuries-old British rule.

Sheffield argues that Austria-Hungary acted "in the full knowledge that Serbia's protector Russia was unlikely to stand by and this might lead to a general European war" and that "Germany gave Austria unconditional support in its actions, again fully aware of the likely consequences". But if Austria-Hungary and Germany were fully aware of the likely consequences, why did this not also apply to Russia, France and Britain?

And if the likely consequences were European War, we also need to ask why that was the case. Take the example of Russia, which we are told was Serbia's protector. Why was Russia Serbia's protector? The idea that Tsarist Russia, that prison house of smaller nations from the Baltic to Central Asia, was deeply committed to the rights of the Serbian people has about as much credibility as the idea that the United States waged the Vietnam War out of its passionate concern for the freedom of the South Vietnamese (who they had been more than happy to hand back to the rule of the French). No, Russia was Serbia's protector for the same reason that Austria-Hungary wanted to crush it: because this served their imperial interests in the area. From the standpoint of its geopolitical interests, Russia, whether Tsarist, Stalinist or run by Putin, has always wanted to control as much of the Balkans and the Black Sea area as possible, regardless of the wishes of the local people. In reality Russia was not in the least forced or obliged to go to war over Serbia; it did so because it calculated that this was in its interests.

Exactly the same applies to France and to Britain. Nothing obliged them to go to war in solidarity with Russia except their own calculation of their own imperialist interests. To the argument that they were "honour bound" to do so because of treaties they had made there is the powerful reply: why did they make those treaties in the first place? Britain, France and Russia were not "natural" or "traditional" allies: for much of the 18th and 19th centuries Britain treated France (not Germany) as its main enemy and they fought several major wars.

Another quite common interpretation is that the War was somehow "an accident" or "mistake" and that the various governments of Europe sleepwalked into war, almost against their best intentions. They favour, as they often put it, the notion of a cock-up to a conspiracy. John Keegan, probably Britain's most eminent military historian, maintains that:

> The First World War was a tragic and unnecessary conflict. Unnecessary because the train of events that led to its outbreak might have been broken at any point during the five weeks of crisis that preceded the first clash of arms, had prudence or common goodwill found a voice.[145]

And Niall Ferguson in *The Pity of War* claimed that, "It was something worse than a tragedy... It was nothing less than the greatest error of modern history".[146] The error, he argued, was on the part of the British government, which should have stood aside and allowed Germany to dominate Europe (including defeating France). This would have produced a "continental Europe...not wholly unlike the European Union we know today—but without the massive contraction in British overseas power entailed by the fighting of two world wars".[147] (Ferguson is a strong supporter of the British Empire.)

Christopher Clark, in *The Sleepwalkers: How Europe Went to War in 1914*, has produced a sustained polemic against the idea of German war guilt and any blame-centred approach:

> [T]he quest for blame predisposes the investigator to construe the actions of decision-makers as planned and driven by a coherent intention. You have to show that someone willed war as well as caused it...the view expounded in this book is that such arguments are not supported by the evidence.
>
> The outbreak of war in 1914 is not an Agatha Christie drama at the end of which we will discover the culprit standing over a corpse in the conservatory with a smoking pistol. There is no smoking gun in this story; or rather there is one in the hands of every major character. Viewed in this light, the outbreak of war was a tragedy not a crime.[148]

The "sleepwalkers" thesis clearly cuts across those who would seek a militaristic or nationalistic "celebration" of the War as a war for "democracy" or "freedom" or those, like the victors at Versailles, who wanted to pin all the blame for terrible slaughter on Germany. Beyond that, however, it can sit with a range of political standpoints. For the right wing Niall Ferguson, it goes along with presenting the War as an error from the point of view of preserving the British Empire. For the military historian John Keegan, who was actually a supporter of the Vietnam War, it permits an air of resigned neutrality and objectivity. At the same time it can be linked to a more radical perspective which condemns the war as the responsibility of stupid and unaccountable crowned heads (of the main protagonists only France was a republic) or depicts it, as in the famous *Blackadder* series, as the fault of a foolish, out-of-date class of aristocrats wedded to a mindless jingoism of king and country for which they were quite happy to sacrifice the great unwashed.

But regardless of the politics with which it is associated the "sleepwalkers" thesis is unconvincing history. Yes, it fits some of the facts of the immediate outbreak of war: the almost accidental character of the assassination in Sarajevo (the Archduke's carriage took a wrong turning into the path of Princip); the fact that many of the leaders on both sides appear to have anticipated only a short war and so on. However, like the

German war-guilt analysis, the "sleepwalkers" thesis shows its inadequacy when we look at the bigger picture.

For a start it is reasonable to ask why, if the war was somehow a mistake, the respective governments, on finding themselves caught up in an ongoing catastrophe, did not extricate themselves from it by making peace? Even in late 1916, after the terrible slaughters of Verdun and the Somme, and even in 1917, after the Russian February Revolution and the fall of Tsarism, these rulers were determined to fight on whatever the human cost. When, after the October Revolution, the Bolsheviks took Russia out of the war, the Entente powers denounced them bitterly.

But the main point is that it is possible to sleepwalk over a cliff only if there is a cliff in the vicinity available to be walked over. It is possible for kings, emperors and politicians to stumble blindly into a catastrophe provided that a catastrophe is waiting to happen, that the necessary conditions for it have been prepared.

In the case of the First World War it is abundantly clear that it was a war which had been prepared over a considerable period and that informed people were well aware that it was coming. The division of Europe into two antagonistic power blocs had developed over decades. The Triple Alliance between Germany, Austria-Hungary and Italy had been formed in 1882 (and survived, at least nominally, until Italy's defection in 1915); the Triple Entente between Britain, France and Russia was initiated by the *entente cordiale* signed in 1904 and formally established in 1907. There was a prolonged naval arms race between Britain and Germany from 1906 to 1914 which involved Britain in the construction of 29 Dreadnoughts (battleships) compared to the 17 built by Germany. And well before the Sarajevo assassination there was a series of "international incidents": the Tangier Crisis of 1905-1906 and the Agadir crisis of 1911 in Morocco, as well as the first and second Balkan Wars in 1912 all had the potential to spark a war.

Above all there is the fact that anti-militarists across Europe were acutely conscious of the approach of war and repeatedly warned against it. In 1907 the congress of the Second International at Stuttgart passed a lengthy anti-war motion stating:

> Wars between capitalist states are, as a rule, the outcome of their competition on the world market, for each state seeks not only to secure its existing markets, but also to conquer new ones. In this, the subjugation

of foreign peoples and countries plays a prominent role... The Congress, therefore, considers it as the duty of the working class and particularly of its representatives in the parliaments to combat the naval and military armaments with all their might...

If a war threatens to break out, it is the duty of the working classes and their parliamentary representatives in the countries involved...to exert every effort in order to prevent the outbreak of war by the means they consider most effective.

And then in 1912 at Basel:

The discussion mainly centred on the threat of world war which was hanging over Europe...it also identified that "the greatest danger to the peace of Europe is the artificially cultivated hostility between Great Britain and the German Empire," which was a reference to the arms race and growth of petty nationalism in these two countries...

Essentially, the congress was called at Basel to reinforce the International's firm stance of "war on war" which had been declared in Stuttgart and Copenhagen, and a call to Socialists to "exert every effort in order to prevent the outbreak of war by the means they consider most effective."[149]

The War, therefore, was anything but accidental or unexpected precisely because it was the culmination of well established imperial rivalries. The final confirmation of the predatory character of the War was provided by the Treaty of Versailles at its conclusion which, in addition to punitive reparations and other penalties, stripped Germany of all its colonies and handed them over not to the indigenous peoples concerned but (under cover of the League of Nations) to the victors.

This vindication of Lenin remains important today and for the future because it serves as a telling warning against being bulldozed by rhetoric and media hype into accepting at face value the justifications for wars furnished by governments. In the modern world where wars have to be fought by ordinary people and governments are, justifiably, nervous if not frightened of their populations, the launching of wars is always accompanied by the deliberate creation of "war fever". Politicians and media combine to depict the enemy as the incarnation of wickedness and evil (Saddam Hussein, the Taliban, Al Qaeda, Isis, etc) and the war as a response to some particular crime or threat (the invasion of

Kuwait, 9/11, "weapons of mass destruction", etc). The war fever and tide of chauvinism generated in 1914 was more intense than anything we have experienced recently, but Lenin stood out against it and cut through it to the underlying realities with unmatched clarity and determination. For us in the world of Donald Trump and Rupert Murdoch this is an exceptionally useful example.

A century of change

When it comes to assessing the contemporary validity and relevance of Lenin's theoretical analysis of the exact nature and structure of imperialism—that is, of the given stage of capitalism which he calls "imperialism"—we face a different problem. Lenin believed that the imperialism he was analysing was capitalism's "highest" or "final" stage and that it was due, shortly, to be overthrown by international proletarian revolution. This did not happen. The fact that it did not happen does not mean that his analysis was foolish or refuted because actually the War *did* turn into a "civil war", first in Ireland, then in Russia and elsewhere. And the War *did* lead to a huge revolutionary wave across Europe which nearly succeeded, as we shall discuss in more detail later in this book. But the fact that the international revolution was defeated means that in assessing the relevance of Lenin's theoretical analysis for today, we have to take account of a century of change.

Capitalism is an exceptionally dynamic system. As Marx put it in the *Communist Manifesto*, "Constant revolutionising of production, uninterrupted disturbance of all social conditions, everlasting uncertainty and agitation distinguish the bourgeois epoch from all earlier ones". It would, therefore, be completely contrary to Marx's, and Lenin's, method to imagine that over a century there would not have been numerous and important changes in the economic and political structure of imperialism. Consider the following (inadequate) list of major events and developments that have played their part in shaping the current structure of world capitalism:

1. The emergence, survival and rise of the Soviet Union;
2. The economic crash of 1929 and the Great Depression of the 1930s;
3. The rise of fascism;
4. The Second World War;

5. The emergence since the Second World War of the United States as the world's overwhelmingly dominant economy;

6. The bi-polar Cold War;

7. The post-war economic boom, the greatest boom in capitalism's history;

8. The colonial revolution (China, Vietnam, Cuba, etc) and the European retreat from direct colonial rule (India, Africa, etc);

9. The emergence of oil as the imperialist commodity par excellence;

10. The end of the boom and return of recurring crises in 1973;

11. The rise of neo-liberalism;

12. The rise or intensification of "globalisation";

13. The collapse of "Communism" in Eastern Europe and Russia;

14. The US bid for a "new world order";

15. The rise of the NICs (Newly Industrialising Countries), above all of China;

16. The serial wars in the Middle East, etc;

17. The crash of 2007-2008 and the great recession.

In view of these developments, and the list could obviously be much longer, it would clearly be foolish to treat Lenin's analysis as an adequate guide to contemporary reality, as foolish as treating Engels's *Condition of the Working Class in England in 1844* as a description of working class life in Manchester today or Trotsky's 1938 text *The Death Agony of Capitalism and the Tasks of the Fourth International* as a picture of the world economy today. In this context, I would refer the reader to two texts which offer extensive and masterly surveys of these changes: Chris Harman's "Analysing imperialism"[150] and Alex Callinicos's *Imperialism and Global Political Economy*.[151] Given the extent of these changes what is really striking is just how much of Lenin's analysis clearly still applies.

For a start, the concentration of production and the rise of great monopolies has obviously continued and these great corporations—the ExxonMobiles, BPs, Walmarts, Texacos, Apples and Microsofts, and the like—continue to dominate the world economy. Secondly, finance capital and the banks continue to play a major role, as was seen in the 2008 crash, and the export of capital also continues to be important.[152] We still have a division of the world into a handful of major imperialist powers and a majority of much poorer and weaker oppressed countries, even if they have formal political independence, though there is also (more than in Lenin's time) a layer of sub-imperial powers with regional ambitions such as Turkey and India. In short, imperialism and imperialist wars are manifestly still with us.

In this context, I want to consider, albeit briefly, four debates which have taken place within and around Marxism that have a substantial bearing on the relevance of Lenin's theory for today. These are: his theory of reformism; the question of dependency theory; the concept of globalisation; and the notion of a unipolar imperial order. All of these topics have been the subject of major studies and would merit at least a chapter each, so my discussion of them is doomed to inadequacy and I try to confine myself to observations that are fairly evident in the light of history.

The problem of reformism

Lenin's theory of reformism/opportunism is in many respects the weakest part of his theory as a whole. As we have seen, he believed the economic and social basis of reformism lay in the ability of the imperialist bourgeoisie, out of its "super-profits", to "bribe" a layer of the working class and its various officials, representatives, etc. Utilising this idea, he contrasts England in the mid- 19th century with the situation "now" (1916):

> It was possible in those days to bribe and corrupt the working class of *one* country for decades. This is now improbable, if not impossible. But on the other hand, *every* imperialist "Great" Power can and does bribe *smaller* strata (than in England in 1848–68) of the "labour aristocracy". Formerly a "*bourgeois labour party*", to use Engels's remarkably profound expression, could arise only in one country, because it alone enjoyed a monopoly, but, on the other hand, it could exist for a long time. Now a "*bourgeois labour party*" *is inevitable* and typical in *all* imperialist countries; but in view of the desperate struggle they are waging for the division of spoils it is improbable that such a party can prevail for long in a number of countries. For the trusts, the financial oligarchy, high prices, etc, while *enabling* the bribery of a handful in the top layers, are increasingly oppressing, crushing, ruining and torturing the *mass* of the proletariat and the semi-proletariat.[153]

This analysis is seriously flawed. In the first place, it was not all confirmed by history. Reformism/opportunism remained dominant in the

British labour movement not just in the 19th century but throughout the 20th century and down to this very day. Moreover, it is not just a question of Britain; reformism, in one form or another, has dominated the entire European labour movement over the last century,[154] including in those European countries that were not major imperialist powers, such as Sweden and Greece. The only exceptions to this were moments of intense revolutionary crisis such as Germany in 1923 or Spain in 1936 (when anarchism was the dominant tendency). Also, reformism has been a force in the working class movements of many countries that were victims of imperialism and particularly in their trade union movements; examples range from Chile and Brazil to South Africa (both under apartheid and after it) and India. Clearly, reformism has much deeper roots than just the bribery of the small upper strata.

Secondly, the notion of "bribery", even understood metaphorically, is unsatisfactory. Of course employers and the bourgeois state can and do bribe and corrupt individual workers (by offering them promotion, etc), individual trade union leaders and MPs, etc, but that is a different matter from "bribing" the whole working class or even a whole layer of it. In reality the way workers internationally have raised their living standards has been through trade union and political struggle—wage claims and parliamentary reforms such as the achievement of the welfare state, etc. It is true that capitalists who are doing well, individually and as a class, may be more willing to make such concessions, as in the post-war boom, than when the system is in crisis and they look to lower workers' living standards. However, this can hardly be described as "bribery" especially given the fact that revolutionary socialists, beginning with Marx and Lenin, have always supported workers' economic struggle. The argument that the working class is bribed by these concessions leads straight to the anti-Marxist or, sometimes, "third worldist" view, already discussed in Chapter 2 above, that the entire Western working class was "bought off" by consumer goods and is no longer a potential force for socialist change.

Thirdly, in the Russian Revolution itself and in the revolutionary wave that swept Europe in 1919-1920 and on many other occasions, it was precisely the better paid skilled workers, such as engineers and metal workers (in the Putilov works, in the Fiat factories in Turin and in the Clyde shipyards) who were the most advanced and most militant, not only in terms of economic struggle but also in political consciousness.

These and other criticisms of Lenin's theory of reformism were first advanced by Tony Cliff in his 1957 article "The Economic Roots of Reformism", which accepted the link between imperialism and reformism but argued that once one looked concretely at how capitalist prosperity (derived from imperialism) affected the British and other European working classes it was clear that it raised the living standards not of a small upper crust but of the class as a whole. In place of Lenin's theory he offered his own account:

> The effects of Imperialism on capitalist prosperity, and thus on Reformism, do not limit themselves to the Imperialist Powers proper, but spread to a greater or lesser degree into all developed capitalist countries. Thus a prosperous Britain, for instance, can offer a wide market to Danish butter, and so spread the benefits derived by British capitalism from the exploitation of the Empire to Danish capitalism...
>
> The expansion of capitalism through imperialism made it possible for the trade unions and Labour Parties to wrest concessions for the workers from capitalism without overthrowing it. This gives rise to a large Reformist bureaucracy which in its turn becomes a brake on the revolutionary development of the working class. The major function of this bureaucracy is to serve as a go-between [between] the workers and the bosses, to mediate, negotiate agreements between them, and "keep the peace" between the classes.
>
> This bureaucracy aims at prosperous capitalism, not its overthrow. It wants the workers' organisations to be not a revolutionary force, but Reformist pressure groups. This bureaucracy is a major disciplinary officer of the working class in the interests of capitalism. It is a major conservative force in modern capitalism.
>
> *But the trade union and Labour Party bureaucracy are effective in disciplining the working class in the long run only to the extent that the economic conditions of the workers themselves are tolerable. In the final analysis the base of Reformism is in capitalist prosperity...*
>
> If Reformism is rooted in Imperialism, it becomes also an important shield for it, supporting its "own" national Imperialism against its Imperialist competitors and against the rising colonial movements.
>
> *Reformism reflects the immediate, day-to-day, narrow national interests of the whole of the working class in Western capitalist countries under conditions of general economic prosperity. These immediate interests are in*

contradiction with the historical and international interests of the working class, of Socialism.[155] [Emphasis in the original]

This analysis constituted an important advance in the understanding of reformism, particularly in the way it focused attention on the role of the trade union bureaucracy which has manifested itself in virtually every country and which Tony Cliff was later to take up and analyse in detail as a phenomenon in its own right.[156] But there remains a problem in linking the prevalence of reformism to periods of capitalist prosperity. There is little evidence that even in periods of recession, austerity and hardship, such as the 1930s, reformism necessarily withers or even starts withering, away. History suggests that rather than being the exception, working class reformist consciousness is more the norm. As I have written elsewhere:

> Most of the time under capitalism, the consciousness of most working class people is reformist: they object to many of the effects of capitalism—this cut, this tax, this policy, this government, etc—without rejecting the system as a whole. Alternatively, they dislike the system as a whole but do not believe they, ie the mass of working people, have the ability to change it. In either case, they look to someone else to do the job for them. Corresponding to this reformist consciousness, there are reformist politicians, parties and organisations who step forward with the message that they are the ones who will deliver the desired change or changes on behalf of the masses. A distinction must, of course, be made between workers with reformist consciousness and leaders or organisations engaged in a reformist political project. With the former their "reformism" tends to be relatively unformed and fluid; it can easily be a bridge to action (a campaign, trade union struggle, etc) which in turn can lead to the development of revolutionary consciousness. With the latter, it is usually more coherent, more set against revolution, and crucially is attached to various institutional and personal privileges (political career, parliamentary seat, trade union office, etc) which give its bearers a certain vested interest in the existing system.[157]

What follows from this is that the dominant consciousness of the working class is likely to remain reformist right up to and even beyond the outbreak of revolution. Only in the course of mass revolutionary struggles will the majority of workers be won to revolution.

However, another aspect of Lenin's theory of reformism *has* stood the test of time and remains very relevant today. This is his designation of reformist leaders as "really allies and agents of the bourgeoisie"[158] within the working class movement and the Labour and Social Democratic parties as "bourgeois labour parties". The truth of this has repeatedly been demonstrated at a number of levels. First, reformist leaders permanently and consistently serve as vehicles for bourgeois ideology within the working class, always propagating ideas such as "the national interest", "the neutrality of the state", "the need to respect the law" and "the necessity and legitimacy of profit". Second, they are happy, indeed desperately anxious, to manage capitalism and in that capacity are willing, almost invariably, to impose cuts and hardship on the working class when the logic of capitalism requires it—the examples of this are legion, from Ramsay MacDonald cutting unemployment benefit in the depths of the Great Depression, to PASOK in Greece or the Labour Party in Ireland in the years following the 2008 crash—while simultaneously joining the bourgeoisie socially and economically.

Third, from the First World War through to today, reformist leaders in all the main countries have almost invariably been staunch supporters of imperialist wars and imperialist alliances such as NATO. Thus, in terms of British Labour leaders, Attlee supported the United States at the start of the Cold War and Britain's manufacture of the atom bomb; Hugh Gaitskell defended, "passionately", the British nuclear deterrent; Harold Wilson supported the Vietnam War; Michael Foot supported the Falklands War; Neil Kinnock supported the first Gulf War; and of course, Tony Blair stood alongside George Bush in leading the drive to the Iraq War. Blair, of course, is exceptionally unctuous and unpleasant, but in substance he is conforming to a pattern that applies internationally. That Jeremy Corbyn has up to now been an exception to this rule is one of the main reasons why not only the capitalist media but also so many of his own MPs and his own cabinet find him so intolerable.

Fourth, in moments of revolutionary upheaval when the fate of capitalism has hung in the balance reformist leaders have often literally collaborated with the state, the capitalists and even outright counter-revolutionaries against the working class and against revolutionaries. The leaders of German Social Democracy collaborating with the proto-fascist *freikorps* in the murder of Rosa Luxemburg and Karl Liebknecht in 1918 is the classic but not the only example of this.

But in noting the historical vindication of Lenin on this point it is important also to stress again that this did not lead him into the ultra-left position of simply equating reformist leaders and "bourgeois labour parties" with the open representatives of capital and the outright capitalist parties (the Tories, Christian Democrats, Conservatives, etc). As he explained in *Left-Wing Communism—an Infantile Disorder,* he always emphasised the need to give these reformists critical support against the right in order to be able to win over the workers who followed them and had illusions in them.

The dependency debate

Lenin believed that the export of capital which, as we have seen, he identified as a key feature of imperialism, would lead to capitalist development in the colonised countries:

> The export of capital greatly affects and accelerates the development of capitalism in those countries to which it is exported. While, therefore, the export of capital may tend to a certain extent to arrest development in the capital exporting countries, it can only do so by expanding and deepening the further development of capitalism throughout the world.[159]

And:

> Capitalism is growing with the greatest rapidity in the colonies and in overseas countries. Among the latter new imperialist powers are emerging (eg Japan).[160]

However, as Chris Harman observes:

> the attraction of Communism to many in the national liberation movements had been because of the perception that capitalism was not producing appreciable industrial advance. In many Third World countries there was a very large urban middle class which suffered from impoverishment, precarious job opportunities and unemployment, as well as political marginalisation by the colonial set-up. The lack of willingness of movements dependent on the local bourgeoisie to wage a consistent and determined struggle against colonialism could attract some of the urban middle class to Communism—provided Communism addressed their concerns about economic development as well as political independence.[161]

This led in 1927-1928 to an unacknowledged abandonment of Lenin's view by the Communist International (under the influence of Stalin) in favour of the position that imperialism was systematically preventing industrialisation in the third world. This was used to justify a much closer alliance with and subordination to the so-called "progressive national bourgeoisie" in the underdeveloped countries than Lenin would have countenanced. There was a convergence internationally between the Comintern view and various radical nationalist economic theories, especially in Latin America, with the emergence of Haya de la Torre's American Popular Revolutionary Alliance (APRA) in Peru and the UN Economic Commission for Latin America led by Argentine economist, Raúl Prebisch. Out of all of this emerged what became known as "dependency theory" which, particularly through the influence of Paul Baran and Paul Sweezy in *Monthly Review*[162] became something like the economic consensus on most of the international left in the post-war period. The central idea of dependency theory was that the advanced capitalist countries, "the core", were systematically impoverishing and obstructing the development of "the periphery". From this it followed that in order to achieve development it was necessary to break away from the international capitalist system:

> The establishment of a socialist planned economy is the essential, indeed indispensable, condition for the attainment of economic and social progress in underdeveloped countries.[163]
>
> Short of liberation from this capitalist structure or the dissolution of the world capitalist system as a whole, the capitalist satellite countries, regions, localities and sectors are condemned to underdevelopment... No country which has been tied to the metropolis as a satellite through incorporation in the world capitalist system has achieved the rank of an economically developed country except by finally abandoning the capitalist system.[164]

This sounds highly revolutionary, but for dependency theorists generally the model for a socialist economy was the Stalinist top-down state planning of the Soviet Union (or Maoist China) and the strategy for achieving this was either a bloc of all classes against the (aristocratic) "oligarchy" or nationalist guerrilla warfare in the countryside á la Cuban Revolution. This was part of a wider transformation of Marxism via Stalinism into third world nationalism that took place in the developing world in the mid-20th century.[165] But for our purposes here, the key thing is that dependency theory has been subject to the verdict of history.

On the one hand, those countries that tried to pursue independent economic development by state planning and cutting themselves off from international capitalism by variations on Stalin's "socialism in one country" (Cuba, North Korea, Vietnam and others) have not achieved it. On the other hand, there are a number of countries that did succeed in achieving substantial development, notably the Asian Tigers (Hong Kong, Singapore, South Korea and Taiwan), and others that have certainly experienced, or are experiencing, serious growth such as Malaysia, Brazil, Mexico, India, Turkey and above all China. Moreover, they have achieved this not by cutting themselves off from the world market but by inserting themselves into it in various ways. These facts decisively refute dependency theory as it was formulated in the 1950s, 1960s, and 1970s.

Having said that, it also needs to be noted that these same facts have also been claimed by the right, by apologists for neo-liberalism and capitalism, to claim that capitalist globalisation is solving the problems of the world and heading towards the abolition of hunger, poverty and a more equal world. This is also untrue. First, the development that has occurred has been very uneven, concentrated in relatively few countries, with large swathes of the world, especially Africa, left behind and effectively excluded from this process. Second, the development has been extremely socially unequal both within the newly industrialising countries themselves and on a global scale, thus leading to the kind of obscene figures regularly cited by Oxfam of eight multi-billionaires possessing as much wealth as the bottom half of the world's population and the like. Third, the development has produced the immense global increase in the size of the working class, and therefore the potential for international socialist revolution, that I outlined in Chapter 1.

Lastly, Lenin, influenced by the example of Japan, (as we have seen) believed the growth of capitalism in the colonies could lead to the emergence of new imperialist powers and thus to new inter-imperial rivalries. This leads to another recent debate about imperialism.

Ultra-imperialism or inter-imperialist rivalry

During the Cold War the view, then dominant on the left, that Russia was socialist or some kind of workers' state and therefore not imperialist[166] led most people on the left to see imperialism at that time as unipolar. There was one supreme imperialist power in the world and that was the United States. All other imperial powers (Britain, France, Germany, Japan, etc) were under its hegemony and likely to remain so. As Harman notes:

[M]ost of the left quietly redefined imperialism so as to refer simply to the exploitation of the Third World by Western capitalist classes, ignoring the drive towards war between imperialist powers so central to Lenin's theory, and in practice seeing the whole system as a version of the ultra-imperialism forecast by Kautsky.[167]

Thus Lukács, in 1967, writes, "We know today that the Leninist thesis that imperialist development leads to world war has lost its general validity in the present".[168] When "communism" collapsed in Eastern Europe and the Soviet Union in 1989-1991 and George Bush Snr proclaimed his "new world order", these ideological tendencies on the left were reinforced. The old debate about ultra-imperialism reappeared in new forms.

In 2000 Michael Hardt and Toni Negri produced their (temporarily) highly influential book, *Empire*. Hardt and Negri contrasted their account of contemporary "empire" to Lenin's (and Bukharin's) theory of imperialism. They argued that globalised capitalism had reached such degree of international integration that the role of nation states had been reduced if not to zero, at least to the level of being "merely instruments to record the flow of commodities, money and populations that they [the multinational corporations] set in motion".[169] They argued:

In contrast to imperialism, Empire establishes no territorial centre of power and does not rely on fixed boundaries or barriers. It is a decentred and deterritorialised apparatus of rule that progressively incorporates the entire global realm within its open, expanding powers. Empire manages hybrid identities, flexible hierarchies, and plural exchanges through modulating networks of command. The distinct national colours of the imperialist map of the world have merged and blended in the imperial global rainbow.[170]

This was powerful rhetoric which certainly captured what was then the zeitgeist, the mood of the moment,[171] in that it appealed to a combination of the infant anti-capitalist or alter-globalisation movement which emerged in the Battle of Seattle in 1999 and which focused on the World Trade Organisation (WTO), the World Bank, the IMF and other transnational institutions, rather than governments, and the resurgent "autonomism" of the Black Block, Ya Basta and the Tute Bianche (White Overalls) who cut a dash on the demos of the time.

Unfortunately, it was weak theory. Firstly, it was empirically false in that most multinational corporations, while operating globally, retained a specific national base. The examples are obvious and legion: ExxonMobil, Microsoft, Apple, Walmart, Texaco, Coca-Cola, General Motors, CitiBank, Goldman Sachs in the United States; BP Royal Dutch Shell, HSBC, Barclays, GlaxoSmithKlein in the UK; Toyota, Honda, Misubishi, Nissan, Hitachi in Japan; Volkswagen, Daimler, BMW, Siemens, Deutsche Bank in Germany; Samsung, Hyundai in South Korea, etc. Moreover, they retain and renew their close ties with the state apparatus and governments of their home base to ensure that it acts as a guardian of their interests both in the home market and globally. Again this is easy to demonstrate factually but Trump's recent appointment of ExxonMobil CEO Rex Tillerson as his Secretary of State seems to sum it up. To put it in more theoretical terms, Hardt and Negri were wrong to ignore or dismiss the trend highlighted by Lenin and Bukharin towards the growing together or merger of monopoly capital and the state: that is, the concept of a tendency, built into capitalism, towards state capitalism.

Secondly, on the basis of this faulty theory, Hardt and Negri developed a political prognosis that not only minimised the role of nation states and therefore of war but more or less proclaimed the impossibility of inter-imperialist conflicts. "The big shift", wrote Negri, "is the impossibility of war between civilized nations".[172] This was "ultra-imperialism" with a vengeance.[173] In the event, as Joseph Choonara has pointed out, "The ink had barely dried [on *Empire*] before the events of 11 September 2001 and the beginning of a new cycle of imperialist wars",[174] specifically the US-led invasions of Afghanistan and Iraq, which brought out for all to see the continuing role of national state machines; of their links to corporations, above all the oil industry; and the continuing relevance of the concept of imperialism.

Much more substantial than Hardt and Negri's notion of empire as "a smooth space" with "no place of power"[175] was the quite widespread view on the left that imperial power was real but concentrated overwhelmingly, almost exclusively, in one place, the United States. This view often drew on the, very fashionable, concept of hegemony to depict the United States as the lone and supreme hegemon beneath whose umbrella all potential imperial rivals (Britain, France, Germany, Japan and so on) were both sheltered and imprisoned. What gave this substance were the hard and indisputable facts that at the time US military spending and capability (measured in terms of hardware) exceeded that of all its potential rivals put together, and still does,[176] and that it stood, and stands, as undisputed leader of NATO, by far the world's largest military alliance .

In the middle of the last decade there was extensive discussion of this unipolar conception of imperialism. For example Perry Anderson wrote:

> Essentially, what we see is the emergence, still in its early stages, of a modern equivalent of the Concert of Powers after the French Revolution and Napoleonic Wars. That is: increasing levels of formal and informal coordination to maintain the stability of the established order, accompanied by traditional jockeying for advantage within its parameters, from which there is no radical discord. The decisions of the Security Council are a principal theatre of this process, currently on display in collective resolutions on Iran. There is, however, one large difference between the Concert of Powers after the Congress of Vienna and its counterpart since Nixon's visit to China and the Congress of Paris. This time a single superordinate power, occupying a position unlike any other, holds the system together. In the days of Metternich and Castlereagh, there was no hegemon comparable to America. With still the world's largest economy, financial markets, reserve currency, armed forces, global bases, culture industry and international language, the US combines assets that no other state can begin to match. The other powers accept its asymmetrical position among them, and take care not to thwart it on any matter to which it attaches strategic importance.[177]

There was also something like a set piece debate between Leo Panitch and Sam Gindin on the one hand and Alex Callinicos on the other. Panitch and Gindin's argument,[178] in essence, was that the classical theory of imperialism as regards inter-imperialist rivalries no longer applied because neo-liberalism, under US leadership, had effectively resolved the economic crisis that beset international capitalism in the 1970s, leaving the United States stronger than ever before and able at a structural level to integrate and control the behaviour of its potential rivals:

> [I]t was after the US applied neo-liberal discipline to itself under the Volcker shock [the dramatic raising of interest rates in 1980-1981] that the international authority of neo-liberalism was established, emulated and generalised. It was this that resolved, for capital, the crisis of the 1970s...
>
> It was precisely through the neo-liberal resolution of that crisis that global capitalism's dynamism and the structural power of the American empire were reconstituted over the last quarter of a century.[179]

While there would be tensions and tactical disagreements, such as France's objections to the Iraq adventure of 2003, there would be no fundamental challenge to "the one imperial state".

In contrast Callinicos asserted that the underlying crisis of capitalism that had started to manifest itself in 1973 was rooted in the tendency of the rate of profit to decline and had not been resolved; that for this and other reasons the position of the United States was much weaker than appeared on the surface; and that in the years ahead there would be increasing economic challenges to US hegemony which would, in turn, generate political and military conflict:

> It is hardly surprising that, in the aftermath of the Cold War, with the US enjoying unparalleled ideological and military supremacy, and Japan and continental Europe in the grip of economic stagnation, even states outside the Western camp such as Russia and China have been very cautious about balancing against the hegemonic power. But will this state of affairs persist? There are already signs that it is beginning to break up. Even Panitch and Gindin can't deny China's potential as a challenger to US domination in Asia, though they are right to say that this potential has yet to be realised. But Russia is also becoming restive, particularly in response to its growing encirclement by pro-Western regimes, thanks most recently to the velvet pseudo-revolutions in Georgia and Ukraine.[180]

Therefore, the "classical" theory of imperialism and imperialist war still stood at least as a relevant point of departure for the analysis of the contemporary world.

Ten years on, we cannot say that history has delivered a conclusive verdict on this question—there hasn't been another world war—but the balance of evidence strongly favours the Leninist as opposed to the ultra-imperialist side of the argument.

First, the economic crash of 2007-2008, followed by the great recession and the extremely slow recovery, demonstrated clearly that neo-liberalism had not resolved the underlying problems of international capitalism or the crisis of profitability that lay at the heart of those problems. Consequently the chronic economic instability which brings with it uneven development and changes in the relative strength of different countries is set to continue.

Second, the long-term relative decline of the United States from its overwhelmingly dominant position in the world economy of the 1950s has not been reversed. Moreover, its strategy of deploying its enormous military power to compensate for its relative economic weakness has run into various difficulties. As we have seen, in terms of weapons stockpiled, the US military arsenal dwarfs all others, but in practice its ability to deploy those weapons effectively is another story. Of course it could, at the push of a button destroy the whole world or any country within it. But the fact is that 16 and 14 years respectively after the invasions of Afghanistan and Iraq, and despite serious attempts to disengage, the United States is still mired in conflict in these countries and this constitutes a substantial defeat. The root of its problem is not military but political—its political unwillingness, ever since Vietnam, to take the major casualties required to subdue determined resistance on the ground.

The seriousness of this state of affairs from the standpoint of US imperialism is illustrated by the cases of Iran and Syria. Had Iraq proved to be the cakewalk anticipated by the neo-cons who dominated US policy under Bush, they would almost certainly have liked to move on to regime-change in Iran. But the combination of their inability to pacify either Afghanistan or Iraq and their fear of global and domestic anti-war protest, as seen in 2003, has made them permanently unwilling to undertake such a risky action. And rightly so. Iran is three times the size and has three times the population of Iraq and a government with more support and legitimacy than Saddam Hussain. A US attempt at occupation would almost certainly be a disaster—for the United States. Instead, Obama found it necessary to come to an accommodation with Iran. In the case of Syria, the United States would probably have preferred to replace the tyrannical dictator, Assad, with a more compliant tyrannical dictator, but actually it found itself less able to intervene in the situation than Putin's Russia. The horrific slaughter of the Syrian civil war left the United States looking impotent.

One consequence of the relative weakness of the United States in the Middle East and elsewhere is the emergence of sub-imperial powers whose scope for action has increased considerably. By sub-imperial powers I mean states which are decidedly weaker, economically, politically and militarily, than the main imperialist states (above all the United States but also Russia, the UK, France, Germany, Japan, China, etc), but nevertheless are independent centres of capital accumulation with their own aspirations to regional hegemony. Turkey, Saudi Arabia and Iran in the Middle East and India in South Asia all fall into this category. None of these states is in a position to challenge the United States head on, but neither is the United States able simply to bend them to its will. This creates an unstable situation with all sorts of potential for conflict and, indeed, regional war.

Fourth, there is the question of the United State's major long-term rivals Russia and China. If the Cold War is seen as at root an ideological conflict (freedom versus totalitarianism, capitalism versus communism, etc) then it can be considered finished business which is unlikely to resurface. But if the ideological conflict is seen, as I believe it should be, as a cloak for an underlying real conflict of interest—in essentially the same sense as the conflict between Britain and France in the 18th and 19th centuries and Britain and Germany in the first half of the 20th century were material conflicts of interest—then it must be expected that over time the conflict between the United States and Russia will re-emerge. And this is exactly what we have seen in recent years as Putin flexes his muscles more and more.

In the aftermath of the collapse of the Soviet Union, the United States was able, via NATO, to extend its hegemony eastwards. But subsequently Putin has been striking back both in Georgia and, more importantly, in Ukraine. This situation is currently masked by the somewhat bizarre phenomenon of Russia's apparent alliance with Trump against Clinton in the 2016 US presidential election, but in the longer term the fundamental geopolitical conflict of interest in the Baltic, in eastern Europe and around the Black Sea is likely to "trump" the relationship with Trump.

Even more important in the long run will be the question of the rise of China which I have already discussed in the Introduction. To repeat, if present trends in economic growth continue, China will match or overtake the United States as the world's biggest economy in 20 to 30 years and this will unavoidably have massive consequences for the geo-political and military balance of power in the world. It will give rise to precisely the kind of "struggle for redivision" of the world that Lenin emphasised as an inevitable feature of imperialism. At present China's international strategy is that it is doing very well out of the present set-up so it has little appetite for confrontation but as it grows more powerful this is highly likely to change. Also it is not just a question of China's attitude. The United States is well aware of the coming challenge to its hegemony and is making its preparations through its "Asian pivot", also discussed in the Introduction.

Of course present trends may not continue. The Chinese economy may falter or even crash but this would only unleash a whole chain of destabilisation on the world, especially as it would be very likely to coincide with, as both cause and consequence, another international recession, especially given the current symbiotic mutual dependence between the US and Chinese economies.

The timescale of two or three decades for US-Chinese economic parity is not very long in terms of world history but it has another significance; it is also the approximate timescale for the arrival of catastrophic climate change. The interaction here is lethal. Imperial rivalry prevents either of the two major contributors to climate change taking the necessary measures to prevent it; its advent will precipitate a multitude of deadly rivalries and conflicts.

In short *Pax Americana* is a utopian or dystopian, call it what you will, illusion. It's not going to happen.

All of this reinforces the contemporary relevance of Lenin's theory of imperialism and especially the anti-imperialist politics he derived from it.

Anti-imperialism today

For would-be revolutionaries and socialists today, uncompromising opposition to imperialism and imperialist wars is an absolute necessity. This was demonstrated by the lamentable trajectory of those former leftists and Marxists who abandoned opposition to imperialism in the name of the supposed threat posed by Islamic fundamentalism and terrorism: a trajectory epitomized by the late Christopher Hitchens (who actually ended up endorsing George Bush) but also by the likes of Fred Halliday, Nick Cohen and Norman Geras. To support imperialist war or "intervention", even or especially when it is dressed up as "humanitarian", is to cross a line towards overall accommodation to the capitalist order from which it is very difficult to draw back.

There are also a plethora of "regional" conflicts in the world today where an understanding of global imperialism and the application of Leninist politics are crucial for a revolutionary socialist position. Most important of these is the ongoing vital question of Palestine. All those, including those on the left, who fail to grasp that the struggle in Palestine is fundamentally an anti-imperialist struggle tend to lose their way on this issue. Either they tend to view the conflict as a local dispute between different religions/races/nations that should learn to "tolerate" each other, or they explain the United States' seemingly unconditional support for Israel in terms of "the power of the Jewish lobby" as though Jewish interests controlled America, if not the world, an idea that leads straight to anti-semitic fantasies and conspiracy theories.

Understanding that Israel is fundamentally an agent of US imperialism in the Middle East (albeit an agent with a degree of autonomy) is also important in terms of the strategy required for Palestinian liberation. It suggests that a free Palestine can be achieved only by defeating Zionism and imperialism. This in turn raises the question of what social force might be able to do this? Clearly this would be well nigh impossible for the Palestinians by themselves, whatever the degree of their heroism, but not so impossible in the context of a Middle Eastern Arab workers revolution and a victorious Arab Spring.

The struggle of the Kurdish people is another example. The Leninist principle of the right of nations to self-determination signifies that the right of the Kurds to their own nation must be supported unconditionally by the working class and socialist movements of Turkey, Syria, Iran and Iraq so as to eventually facilitate the unity of working people in the Middle East. The same basic principles apply, with varying degrees of emphasis, to Catalan and Basque independence in the Spanish state, and to Scottish independence and Irish reunification in relation to Britain.

Moreover as the general decay of European capitalism develops, it is more than likely that the EU will be subject to more and more stresses and strains and new "national questions" will emerge demanding a socialist response. The starting point for that response will be the theory of imperialism and the politics of anti-imperialism developed above all by Lenin combined, of course, with the study of the current concrete reality.[181]

3

The state and revolution today

THE *State and Revolution* is the most famous and important of all Lenin's many works. Its importance to Lenin can be judged by when it was written—August and September 1917 while he was in hiding, at the time of the Kornilov coup and on the eve of the insurrection, a time when it can be imagined he had rather a lot to do and a lot on his mind.[182] Its importance is also clear from what he said in a note to his close associate Kamenev written in July 1917 when he had good cause to fear for his life:

> *Entre nous*: if they do me in, I ask you to publish my notebook: "Marxism on the State" (it got left behind in Stockholm). It's bound in a blue cover. It contains a collection of all the quotations from Marx and Engels, likewise from Kautsky against Pannekoek. There are a number of remarks and notes, and formulations. I think it could be published after a week's work. I believe it to be important, because not only Plekhanov but also Kautsky have bungled things. The condition: all this is absolutely *entre nous*![183]

The objective historical importance of *The State and Revolution* is also clear. It was the theoretical foundation of the central slogan of the Revolution, "All power to the Soviets", and thus of the Revolution itself. And here it must be remembered that the idea of soviet power was not only the central aspiration of the Russian working class in 1917 but also the key element in its appeal to the international working class. From Berlin and Turin to Limerick, workers who aimed to follow in Russia's footsteps formed or tried to form "soviets" (workers' councils).

The State and Revolution draws the sharpest and clearest theoretical dividing line between reformist and revolutionary socialism, and between the Marxism of the Second and of the Third International, between Social Democracy and Communism. That split had already occurred over the question of the First World War, of course, but it was *The State and Revolution* that completed the break and, as it were, hammered it home, especially for the period when the war was over and revolution was on the agenda across Europe. Was the goal of the working class movement to win a parliamentary majority for a socialist party so that it could take control of the state and thus transform society in a socialist direction, as the German Social Democratic Party, the British Labour Party and the parties of the Second International argued? Or was the goal, as the parties of the Third or Communist International maintained, to prepare and organise for a working class uprising which would destroy the existing state apparatus, including its parliament, and replace it with a "soviet" state, a state based on workers' councils?[184]

The State and Revolution was the fundamental text of this historic fork in the road. And it continued to be regarded as an authoritative, almost sacred, text of the international Communist movement long after that movement had abandoned its central positions in practice.[185] Some idea of the work's ongoing prestige can be gleaned from the fact that such leading political theorists of the time as Lucio Colletti and Ralph Miliband both devoted substantial and largely approving essays to it in the early 1970s.[186]

However, it is not *The State and Revolution*'s historic significance that is my main interest here. Rather, my concern is with its contemporary relevance. Are its main theses (still) valid and can and should they be regarded as a guide to action now and in the immediate future? In order to answer this question it is first necessary to set out a summary of Lenin's argument.

He begins with the assertion that the state is not an eternal institution but the product of the division of society into classes. He quotes from Engels's *The Origin of the Family, Private Property and the State*:

> [The state] is a product of society at a certain stage of development; it is the admission that this society has become entangled in an insoluble contradiction with itself, that it has split into irreconcilable antagonisms which it is powerless to dispel. But in order that these antagonisms, these classes with conflicting economic interests, might not consume themselves and society in fruitless struggle, it became necessary to have a power, seemingly standing above society...and alienating itself more and more from it...the state.[187]

This, says Lenin, "expresses with perfect clarity the basic idea of Marxism with regard to the historical role and meaning of the state" which he stresses is that the state is "a product and a manifestation of the *irreconcilability* of class antagonisms".[188] Lenin then contrasts this with "bourgeois and particularly petty bourgeois ideologists" who have "corrected" Marx "to make it appear that the state is an organ for the reconciliation of classes" whereas "According to Marx, the state is an organ of class *rule*, an organ for the *oppression* of one class by another".[189] He elaborates on this point, again referencing Engels, by stressing that the essence of the state consists of "special bodies of armed men having prisons, etc at their command".[190]

From this Lenin draws the obvious conclusion that the modern state is a capitalist state, serving the interests of the capitalist class. This conclusion had, of course, already been drawn repeatedly by Marx and Engels including in *The Communist Manifesto:* "The executive of the modern state is but a committee for managing the common affairs of the whole bourgeoisie." But Lenin drives it home. He stresses that Marx's dictum applies even to the most democratic republic with full universal suffrage:

> [T]he omnipotence of "wealth" is more certain in a democratic republic... A democratic republic is the best possible political shell for capitalism, and, therefore, once capital has gained possession of this very best shell...it establishes its power so securely, so firmly, that no change of persons, institutions or parties in the bourgeois-democratic republic can shake it.[191]

Universal suffrage is also, says Lenin, an instrument of bourgeois rule, "a means to decide once every few years which member of the ruling class is to repress and crush the people"[192] in contrast to "the false notion that universal suffrage 'in the present-day state' is really capable of revealing the will of the majority of the working people and of securing its realization."[193] And he emphatically concludes, "Bourgeois states are most varied in form, but their essence is the same: all these states, whatever their form, in the final analysis are inevitably *the dictatorship of the bourgeoisie*".[194] [Emphasis in original]

So far Lenin has been summarising, albeit in markedly more vehement language, the "orthodox" Marxist position on the state. By orthodox I mean not just the actual views of Marx and Engels but what was considered orthodox by the leading parties and leading Marxists of the Second International, that is by German Social Democracy, Karl Kautsky, George Plekhanov and the like. ("It is not denied [by the Kautskyites] that the state is an organ of class rule or that class antagonisms are irreconcilable".)[195] But at this point Lenin makes a decisive move beyond "the orthodoxy", that is the orthodoxy of the Second International.

He bases himself on the observation of Marx and Engels in their 1872 Preface to *The Communist Manifesto* that "One thing especially was proved by the Commune, viz, that 'the working class cannot simply lay hold of the ready-made state machinery and wield it for its own purposes'".[196] He then notes that this comment has generally been interpreted (by the Marxists of the Second International) to mean that Marx is emphasising "the idea of slow development" but:

> As a matter of fact *the exact opposite is the case*. Marx's idea is that the working class must *break up*, smash the "ready-made state machinery" and not confine itself to laying hold of it.[197]

Lenin backs up his interpretation with quotations from the *18th Brumaire of Louis Napoleon* and Marx's 1871 "Letter to Kugelman".[198]

It is this idea—the impossibility of the working class "taking over" the existing state machinery and the absolute necessity of destroying it—which is the central, the key, idea in *The State and Revolution* and its decisive innovation. True, this idea is already present in Marx and Engels, as Lenin insists and demonstrates, but it is in a sentence here and a sentence there. It is Lenin who "discovers" this point which had hitherto been lost or ignored, grasps its significance and gives it such emphasis as to make it unavoidable and unignorable. The phrases, "the destruction of the apparatus of state power", "abolishing the bourgeois state", "destroying the state machine", "smashing the state" are repeated again and again and driven home with a force that is both characteristic of Lenin's writing and almost unique to it.

The significance of this point is that it contradicts the entire previously dominant strategy of the international socialist movement. That strategy, exemplified in the practice of the SPD but also pursued, albeit with national variations, by all the major socialist parties of Europe, was to win governmental power through the accumulation of votes and then use that governmental power to take control of the existing state apparatus (a process often described as "the conquest of state power") which in turn was to be used to transform society.

The question of "smashing the state" is obviously linked to the question of violent revolution, which Lenin also advocates—it is hard to see how the state machine can be "smashed" without any physical and extra-legal confrontation, especially as "special bodies of armed men" constitute the essence of the state—but is nevertheless not identical to it and is, in fact, more important. On the one hand, as October 1917 showed, it may be possible to destroy the existing state apparatus (by winning over the rank and file of the armed forces, etc) with relatively little violence. On the other hand, it is possible to have a violent revolution, an armed struggle, which preserves and "takes over" the existing state apparatus (albeit the outcome of this operation will be some form of capitalism—perhaps state capitalism—not workers' power or socialism).

Taking over the state machine, either by parliamentary or military means, is a strategy in which leaders at the top, whether they are MPs or guerrilla leaders (Alexis Tsipras or Fidel Castro) play the active and predominant part while the mass of the working class are reduced to a supporting role. In contrast "smashing the state" puts a premium on initiative and mass action from below. It is necessary, through force of numbers, to drive the police off the streets and seize police stations; to go to the barracks and win over the soldiers; to form local committees which control areas; and to commandeer buses and trains and such like. All of this requires a risen working class acting in its workplaces and neighbourhoods.

This becomes particularly clear when we examine the next question addressed by Lenin which follows directly from dismantling the capitalist state: namely, "What is to Replace the Smashed State Machine?"

As Lenin points out, Marx had already given a "general" answer to this question in *The Communist Manifesto*: "the proletariat organised as the ruling class...winning the battle of democracy". But because Marx "did not indulge in utopias", a concrete answer as to "the specific forms this organisation would assume" had to wait for "the *experience* of the mass movement".[199] This was provided by the Paris Commune of 1871 when the working class of Paris rose up, took control of the city and held it for 74 days until brutally suppressed by the French government based in Versailles.

Using Marx's analysis of the Commune in *The Civil War in France*,

Lenin identifies a number of key features of the new state that will supplant the old capitalist state. They are: "suppression of the standing army, and its replacement by the armed people... The police...turned into the responsible and at all times revocable instrument of the Commune";[200] the Commune to be formed of "municipal councillors, chosen by universal suffrage in the various wards of Paris, responsible and revocable at any time"; "the officials of all other branches of the administration" to be similarly subject to recall; and "the privileges and representation allowances of the high dignitaries of state" to be abolished and "From the Commune downwards, public service to be done at workmen's wages".[201]

Commenting on these measures, Lenin writes:

> The Commune, therefore, appears to have replaced the smashed state machine "only" by fuller democracy: abolition of the standing army; all officials to be elected and subject to recall. But as a matter of fact this "only" signifies a gigantic replacement of certain institutions by other institutions of a fundamentally different type. This is exactly a case of "quantity being transformed into quality": democracy, introduced as fully and consistently as is at all conceivable, is transformed from bourgeois into proletarian democracy; from the state (= a special force for the suppression of a particular class) into something which is no longer the state proper.[202]

Against anarchism, Lenin insists that a state, the dictatorship of the proletariat, is still necessary "to suppress the bourgeoisie and crush their resistance" and argues that one of the reasons for the Commune's defeat "was that it did not do this with sufficient determination".[203] But because this new state represents the interests of the majority against the minority (of exploiters) and because it will increasingly involve that majority in its day-to-day work it will already be *starting* to wither away. Lenin strongly emphasises the anti-bureaucratic character of the new state. He accepts that:

> Abolishing the bureaucracy at once, everywhere and completely, is out of the question. It is a utopia. But to smash the old bureaucratic machine at once and to begin immediately to construct a new one that will make possible the gradual abolition of all bureaucracy—this is not a utopia, it is the experience of the Commune, the direct and immediate task of the revolutionary proletariat.[204]

It is this semi-state which, Lenin says (again following Marx and Engels), will wither away completely with the achievement of "complete communism" by which he means a society without class divisions or class struggle and based on the principle (taken from Marx's *Critique of the Gotha Programme*) of "From each according to his ability, to each according to his needs!"

> We set ourselves the ultimate aim of abolishing the state, ie, all organized and systematic violence, all use of violence against people in general. We do not expect the advent of a system of society in which the principle of subordination of the minority to the majority will not be observed. In striving for socialism, however, we are convinced that it will develop into communism and, therefore, that the need for violence against people in general, for the *subordination* of one man to another, and of one section of the population to another, will vanish altogether since people will *become accustomed* to observing the elementary conditions of social life *without violence* and *without subordination*.[205]

This is far from being all that is contained in this remarkable book but it is, I hope, a fair summary of its central argument, an argument which is, at least in its own terms, rigorously consistent. There is, however, an important omission in *The State and Revolution* and it is one that Lenin himself draws attention to, namely the experience of the Russian Revolution itself. The reason for this omission is that Lenin was planning a chapter on it but was unable to write it because he was "'interrupted' by a political crisis—the eve of the October Revolution of 1917".[206] As a consequence there are only a couple of passing references to what would probably have been central to that chapter—the role of the soviets or workers' councils. Actually the passing remarks themselves point to that centrality. Thus:

> [T]he bourgeois ideologists...substitute arguing and talk about the distant future for the vital and burning question of present-day politics, namely, the expropriation of the capitalists, the conversion of all citizens into workers and other employees of one huge "syndicate"—the whole state—and the complete subordination of the entire work of this syndicate to a genuinely democratic state, *the state of the Soviets of Workers' and Soldiers' Deputies*.[207] [Emphasis in original]

And:

[T]he entire class-conscious proletariat will be with us in the fight—not to "shift the balance of forces", but to overthrow the bourgeoisie, to destroy bourgeois parliamentarism, for a democratic republic after the type of the Commune, or a republic of Soviets of Workers' and Soldiers' Deputies, for the revolutionary dictatorship of the proletariat.[208]

Moreover, as we have seen, the question of soviet power lay at the heart of all Lenin's theory and practice in 1917. It is therefore useful to note how certain features of the Russian soviets added significantly to and developed beyond the experience provided by the Commune and reasonable to consider these features as an aspect of Lenin's theory of the state.

First, we should note that whereas the Commune was established only after the insurrection and the assumption of power by the working class (at least in Paris), the soviets, both in 1905 and 1917, made their appearance before the conquest of power (though after the uprising that overthrew the Tsar). The soviets emerged not in the first instance as a new state but as an expression of and means of coordinating the revolutionary struggle, which was also the *embryo* of a new state. This created a period of dual power in which the undermining and "smashing" of the bourgeois state was greatly facilitated by the possibility of winning the workers, soldiers and sailors over to accepting the authority of the soviets as "their" government. It also created the possibility of first popularising the idea of soviet power internationally and then agitating for and actually establishing soviets or similar organisations in revolutionary and pre-revolutionary situations in other countries *prior* to the insurrection.

Second, whereas the Commune was based on elections in municipal wards, that is on geographical constituencies, the soviets were based on the election of delegates from workplaces and soldiers' and sailors' units. This difference reflected economic development. In Paris in 1871 industrial production was generally small scale and the working class was predominantly located in small workshops. In Petrograd and Moscow, despite the overall backwardness of Russia, there were numerous factories some of which, like the Putilov works, were among the largest in the world. It also reflected the huge role in the revolution played by the soldiers and sailors of the vast conscript army, itself the product of the industrial scale mobilisation for total war.

But this shift from areas to workplaces and barracks as the main unit of representation constituted a major advance in working class democracy. It meant that the election of a deputy could be the outcome of a collective discussion and debate rather than of individualised, atomised, voting. It also made exercising the right of recall much easier and more effective. Because in a "parliamentary" constituency the electors are not a collective and do not assemble or meet on a regular basis it is very difficult to recall a representative. But with workplace elections the electors are a collective and can recall their delegate by simply holding a workplace meeting. This is not just a question of dealing with deputies who "sell out"; it also makes it possible for the soviet to reflect shifts in the views of the workers. This is very important in the midst of a revolution when, precisely because the masses are involved in daily struggle, the consciousness of the working class is changing very rapidly. And clearly workplace-based election reinforces the class character of the democracy, of the new state.

Lenin, in his 1918 polemic with Kautsky, put it this way:

> The Soviets are the direct organisation of the working and exploited people themselves, which *helps* them to organise and administer their own state in every possible way. And in this it is the vanguard of the working and exploited people, the urban proletariat, that enjoys the advantage of being best united by the large enterprises; it is easier for it than for all others to elect and exercise control over those elected. The Soviet form of organisation automatically helps to unite all the working and exploited people around their vanguard, the proletariat. The old bourgeois apparatus—the bureaucracy, the privileges of wealth, of bourgeois education, of social connections, etc (these real privileges are the more varied the more highly bourgeois democracy is developed)— all this disappears under the Soviet form of organisation... Indirect elections to non-local Soviets make it easier to hold congresses of Soviets, they make the *entire* apparatus less costly, more flexible, more accessible to the workers and peasants at a time when life is seething and it is necessary to be able very quickly to recall one's local deputy or to delegate him to a general congress of Soviets.[209]

And even when in 1920 he is arguing in favour of participating in bourgeois parliaments Lenin still insists:

[O]nly workers' Soviets, not parliament, can be the instrument enabling the proletariat to achieve its aims; those who have failed to understand this are, of course, out-and-out reactionaries, even if they are most highly educated people, most experienced politicians, most sincere socialists, most erudite Marxists, and most honest citizens and fathers of families.[210]

So, with this addition, we can turn to our central question: is the argument of *The State and Revolution* valid today? Can it and should it serve as a guide to action for 21st century workers and socialists?

Arguments against Lenin's theory

The question of the state, its nature, role and legitimacy, has been at the centre of political philosophy and political theory from at least Hobbes's *Leviathan* in the 17th century, if not Plato's *Republic*, and has continued to be so up to the present, including in recent major academic debates. A comprehensive survey of this debate is obviously beyond what is possible in this work. Instead I'm going to focus on six positions, each of which constitutes an explicit or implicit critique of, and alternative to, the Leninist theory of the state and each of which has a certain resonance and currency in society today and in contemporary movements for social change. The positions are: 1) that universal suffrage gives democracy; 2) the pluralist theory of power; 3) Foucault's theory of power; 4) the autonomist/anarchist critique; 5) the "Gramscian" critique; and 6) Poulantzas's critique. I will then consider the positive relevance of Lenin's view in relation to recent and future struggles.

Universal suffrage

By far the most important argument against the Leninist (and Marxist) theory of the state is that the existence of universal suffrage (along with parliamentary government and "free and fair" elections) is democracy and ensures that the state apparatus (the police, armed forces, judiciary, civil servants, etc) is politically neutral and serves the people.

This is not an academic theory—it is seldom put in theoretical form and is very hard to defend as such or support with empirical evidence—but it is something much more powerful than that. It is the absolutely dominant position supported by the entire European and North

American political establishment and most of the global establishment as well, and accepted as more or less self-evidently true by almost all the media, along with most of the education system or systems. Crucially, and this is very important for the maintenance of consensus in this matter, it is also accepted by the majority of the main "opposition" parties and movements. To be specific, it is accepted by most of the social democratic parties and trade unions, or at least their leaderships. (I do not want to exaggerate the extent to which this view is actually accepted at the base of society. In fact it is clear that large numbers of working class people reject the "official" view of the political structure and believe that "*they* (the politicians and "high-ups") are all the same" and "all in it for themselves" and see the police as their enemy. Then there is another layer of people who half believe these things and half accept the official narrative.)

As a result this view becomes the taken-for-granted assumption, the "common sense", on which almost all political discourse is based and within which it is framed. More than that, it takes on, and is actively given, a normative character. To dissent from it is not merely to hold a different or even a mistaken view, it is to be an opponent of democracy as such and anti-patriotic, disreputable to say the least and quite possibly "evil". One consequence of this is that many political figures on the left who personally and privately do not believe in the class neutrality of the state and its institutions, nevertheless feel obliged, for fear of the scandal or loss of public sympathy, to speak publicly as if they do.

To see how this works, imagine if in the British House of Commons a leading left wing politician, probably a member of the Labour Party, maybe even its leader, were to respond to comments from the Tory front bench about sending "our boys" to the Middle East to serve their country, by saying, "I do not accept that the armed forces are 'our boys' or serve the British people; they are an instrument of the British capitalist class being deployed abroad in the interests of imperialism and at home to hold down the working class". The response would, of course, be ferocious and the ferocity would not at all be confined to the Tories but would be expressed with equal rage by numerous Labour MPs and by virtually the entire mass media. It would be the same if analogous comments were made about the police (say after a riot or confrontation with a demonstration or a police killing) or about judges if they ruled against workers in an industrial dispute. I give a British example but it would be the same in all countries.

However, the fact that a theory or view is widely imposed and widely accepted obviously does not make it valid and in this case the claim that universal suffrage and parliamentary government deliver real democracy, governments or states that represent the interests or wishes of the majority, will not withstand critical examination.

In the first place, no election taking place in a capitalist society is fought on a level playing field. By their very nature political parties that represent the interests of the rich and the corporations, together with the upper middle classes, have enormously more money and resources at their disposal than do parties which rely mainly on the support of the working class and the poor. This makes a big difference in election campaigns.

An election campaign involves the production and organisation on a large scale of leaflets, posters, billboard adverts, newspaper and TV advertising, public meetings across the country and so on, all of which costs money. It is true that a workers' party, a party of "the people", will have more volunteers, more "foot-soldiers", than a party of the rich but apart from rare and very exceptional circumstances the resources of the bourgeois parties will far outweigh those of the workers' parties or the left. And the more important and the larger the scale of the election the more this disparity between the resources of the corporations and the "ordinary" people makes itself felt: the US presidential election being an extreme case in that it is close to impossible to mount a credible national campaign without major corporate sponsorship. The only significant counterweight to this huge imbalance is the funding of many social democratic parties by the trade unions but obviously this is not, and cannot be, enough to achieve parity.

Moreover this funding comes with a price. In practice the political use of trade union money and resources, which far exceed that of any other tendency in the working class movement, is heavily influenced by the trade union bureaucracies and is deployed, by and large, to prevent social democratic parties moving too far to the left.

Also elections take place in the context of and under the influence of a mass media that is heavily biased against the left and socialism. This is inevitably the case because: a) most of the media is owned and controlled by big business and run as a business; b) even when the media is state owned, like the BBC, it is still controlled from above by people committed to the status quo; and c) the media operates on the basis of concepts of "objectivity" which take capitalist social relations for granted and regard "the middle ground" as somewhere between George Bush and Hilary Clinton or David Cameron and Tony Blair, and of "news values" which systematically combine the political agenda of the government/state with celebrity culture "infotainment".[211] Moreover this media bias is only one (important) aspect of wider capitalist hegemony which operates both globally and in every nation state through a multitude of institutions including the education system and most of the various churches. In 1845, in *The German Ideology*, Marx and Engels wrote:

> The ideas of the ruling class are in every epoch the ruling ideas, ie the class which is the ruling material force of society, is at the same time its ruling intellectual force. The class which has the means of material production at its disposal, has control at the same time over the means of mental production, so that thereby, generally speaking, the ideas of those who lack the means of mental production are subject to it.[212]

Today, in the age of Disney and Murdoch, CNN and Berlusconi, this is as true as it was then. And the consequence of all these factors, which reinforce each other, is that it is very difficult for any left wing party, any party that stands to the left of "mainstream" social democracy and is actually, or aspires to be, anti-capitalist to overcome all these obstacles and win an election. It can be done of course, as the election of Syriza in Greece in January 2015 shows. But, as the subsequent fate of the Syriza government also shows, this is far from the end of the story.

Having won a general election and having formed a government such a would-be anti-capitalist party finds itself in the position of being in office but not in power.

First and foremost, such a government is not in control of the national economy. The bulk of industrial and financial capital which between them dominate the economic life of the country will be, in so far as a government is or is perceived to be anti-capitalist, in the hands people hostile to it. Second, it is not at all, not even nominally, in control of the global economy on which it is likely to be heavily dependent and with which it is likely to be deeply enmeshed. This will almost certainly include a considerable number of multinational corporations with substantial investment in the country and in many cases will involve all sorts of specific ties, obligations, debts, etc, to institutions such as the IMF, the World Bank, or the European Central Bank. Our would-be anti-capitalist government would also face the hostility of numerous and very powerful foreign governments who would be working in concert with the aforementioned corporations, banks and international institutions.

Between them these forces have the ability to make life extremely difficult for any government that wishes to act against their interests. They can, for example, go on investment strike or simply lower their level of investment. They can close down operations and relocate to countries they feel are more "business friendly". Both of these courses of action can be presented as simple "business" decisions rather political interventions, but both can have the effect of seriously damaging the economy and increasing the level of unemployment. They can also provoke a run on the banks or speculation against the national currency. Moreover, they can do these things secure in the knowledge that the bulk of the media will blame the left government for the economic hardship which ensues.

So what resources will our elected radical government have at its disposal to deal with this very hostile environment? It will, of course, have "moral" and legal authority. Where "the public" or "ordinary people" are concerned that moral authority may be, probably will be, very high but it is not the opposition of ordinary people that we are talking about; the problem is opposition and indeed sabotage by bankers and corporations and it seems highly unlikely that the government's democratic or moral authority would cut any ice whatsoever with such people.

In 2015 the Greek Syriza government, generally perceived as radical and left wing at the time, received a dramatic democratic endorsement from the Greek people with a 60 percent *"Oxi"* (No) vote in the referendum on the Troika's austerity memorandum. Did Mario Draghi and the European Central Bank bat an eyelid? Of course not. They simply piled on the pressure—pressure which, sadly, swiftly broke Syriza's resistance. No senior banker or corporate CEO worth his or her immense salary would do otherwise.

So what of the government's legal authority? Constitutionally such a government would have the power, provided it commanded a majority in parliament, to pass laws that would be legally binding on companies and financial institutions operating on its territory. But how would it be able to administer and enforce such laws? In so far as it operated as a "normal" (constitutional) government, it would run the country and enforce the laws passed by parliament by means of the existing state apparatuses. It would use the existing government departments, with their established teams of civil servants, and it would, if necessary, deploy the existing courts, police and, as a last resort, the military to secure compliance. In theory these apparatuses would be constitutionally obliged to follow the orders of the democratically elected government, but would they do so in practice?

To answer this question we shall consider three things: a) the nature and composition of the state apparatuses; b) the nature of the challenge being posed by the government; and c) the historical experience of the state's relationship to left governments.

The first thing to note is that state apparatuses, with very few exceptions, are hierarchical organisations. The democratic elective principle applies, as a rule, only to parliaments (and local councils). The armed forces, police, judiciary, prisons, civil service and so on are based on appointment, discipline and subordination. Unless there is mutiny in the ranks, their behaviour is determined by those who run them.

The next thing to note is that those who head these institutions are highly paid. They are not highly paid compared to CEOs in the private sector, still less compared to major capitalists but they are paid far, far above the average wage. In the United States an army general earns about US$180,000 a year plus considerable perks; a police chief in a major city earns over US$190,000 and federal judges between US$220,000 and US$250,000. In Britain a brigadier earns over £100,000 and General Sir Peter Hall, Head of the Army, receives £180,000 plus a flat in Central London. General Sir David Richards, Chief of Defence Staff, gets £256,000 a year with an apartment in Kensington Palace (a royal palace and official residence of the Duke and Duchess of Cambridge). Pay for police chiefs in Britain ranges from over £280,000 for the Metropolitan Police Commissioner to about £170,000 for an average Chief Constable. British judges average between £200,000 and £250,000 a year. In 2010 the *Guardian* reported that Prime Minister David Cameron had data published about the salaries of top civil servants:

The data lists the names of some 170 senior civil servants who earn over £150,000, more than the prime minister. Top of the list is John Fingleton, the chief executive of the Office of Fair Trading, who earns up to £279,999 a year. Other high earners include David Nicholson, the chief executive of the NHS, who earns between £255,000 and £259,999 and Joe Harley, IT director general and chief information officer for the Department for Work and Pensions. The Ministry of Defence has the largest number of high earners, with no less than 28 of its civil servants making the list, along with 21 from the Cabinet Office.[213]

These facts are hardly surprising. Rather, it would be astonishing if they were otherwise in any stratified society. Nevertheless they are worth reflecting on because they have important political implications. It is one of the most basic facts of political life, observable in voting behaviour across the world, that high earners tend to be "right wing" or "conservative" in their views. Moreover, these state officials are overwhelmingly drawn from very privileged backgrounds. This is true internationally but the British case is particularly illustrative because of the role of private, fee paying education. As Owen Jones has noted:

> Only 7 percent in Britain are privately educated, and yet this section of society makes up 71 percent of senior judges, 62 percent of the senior armed forces and 55 percent of permanent secretaries. It is quite something when the "cabinet of millionaires" is one of the less unrepresentative pillars of power, with 36 percent hailing from private schools.[214]

Obviously incomes, background and education will all shape the outlook and behaviour of those who run the apparatuses of the state. But there is more involved than these standard "sociological" influences. The state machine of every capitalist society consists of a set of institutions that has been shaped historically over a lengthy period of time (in the case of Britain more than 400 years) to serve the interests of that capitalist society and its dominant class. In the course of that history it has developed a tradition, an ideology and an ethos which fits this purpose and which, for example, identifies being "politically neutral" with being "above politics" (like the monarchy) and with the need to defend "the country" regardless of and, if necessary, against "irresponsible" and "here today, gone tomorrow" politicians.

Given the already noted hierarchical character of these institutions, it would be more or less impossible for anyone who did not share this ideology and ethos, who was not "responsible" and "reliable", to be appointed to senior positions. In other words, everything we know about the nature of senior figures in the state suggests that they certainly could not be relied on simply to do the bidding of a left or radical government or to defend that government if it found itself in conflict with major national and international capitalist interests.

This is where we have to consider the nature and degree of challenge represented by our putative elected "left" government. Obviously this challenge can exist at many points on a spectrum, but broadly I would suggest there are four possible "scenarios".

First, the government offers only a very mild challenge to the system and the ruling class. It makes clear that it has no intention of trying to "overthrow" or "fundamentally transform" capitalism and that it completely accepts the established structures and rules of the existing state. All it aspires to is to run capitalism in a way that is somewhat more humane and more favourable to the lower orders. Second, the government does not attempt to end capitalism, even gradually, but is nonetheless committed to a policy or set of policies which the capitalist class considers seriously against its interests (for example outright opposition to austerity, or large scale disarmament and opposition to NATO membership). Third, behind or under the auspices of the government a mass movement is developing which the capitalist class fears and which it believes is in the process of getting out of control and moving in a revolutionary direction. Fourth, the elected left government really does want to bring about an end to capitalism and a transition to socialism and sets about introducing anti-capitalist measures.

In terms of historical experience the first scenario—very little real challenge—is, by far, predominant. This is the norm for the large majority of social democratic and labour governments in Britain, France, Germany, Spain, Italy, Greece, Scandinavia and elsewhere (which is precisely why they are now frequently thought of as "mainstream" rather than "left" and certainly not "radical left"). In these cases the government may come under pressure from the state apparatuses, sometimes very strong pressure, behind the scenes. But this pressure is often acceded to and publicly the appearance of business as usual, of the state as the politically neutral servant of the government, is maintained. At the opposite end of the spectrum, the scenario of a determined challenge to the very existence of capitalism by an elected left government is not just rare, but as far as I can see historically non-existent. I am speaking here of deeds not words, of course, but there is simply no example of a radical left government embarking on a serious legislative assault on the foundations of capitalism. How the state would respond to such a development must therefore remain a matter of speculation rather than hard fact, but we can get a pretty good idea from how it has responded to the second and third scenarios of which we do have historical examples.

One such example is the Curragh Mutiny in Ireland in 1914. Strictly speaking this occurred before the introduction of full universal suffrage (in 1918 and 1928) and was directed at a Liberal, not a left, government. Nevertheless it is a revealing episode. The Liberal government, led by Prime Minister Herbert Asquith, was in favour of granting Ireland Home Rule. The Ulster Unionists were vehemently opposed and created the paramilitary Ulster Volunteer Force (UVF) to resist. With Home Rule due to become law in 1914, the British Cabinet discussed military action against the Ulster Volunteers. Faced with this prospect, the officers of the British Army stationed at the Curragh, after consultation with senior officers in London, rebelled. Technically, they avoided the offence of mutiny by collectively resigning their commissions. Within three days the government capitulated and accepted there could be no action against the Ulster Volunteers. In the event Home Rule was shelved because of the outbreak of the First World War, but the Curragh incident had a lasting effect on British policy and paved the way for the partition of Ireland in 1921. It was a graphic illustration of the willingness of a key component of the state machine to act against the declared will of a "democratically" elected parliament and government.

Two even more telling examples are provided by Spain in 1936 and Chile in 1973. The Spanish Popular Front government took office on 16 February 1936, as a result of its general election victory. The Popular Front comprised two liberal (bourgeois) republican parties, the Spanish Socialist Party (a far left social democratic party), the Spanish Communist Party, a section of the anarcho-syndicalist CNT and the formerly Trotskyist and avowedly revolutionary Marxist, POUM. In itself this government had no plans to challenge or abolish capitalism in Spain but it came to power on the basis of six years of intense class struggle which included the overthrow of the Spanish monarchy in 1931 and the uprising of the Asturian miners in 1934.

To the Spanish ruling class this was unacceptable and it reacted in July 1936 by backing a fascist coup led by four generals including General Francisco Franco. The coup was mounted from within the Spanish state apparatus using the army. It succeeded in about half of Spain, while in the other half it was resisted by mass workers' action from below, with the workers effectively taking power in Barcelona and elsewhere. The country was thus split in two and the Spanish Civil War began. After three years of intense and bitter fighting the fascist forces, armed and assisted by Hitler and Mussolini, were triumphant. After their victory they exacted a terrible revenge slaughtering up to 200,000 of their opponents.

Chile in 1970 saw the election of the Popular Unity government led by Salvador Allende. Popular Unity resembled the Spanish Popular Front of the 1930s in that its core consisted of an alliance between the Communist Party and the Socialist Party (Allende was from the Socialist Party) with liberal Radicals. In office, Allende and Popular Unity pursued policies of limited nationalization, social reform and Keynesian economic expansion. They did not, however, challenge the Chilean state apparatus or military, hoping instead to win their support or at least to neutralize them. For a year or so the government's economic strategy seemed to be working—the economy grew and working class living standards were raised—but in 1972 Chile went into economic crisis and experienced raging inflation.

The Chilean working class responded to this with mass resistance in the form of major strikes and demonstrations and the organization of *cordones* (industrial coordinating networks), which were embryonic workers' councils, combined with demands that the pace of change should be speeded up. At the same time, the right increased their mobilisation against the movement and the government and began preparations for a coup. Allende temporized. 1973 saw two unsuccessful coup attempts but Allende still did not break with the military or arm the workers. On 11 September the infamous General Pinochet, whom Allende had made Commander-in-Chief of the Chilean Army on 23 August, staged a successful coup (with the backing of the United States) which claimed the lives of Allende himself and 30,000 Chileans, establishing a brutal military dictatorship that ruled Chile for 17 years.

From the point of view of this discussion, what is significant is that in both these cases the coups were led and executed by the military, ie from within the existing state apparatus, that showed itself quite willing to overrule the results of universal suffrage when it deemed this necessary "in the interests of the nation".

In view of this history, the recent threat of mutiny against a Jeremy Corbyn led Labour government by an anonymous serving general is a serious warning:

> A senior serving general has reportedly warned that a Jeremy Corbyn government could face "a mutiny" from the Army if it tried to downgrade them. The unnamed general said members of the armed forces would begin directly and publicly challenging the labour leader if he tried to scrap Trident, pull out of Nato or announce "any plans to emasculate and shrink the size of the armed forces.".... "The Army just wouldn't stand for it. The general staff would not allow a prime minister to jeopardise the security of this country and I think people would use whatever means possible, fair or foul to prevent that. You can't put a maverick in charge of a country's security. There would be mass resignations at all levels and you would face the very real prospect of an event which would effectively be a mutiny".[215]

We are told that this "anonymous" general had served in Northern Ireland (obviously the press, who were used to give wide publicity to this "leak", knew his identity) and the prediction of "mass resignations... which would effectively be a mutiny" directly evokes the tactic used in the Curragh a century ago.

For all these reasons—the influence of money and resources on the electoral process; the ideological hegemony of the bourgeoisie; the hierarchical, privileged and conservative character of the state apparatuses; and the clear historical experience—we can see that Lenin's (already quoted) description of the idea "that universal suffrage 'in the present-day state' is really capable of revealing the will of the majority of the working people and of securing its realization" as a "false notion"[216] still holds true today.

What is also clear is that the advent of universal suffrage has not changed or prevented the systematic use of the state machine—especially the police, courts, special agencies and, sometimes, the army—to harass and repress the working class and other oppressed people. This is very much the daily experience of working people whether they are in the Paris *banlieues*, the US ghettos and the estates of Clondalkin and Balleyfermot (working class communities in Dublin) and of strikers, demonstrators and protesters in every country. And even when it is not in anyway theorised or politically articulated, this experience produces a quite different attitude to the police (especially) and other state representatives in working class communities where they tend to be instinctively distrusted or even hated, as compared to the attitude in middle class communities where they are more often seen as protectors and allies.

Moreover, this everyday antagonism also regularly escalates, primarily at the behest of the ruling class, into atrocities, outrages, killings and even massacres. Historically speaking the examples of this are far too numerous to list. Nevertheless here are a few examples that spring immediately to mind and all of which occurred in "democracies" with universal suffrage: the slaughter of the Asturian miners in 1934 (5,000 killed); the behaviour of the CRS (the French riot police) towards French students in May 1968; the Chicago police riot in 1968; Bloody Sunday in Derry in 1972; the role of the British police in the Miners' Strike of 1984-1985; the behaviour of the Italian police in Genoa in 2001; the Marikana miners massacre in South Africa in 2012; and the killing on a daily basis of unarmed black people by US police in contemporary America.

The last two examples are particularly telling because they follow on the heels of "democratic" and anti-racist victories—the defeat of Apartheid in South Africa and the election of Barack Obama as the first Black US President—which, if democracy lived up to its name and the forces of the state were really subordinate to the electoral process, would have made such events unthinkable.

In sum, the class nature of the state in capitalist society is not changed in any *fundamental* way by the advent of universal suffrage.

The pluralist theory of power

The pluralist theory of power serves as a kind of sociological complement to the arguments that universal suffrage and the parliamentary system provide real democracy and the state serves all the people. Historically it has its roots in the work of the "elite theorists" such as Vilfredo Pareto (1848-1923), Gaetano Mosca (1858-1941) and Robert

Michels (1876-1936) who, at the beginning of the 20th century, rejected any possibility of equality or a classless society in favour of the view that social inequality and hierarchy were part of human nature and saw history as an unending struggle between different elites. Elite theory in its original form had clear affinities with fascism, especially Italian fascism, in that if democracy and equality were illusions the best that could be achieved was rule by a strong, vigorous, dynamic elite.

After the Second World War elite theory was subject to a development and revision known as "elite pluralism", or "pluralism" for short, that rendered it more compatible with democracy. Through the work of political scientists and sociologists such as Robert A Dahl, Arnold Rose and Raymond Aron, it emerged in the 1950s and 1960s as the hegemonic theory of power and the state in academic social science. Moreover, it remains to this day the perspective underlying much media coverage of politics and current affairs.

Pluralism does not make any simple claim that universal suffrage delivered "rule by the people". Rather it maintains that all social and political life is dominated by elites but that what exists in "liberal" Western societies is not a single elite or ruling class but a plurality of separate elites such as the legal elite, the financial elite, the industrial elite, the military elite, the media elite, the medical elite, the trade union elite and so on. Rather than working in concert these different elites compete with one another for influence and in this process of competition it is the function of government and state to act as an "honest broker" between these groups, ensuring no single one achieves undue dominance. Government becomes, as Raymond Aron (and many others) put it, "a business of compromise".

In this scheme of things the fact that the government is elected by popular vote in free elections doesn't produce direct popular rule but it allows for a kind of limited negative democracy which rules out extremes or dictatorship and enables the people to choose between different packages of elite influence within a more or less stable system. In pluralist thinking an important role is played by mass political parties and major "interest" or "pressure" groups.

Dahl, probably the best known proponent of pluralism, claims that this produces a political system in which "all the active and legitimate groups in the population can make themselves heard at some crucial stage in the process of decision" and:

There are a number of loci for arriving at political decisions; that business men, trade unions, politicians, consumers, farmers, voters and many other aggregates all have an impact on policy outcomes; that none of these aggregates is homogeneous for all purposes; that each of them is highly influential over some scopes but weal over many others; and that the power to reject undesired alternatives is more common than the power to dominate over outcomes directly.[217]

Clearly this analysis stands in complete contrast to Lenin's view that "Bourgeois states are most varied in form, but...in the final analysis are inevitably *the dictatorship of the bourgeoisie*", but it fitted extremely well with the needs of Western Cold War ideology in terms of the opposition that was then constructed in academic social science between "pluralism" (us) and "totalitarianism" (them).[218] It also closely corresponds to the way politics appeared and still appears today from the vantage point of the US Congress or the House of Commons and the newsrooms of the BBC or other "impartial" state broadcasters.

Despite its prevalence the pluralist theory is easily rebutted from a Marxist standpoint.[219] First, operating in its own terms, it is evident that even if we accept the notion of competing elites these elites are very far from equal in power or influence. Some, most obviously the financial and industrial elites (the banks and major corporations), have immensely more wealth, resources and power than others, say the trade union elite (trade union officials) or the medical elite (consultants and hospital managers). Moreover we can see that the basis of this disparity is class. It is the respective class positions of top bankers and industrialists (members of the capitalist class proper—the 1%) that give them so much more power than trade union officials or doctors.

Secondly, the large majority of members of almost all the elites (with the exception of trade union officials) are drawn from similar upper class backgrounds, went to similar predominantly upper class educational establishments (Eton, Winchester, Oxford, Cambridge, Yale, Harvard, the Ecole Normale Superior and so on) and mix in similar social circles. And to rise to their elite positions they are extremely likely to have to hold political and social attitudes which fall within a fairly restricted range (roughly right wing conservative to right wing social democrat with a strong bias towards the former).

Third, these considerations, which apply to almost all the elite members except the trade unions, also apply overwhelmingly to the senior figures in the state apparatus and most top politicians—as I have shown in the previous section on universal suffrage.

Fourth, and most important of all, all the rival elites are governed by the same economic logic of capitalist competition (competitive capital accumulation) which also governs the behaviour of the government and the state, even when the government members and the state managers do not happen to be drawn from the capitalist class.

Once again the only significant exception to this is the "elite" of the trade union movement which, even if its leaders and officials are highly paid compared to their members and have "soft" jobs which erode their militancy, nevertheless represent (albeit often unsatisfactorily) a different and opposed class interest. It is a feature of pluralist theory that reveals its apologetic character that it masks this distinction between trade unions and other interest groups, passing them off as similar in character.[220]

Finally, it is true that sometimes different elites compete with one another for influence and occasionally clash, but this no more contradicts the fact that they are different fractions of the same dominant class than the competition between BP and Shell or Toyota and Volkswagen prevents their shareholders and CEOs being members of the same bourgeoisie. And when the state and government mediates between these rivals and competitors it is acting not as an "honest broker" between them and "society as a whole" but between them on behalf of *the capitalist class* as a whole. As Marx put it, "The executive of the modern state is but a committee for managing the common affairs of the whole bourgeoisie."

The Foucault critique

If the argument about universal suffrage is the dominant argument against the Leninist view of the state in mainstream political discourse, a different argument has been particularly influential in the academic world in recent decades and has also found a resonance in various forms of left practice. This is the theory of and approach to power derived from the work of Michel Foucault. It could also be called the Foucault-Nietzsche-anarchist critique because it has its philosophical roots in Nietzsche and because in terms of its influence on political practice it has often been associated with anarchist or autonomist currents.

It is, for a number of reasons, not easy to deal with this critique within the framework of this study. Foucault never presented his position "systematically" and certainly not in any set piece critique of Lenin. Rather, it emerges as an inference from a number of his historical studies of the clinic, the prison and so on with the anti-Leninist conclusions being drawn mainly by other hands. As for its Nietzschean roots, they are largely implicit rather than explicit and since they constitute a profound challenge not just to the Leninist theory of the state but to Marxism and even socialism as a whole, they call for a much more wide-ranging debate than is possible here. Finally, when it comes to anarchist/autonomist practice (or grassroots reformist practice) it is obvious that Foucault is only one influence among many, ranging from Bakunin and Kropotkin to John Holloway and Hardt and Negri). Nevertheless the argument is important and needs to be addressed.

Foucault differs sharply from Nietzsche in terms of his political sympathies, which were radical and on the side of the oppressed rather than aristocratic and elitist. Nevertheless there is a real link in terms of Nietzsche's theory of "the will to power" which provides a foundation for Foucault's insistence on the primacy and ubiquity of power struggles and their independence from economics. For Nietzsche the will to power was the driving force of all human behaviour and history, if not of the universe:

> My idea is that every specific body strives to become master over all space and to extend its force (its will to power) and to thrust back all that resists its extension. But it continually encounters similar efforts on the part of other bodies and ends by coming to an arrangement ("union") with those of them that are sufficiently related to it; thus they then conspire together for power. And the process goes on.[221]
>
> [Anything which] is a living and not a dying body...will have to be an incarnate will to power, it will strive to grow, spread, seize, become predominant—not from any morality or immorality but because it is *living and because life simply is will to power.*[222]

Three short observations on this perspective: a) as it stands in Nietzsche it is simply an assertion, unsupported and untested by any evidence; b) if it is true, it rules out the possibility of human, or proletarian, liberation, offering the prospect only of an endless series of struggles in which oppressor and oppressed from time to time switch places; and c) within the theory there is no reason to side with the oppressed, indeed it would seem more logical to side with the oppressor as Nietzsche generally did.

The essence of the Foucault-based critique is that, contrary to Lenin (as he is often, but wrongly, understood), power is not concentrated in the state or state machine but is everywhere in society: in the school, the office, the prison, the hospital, etc. Power is not a "thing" which can be seized or smashed; it is a social relation embodied in "dividing practices...examples are the mad and the sane, the sick and the healthy, the criminals and the "good boys". What is needed, therefore, is:

> [A] new economy of power relations, a way which is more empirical, more directly related to our present situation, and which implies more relations between theory and practice. It consists of taking the forms of resistance against different forms of power as a starting point. To use another metaphor, it consists of using this resistance as a chemical catalyst so as to bring to light power relations, locate their position, and find out their point of application and the methods used. Rather than analyzing power from the point of view of its internal rationality, it consists of analyzing power relations through the antagonism of strategies.
>
> For example, to find out what our society means by sanity, perhaps we should investigate what is happening in the field of insanity.
>
> And what we mean by legality in the field of illegality.
>
> And, in order to understand what power relations are about, perhaps we should investigate the forms of resistance and attempts made to dissociate these relations.
>
> As a starting point, let us take a series of oppositions which have developed over the last few years: opposition to the power of men over women, of parents over children, of psychiatry over the mentally ill, of medicine over the population, of administration over the ways people live.[223]

This theoretical approach, this methodology, implies, despite Foucault's refusal of the role of "leader" or "strategist", a definite practical strategy, "Every power relationship implies, at least *in potentia*, a strategy of struggle". And the strategy is precisely to focus on the "series of oppositions" listed above, more or less as ends in themselves:

> The aim of these struggles is the power effects as such. For example, the medical profession is not criticized primarily because it is a profit-making concern but because it exercises an uncontrolled power over people's bodies, their health, and their life and death...

> To sum up, the main objective of these struggles is to attack not so
> much "such or such" an institution of power, or group, or elite, or class
> but rather a technique, a form of power.[224]

Out of these various struggles it is hoped that the *episteme* (dominant system of "power-knowledge") of the age will be fundamentally
transformed.

In responding to Foucault it should be stated clearly that his historical studies yield numerous insights of value to socialists and
revolutionaries (for example on the question of mental illness). What I
want to contest is not the value of his researches but the counter-position of his analysis of power to that of Marx and Lenin and the idea that
the strategy deriving from this constitutes a viable alternative to the
Leninist strategy of smashing the capitalist state.

The first thing to say is that the Foucault-based critique seems to rest
on a misreading or misunderstanding of Marx and Lenin. Neither Marx
nor Lenin viewed the state or the state machine as a "thing" or "instrument", like a gun or a motor car, as opposed to a relation between
people. The fact that Lenin stresses the impossibility of "taking over the
state" and the need to smash it shows this because "things" or instruments like guns and motor cars clearly can and will be taken over by the
working class and wielded for their own purposes. The Leninist strategy
for smashing the state also shows it because it is a strategy of dismantling
the core of the state apparatus, its "armed bodies of men", by creating a
class split in the army, turning the rank and file against the officers and
winning them over to the revolution. Moreover, the aim is to replace the
capitalist state apparatus with a new state apparatus characterised by
radically different power relations between people—democratic election, recallability, workers' pay and so on.

Secondly neither Lenin nor Marx thought that state power was the
only or even main form of power in society. On the contrary, the
essence of their theory was that state power, for all its relative autonomy, was ultimately an expression of class power the basis of which lay
in control of the means and process of production. Consequently the
observation that there are power relations in, for example, every workplace (and hospitals, clinics, schools, offices and prisons are all
workplaces) is hardly news to Lenin or any serious Marxist. The real
difference between Foucault and Lenin/Marx here is that Foucault

sees, for example, the power of medical consultants not just as relatively autonomous but as completely separate from the capitalist economy and the capitalist state: "the medical profession is not criticized primarily because it is a profit-making concern but because it exercises an uncontrolled power over people's bodies". And on this Foucault is surely wrong. There is a clear and demonstrable connection (both in terms of personnel and function) between the power position and behaviour of, to name but a few, hospital directors and consultants, prison governors, head teachers, office managers and university principals, and the class power and requirements of the bourgeoisie.

Moreover, recognition of the existence of power in a multitude of locations and institutions does not make all these centres of power equal in degree or importance. Clearly the power of a schoolteacher over her pupils or a doctor in relation to her patients is real, but it is in no way comparable to the power of the state machine, especially—and this is the key strategic point—when it comes to dealing with a mass working class movement. It was not a cabal of doctors and psychiatrists who crushed the Paris Commune, handed power to Hitler, broke the Asturias miners' strike and defeated the Spanish Revolution, overthrew Allende's Popular Unity government, shot down unarmed protesters in Derry or broke the million-strong movement in Tiananmen Square. It was, respectively, the French, German, Spanish, Chilean, British and Chinese state forces. The reason for Lenin's intense focus on the state in *The State and Revolution* was because after three years of world war and in the midst of a revolution the question of the state had become the main question of the day as he, himself, spelt out in the Preface to that work:

> The question of the state is now acquiring particular importance both in theory and in practical politics... The world proletarian revolution is clearly maturing. The question of its relation to the state is acquiring practical importance.

And again:

> The question of the relation of the socialist proletarian revolution to the state, therefore, is acquiring not only practical political importance, but also the significance of a most urgent problem of the day, the problem of explaining to the masses what they will have to do before long to free themselves from capitalist tyranny.[225]

In terms of its practical and strategic implications Foucault's theory of power points towards and seems to fit with both identity-based politics and local community campaigns. In such contexts it can supply these campaigns with a wider "revolutionary" or "anarchist" gloss while at the same time dovetailing with a kind of do-it-yourself reformism. Where it fits much less well is with national trade union struggles, national and international anti-war movements, the global question of climate change and, above all, any kind of mass revolutionary situation in all of which the issue of government/state power is unavoidably central. In practice, therefore, the role of a Foucault-influenced strategy is most likely to be that of adjunct or subordinate element within an overarching reformism.

Anarchist and autonomist critiques

Ever since Bakunin clashed with Marx in the First International in the mid-19th century, anarchists have critiqued Marxists as authoritarian and "statist" and there is no Marxist about whom these objections have been so vigorously made as Lenin. The essence of the anarchist position has been and remains opposition to all forms of government and state on principle. As Bakunin put it:

> With the cry of peace for the workers, liberty for all the oppressed and death to rulers, exploiters and guardians of all kinds, we seek to destroy all states and all churches along with all their institutions and laws, religious, political, juridical, financial, police, university, economic and social, so that the millions of deceived, enslaved, tormented and exploited human beings, liberated from all their directors and benefactors, official and officious, collective and individual may breathe at last with complete freedom.[226]

And:

> We do not accept, even for the purposes of a revolutionary transition, national conventions, constituent assemblies, provisional governments, or so-called revolutionary dictatorships.[227]

Thus anarchists vehemently rejected Lenin's insistence on the need for a new workers' state, the "dictatorship of the proletariat", to replace the capitalist state.

There are philosophical affinities between the classical anarchist identification of power as such as the root of all evil and the Nietzsche/ Foucault view referred to above, with the difference that anarchists place a minus sign where Nietzsche places a plus. But where Lenin's theory of the state and questions of revolutionary strategy are concerned the central issue is this: is it possible for the working class and revolutionaries, not in relation to the classless society of the future, but in the midst of and immediate aftermath of revolution to renounce all use of state power or would this be a recipe for defeat?

The fundamental problem with the anarchist position is that the class struggle, which has formed the material basis for the existence of states for at least 5,000 years, does not cease in the face of a successful workers' uprising in one city or one country. On the contrary, as the history of all revolutions shows, it continues with great intensity as the international capitalist class attempts to roll back and undermine the revolution. How can these attempts be resisted and the construction of a socialist economy be embarked upon without the aid of a state apparatus: that is, without special bodies of armed men and women (militia/ red guards/prisons/courts of justice, etc) and without state ownership and administration of key industries and services (transport, health, education, welfare and so on)?

There are numerous anarchist critiques of Leninist and Bolshevik authoritarianism but very few anarchist attempts to answer these basic and simple questions. One example is by Alexander Berkman, who was in Russia between 1919 and 1921, in his primer *What is Communist Anarchism?* which concludes with a chapter on "Defense of the Revolution".

Berkman argues that the revolution must be defended "by armed force...if necessary", but:

> [T]he social revolution must be Anarchistic in method as in aim. Revolutionary defense must be in consonance with this spirit. Self-defense excludes all acts of coercion, of persecution or revenge. It is concerned only with repelling attack and depriving the enemy of the opportunity to invade you.

> How would foreign invasion be resisted?

> By the strength of the revolution. In what does that strength consist? First and foremost in the support of the people, in the devotion of the

industrial and agricultural masses... Let them believe in the revolution and they will defend it to the death...

The armed workers and peasants are the only effective defense of the revolution... By means of their unions and syndicates they must always be on guard against counter-revolutionary attack. The worker in factory and mill, in mine and field, is the soldier of the revolution. He is at his bench or plough or on the battlefield according to need.[228]

Berkman repeats this idea again and again:

Understand well that the only really effective defense of the revolution lies in the attitude of the people...the strength of the revolution is organic not mechanistic... Let the people feel that it is indeed their own cause which is at stake and the last man of them will fight like a lion in its behalf.[229]

These noble sentiments are, of course, at some level true but as an argument *against* the need for a workers' state they are seriously unconvincing. The first paragraph quoted contains a distinction between self-defence and "coercion" which is unsustainable in a revolution or civil war. Any revolution, if it is to be successful, must engage in a degree of coercion both in the act of insurrection itself and in the transition period that follows it.

In general Berkman's argument resembles that of naïve and idealistic would-be revolutionaries who say, "If everyone in the country went on strike the government would be forced to give in, so its obvious we call a general strike tomorrow". Of course if every worker is a "soldier of the revolution...at his bench or plough or on the battlefield according to need", then there would indeed be no problem. Unfortunately the experience of every struggle, every strike and every revolution is that the consciousness and commitment of the working class and, more broadly, of "the people" develops unevenly. If no workers ever scabbed on strikes there would be no need for picket lines. If no workers ever served in the police or army or fought for the counter-revolution there would be no need for barricades or workers' militia and if all the revolutionary workers simply arrived "on the battlefield according to need" without a party or state to organise this, then revolution would be a very easy and simple matter.

Berkman shows some awareness of the problem when he writes,

"The military defense of the revolution may demand a supreme command, coordination of activities, discipline and obedience of orders". But he doesn't think this through or realise that this precisely implies the need for a state apparatus. Rather, he falls back, again, on vague formulae about these (the supreme command, obedience to orders, etc) proceeding "from the devotion of the workers and peasants".[230]

An interesting parallel with Alexander Berkman is provided by the Organisational Platform of the Libertarian Communists, the founding document of so-called Platform Anarchism written by Nestor Makhno and others, on the basis of the actual experience of the Russian Revolution. The social revolution, they say:

> which threatens the privileges and the very existence of the non-working classes of society, will inevitably provoke a desperate resistance on behalf of these classes, which will take the form of a fierce civil war... As in all wars, the civil war cannot be waged by the labourers with success unless they apply the two fundamental principles of all military action: unity in the plan of operations and unity of common command...

Thus, in view of the necessities imposed by military strategy and also the strategy of the counter-revolution, the armed forces of the revolution should inevitably be based on a *general revolutionary army with a common command and plan of operations.* [231] [my emphasis]

Here, too, on the basis of the Russian experience, ie the experience of a real revolution, anarchists have conceded the essence of the Marxist argument for a workers' state. They deny this saying they reject "the principle of authority...and the state" but their denial is in vain. Like it or not, a revolutionary workers' army "with a common command" implies a state, just as it implies a certain amount of "authority". No amount of word play will get round this.

If post-revolution civil war poses this question most sharply, it is nevertheless the case that the same arguments apply to post-revolution running of the economy. Certainly if the whole "community" or "all the people" or even all of the workers and lower middle classes of the nation (or the world) were completely united and equal in their consciousness and devotion to the libertarian socialist/anarchist cause, there would be no call for a state. Indeed full communism could be established immediately. But in reality this is not going to be the case and operating even something as basic as the railways will require that, as well as being run under workers' control, it is "owned" by a national authority—the workers' state. The only alternative would be that each enterprise (each railway station or section of track) would be owned by its workforce, but this would invite disunity and competition between enterprises and clearly be a recipe for disaster.

Another variant of the anarchist critique—one associated with autonomist currents, such as that around Toni Negri—was presented by John Holloway in his 2002 book *Change the World Without Taking Power*. Basing himself in part on the experience of the Zapatistas in Mexico and partly on tendencies in the post-Seattle anti-capitalist movement, Holloway argues that focusing on the state has been the fundamental weakness of the socialist movement, reformist and revolutionary alike who "despite all their differences, both aim at the winning of state power". The whole idea of capturing state power is wrong because state apparatuses are integrally tied to authoritarian capitalist social relations and so "capturing" them would result in replicating the oppression the movement was trying to overcome:

> The orthodox Marxist tradition, most clearly the Leninist tradition, conceives of revolution instrumentally, as a means to an end. The problem with this approach is that it subordinates the infinite richness of struggle, which is important precisely because it is a struggle for infinite richness, to the single aim of taking power. In doing so, it inevitably reproduces power-over (the subordination of the struggles to the Struggle) and ensures continuity rather than the rupture that is sought. Instrumentalism means engaging with capital on capital's own terms, accepting that our own world can come into being only after the revolution. But capital's terms are not simply a given, they are an active process of separating. It is absurd, for example, to think that the struggle against the separating of doing can lie through the state, since the very existence of the state as a form of social relations is an active separating of doing. To struggle through the state is to become involved in the active process of defeating yourself.[232]

Instead of focusing on the state, Holloway proposes developing non-capitalist social relations in the here and now in "autonomous" spaces, such as the Zapatista liberated zone in Chiapas in southern Mexico. The Occupy movement, as it developed in the United States and elsewhere in 2011, came long after Holloway's book but there are obvious parallels in terms of the strategy pursued—the establishment, albeit in city centre squares as opposed to the remote jungle, of autonomous spaces.

As a theoretical critique of Leninism Holloway's work suffers from a major defect in that in assimilating Leninism to social democracy and reformism on the basis that they all aim at capturing the state he fails to even register the crucial distinction, absolutely central, as we have seen, to *The State and Revolution*, that the capitalist state is not to be taken over or "captured" but smashed. Consequently Holloway's argument that Lenin and Leninists do not recognise how embedded the state is in capitalist social relations misses its mark.

Occupying spaces, whether in Chiapas or Tahrir Square, Puerto Del Sol or Wall St, can play an important role in the revolutionary struggle, but posing it as an *alternative* to the struggle for state power (that is, the struggle to smash the capitalist state and establish a workers' state) is a false strategy. These occupations are or can be hugely inspirational but what they do not do is establish any sort of control over society's main productive forces or accumulations of wealth and thus, in themselves, they are not able to transform economic and social relations of production. Moreover, even if such a strategy aims at avoiding confronting or trying to defeat the state this does not mean that the state will ignore or tolerate the "occupiers". Of course, it may do so for a while, especially if it judges it best to allow the movement to run out of steam. But, sooner or later, if it is not "smashed", the state will use its bodies of armed men to reclaim the "autonomous spaces", as it did with the Occupy movement and with Tahrir Square.

Gramsci versus Lenin?

Incarcerated by Mussolini, the great Italian Marxist, Antonio Gramsci, embarked on an analysis of the causes of the defeat, in the period 1919-1922, of the Italian Revolution and of the revolution in Europe, compared to its success in Russia. Gramsci had played an important role in this revolution as acknowledged intellectual leader of the workers of Turin and of the workers' councils movement and he emerged in 1921 as a founder of the Italian Communist Party (PCI).

His reflections were many sided. They included a philosophical critique of the passive fatalistic and economic determinist Marxism of the Second International and of the Italian Socialist Party in particular (which, he believed underpinned its disastrous failure to act at decisive moments in the struggle) and of what he saw as the mechanical materialism of Bukharin's book on historical materialism, along with a rejection of the rigid ultra-leftism of the early PCI leader Amadeo Bordiga, who saw little difference between fascism and bourgeois democracy, and numerous observations and insights into the dynamics of Italian history. He also made the following observation about the difference between the social structure of Russia and of the West:

> In Russia the State was everything, civil society was primordial and gelatinous; in the West, there was a proper relation between State and civil society, and when the State trembled a sturdy structure of civil society was at once revealed. The State was only an outer ditch, behind which there stood a powerful system of fortresses and earthworks.[233]

This difference necessitated, Gramsci argued, a strategic shift from emphasis on what he called "the war of manoeuvre" to emphasis on "the war of position".[234] This was a military analogy referring to the change in the First World War from armies moving across country to engage in set piece battles to long drawn out trench warfare. What exactly this meant in terms of political strategy was never systematically explained by Gramsci and remains highly debateable, but scattered comments suggest: a) that it implied a rejection of the idea that (after 1921) an immediate insurrectionary offensive or conquest of power was on the cards;[235] b) that the balance of party work between propaganda and agitation needed to alter in the direction of propaganda so as to create a substantial layer of organic worker intellectuals;[236] c) that to "become the leading and ruling class" the proletariat must create "a system of class alliances which enables it mobilise the majority of the working population against capitalism and the bourgeois state";[237] and d) that it implied a long drawn out war of attrition or "reciprocal siege" demanding "immense sacrifices" and therefore requiring an "unprecedented concentration of hegemony".[238]

The concept of hegemony, cited here, is by no means exclusive or original to Gramsci,[239] but it is, of course, particularly associated with him. Its precise meaning or interpretation is part of the debate we are about to embark on but for the moment let's say simply that it means leadership or dominance, and especially ideological or moral leadership, in relation to class struggle and the ability of a ruling class (or a revolutionary would-be ruling class) to win widespread acceptance of its rule/leadership as legitimate or inevitable.

What makes it necessary to consider these Gramscian themes here is that over the last 40 or 50 years they have been repeatedly made the point of departure for an analysis of the state and a political strategy that has been explicitly anti-Leninist in that it has rejected any notion of insurrection or (violent) revolution, any goal of "smashing the state", in favour of a perspective which puts far more emphasis on the role of ideological hegemony than it does on force in securing capitalist rule and replaces the notion of any decisive confrontation with the state with a strategy of gradual transformation of the state and society by means of a "long march through the institutions" of civil society.

The two main arenas within which this allegedly Gramscian perspective, which I shall call Gramscism, was developed were the left of academia, where Gramsci was immensely popular not to say "hegemonic" and, in terms of practical politics, the European Communist Parties or Eurocommunism as it came to be known. In Britain an important role was played by the Communist Party of Great Britain's theoretical journal *Marxism Today*, whose most important intellectual figures were Eric Hobsbawm and Stuart Hall.[240] In Europe, key proponents were the Italian Communist Party (PCI) and the Spanish Communist Party under the leadership of Enrico Berlinguer and Santiago Carillo, respectively.[241] In all these cases, Gramscian terminology was adopted within a political framework and perspective which was already, and had been for many years, explicitly reformist, in the sense of being committed to a peaceful parliamentary road to socialism. Moreover, it was generally employed to legitimate, even within that reformist framework, a significant shift towards the political centre, including the PCI's "historic compromise" with Christian Democracy and *Marxism Today*'s advocacy of "New Times" and a deal between the Labour Party and the Social Democrats.

An idea of the distance travelled from classical Leninism in the name of Gramsci is indicated in this claim by Ernesto Laclau and Chantal Mouffe:

> From the Leninist concept of class alliances to the Gramscian concept of "intellectual and moral" leadership, there is an increasing extension of hegemonic tasks, to the extent that for Gramsci social agents are

not classes but "collective wills"... There is, then, an internal movement of Marxist thought from extreme essentialist forms—those of Plekhanov, for example—to Gramsci's conception of social practices as hegemonic and articulatory, which virtually places us in the field, explored in contemporary thought, of "language games" and the "logic of the signifier".[242]

Historically and theoretically this whole attempt to enlist Gramsci's undoubted insights for anti-Leninist and reformist purposes has been subject to severe and, indeed compelling criticism by, amongst others, Chris Harman, Ernest Mandel and Peter Thomas.[243] What follows is a brief summary of the case against Gramscism.

Gramscism rests, first and foremost, on a radical distortion and misuse of the historical Gramsci. Gramsci was a thoroughgoing revolutionary who split from the Italian Socialist Party to found the PCI in 1921 on an explicitly Leninist basis. In *The Lyons Theses* of 1926, Gramsci's last major work before his imprisonment, he unequivocally reaffirmed his Leninism, writing:

> The transformation of the communist parties...into Bolshevik parties can be considered the fundamental task of the Communist International.[244]
>
> There is no possibility of a revolution in Italy which is not a socialist revolution...the only class which can accomplish a real, deep social transformation is the working class.[245]
>
> It's [the PCI's] fundamental task...to place before the proletariat and its allies the problem of insurrection against the bourgeois state and of the struggle for proletarian dictatorship...[246]
>
> The Communist Party links every immediate demand to a revolutionary objective; makes use of every partial struggle to teach the masses the need for general action and for insurrection...[247]

The whole Gramscist appropriation of Gramsci is therefore predicated on the notion that he abandoned this revolutionary and insurrectionist perspective while in prison. No biographical evidence has ever been presented to prove or even seriously support such a notion. Rather, Gramscism has rested on exploiting the ambiguous and, often opaque, formulations to be found in the *Prison Notebooks*, disregarding the known fact that Gramsci adopted this "Aesopian" language in order to deceive the prison authorities. But even here what Gramsci actually writes contradicts the reformist interpretation put on it.

Gramsci writes of the war of manoeuvre and the war of position but they are both forms of [class] *war*. He writes that, "the supremacy of a social group manifests itself in two ways, as 'domination' and as 'intellectual and moral leadership'".[248] In the analysis of the "relation of forces" in a particular conjuncture he identifies three "moments or levels":

> 1. A relation of forces which is closely linked to the structure independent of human will…the level of development of the material forces of production [which] provides a basis for the emergence of the various social classes… 2…the relation of political forces; in other words…the degree of homogeneity, self-awareness and organisation attained by the various social classes… 3…the relation of military forces which from time to time is directly decisive.[249]

And he says, "Historical development continually oscillates between the first and the third moment, with the mediation of the second".[250] He calls for a "dual perspective" involving "force and consent, authority and hegemony, violence and civilisation".[251]

In the face of this repeated emphasis on the *combination*, ie dialectical interaction, of force and consent, domination and moral leadership, economic structure, politics and military force, the proponents of Gramscism have one-sidedly abstracted and emphasised "hegemony" or ideological leadership in such a way as to minimise or disappear altogether the role of both economic struggle (strikes, etc) and revolutionary insurrection to smash the state and thus counterpose Gramsci to Lenin.

Equally erroneous has been their tendency to treat pre-Gramscian Marxism—the Marxism of Marx and Engels, Lenin, Luxemburg and Trotsky—as if it was generally characterised by crude mechanical economism and an emphasis on physical force with little or no awareness of the role of ideology—as if, in other words, *The German Ideology*, *The Eighteenth Brumaire* and Engels's late letters on historical materialism had not been written; as if Lenin, Luxemburg and Trotsky had not read them and not written their own non-economistic texts such as *What is to be Done?* and *The History of the Russian Revolution*;[252] and as if the concept of hegemony had not been in common usage in the Bolshevik Party. By contrast Gramsci himself more than once referred to Lenin as the originator and developer of the concept of hegemony.[253]

Instead of Gramsci's insights and observations on the question of hegemony constituting an alternative to, or critique of, Lenin's theory of the state and revolution, as the proponents of Gramscism have suggested, it is clear that Gramsci himself saw them as a supplement or addition to Leninism, a development of Leninism on the basis of Leninism itself. This is evidenced not only by Gramsci's invariably favourable references to Lenin as the "last great theoretician" and so on, but also quite explicitly in the statement "the greatest modern theoretician of the philosophy of praxis...constructed the doctrine of hegemony as a complement to the theory of the State-as-force".[254]

But leaving aside these textual and historical debates about Gramsci's relation to Lenin, what is abundantly clear is that the contemporary capitalist class maintains its rule/dominance/hegemony by a complex combination of ideological consent and physical force both of which rest upon and also reinforce its economic power. Take for example two basic ideas which are essential to bourgeois hegemony, respect for (capitalist) property and respect for the (capitalist) law. Both these ideas are systematically promulgated by the education system, the media, the church and many other institutions and, in normal times, are widely accepted by most, though not all, working class people. But they are both continuously backed up by force; by the police, courts, prisons and so on. How long would respect for property and the law survive if this were not so, if it were possible to defy the law with impunity? Conversely it is also evident that capitalist rule which rested on pure force alone with no ideological consent would be incredibly vulnerable.

In reality the balance between force and consent is continually shifting. Most of the time, and especially in periods of relative social peace, the element of consent is to the fore, with force remaining in the background. But this does not mean that force has lost its importance because as consent starts to break down the use of force can increase and then predominate.

Consequently a strategy, such as that proposed by the proponents of Gramscism, which focuses entirely on the struggle for ideological hegemony and ignores the question of force, of the need to smash the capitalist state, is in reality a reversion to pre-Leninist reformism and deeply irresponsible. It is akin to marching one's army into battle with no plan of action should the enemy actually open fire.

A further question which has to be considered in relation to Gramsci's ideas is the extent to which it is possible to build socialist counter hegemony within and under capitalism, ie before the conquest of political power. I will return to this important strategic question in later chapters.

Carrillo, Poulantzas and Eurocommunism

The last alternative to Lenin's theory of the state that I shall address is that of the Spanish Communist Party leader Santiago Carrillo and the Greek-French theorist Nicos Poulantzas, who between them most clearly developed the Eurocommunist position on the state. What makes them particularly relevant today is their influence on Syriza in Greece.

Whereas the "Gramscist" project involved a serious misrepresentation of Gramsci, Carrillo, in his landmark 1977 work *Eurocommunism and the State*, made no secret of his departure "from some of Lenin's theses" which "are out of date".[255] At the start of the book Carrillo speaks of "the revolutionary movement" and "the revolutionary process" and insists that "the State apparatus as a whole continues to be the instrument of the ruling class... This is a Marxist truth".[256] But as the book develops he progressively strips away and discards all the revolutionary conclusions that Lenin (and Marx) drew from this "truth".

Carrillo takes as his point of departure Louis Althusser's famous essay on "Ideology and Ideological State Apparatuses"[257] (along with the kind of interpretation of Gramsci already discussed) and argues that:

> *The strategy of revolutions of today, in the developed capitalist countries, must be oriented to turning these ideological apparatuses round, to transform them and utilise them—if not wholly then partly—against the State power of monopoly capitalism.*[258] [Italics in original]

He then insists that "modern experience has shown that this is possible" and discusses in turn each of Althusser's ideological state apparatuses (the church, the education system, the family, the law, politics and the media) claiming that in each there are observable signs of change and division (this was in 1976) which make their progressive transformation possible. As evidence he sights the emergence of modernising and radical forces within the Catholic Church, the fact that " Today the universities and educational centres...frequently become centres of opposition to capitalist society",[259] the crisis and transformation of the traditional family and so on.

These accounts are followed by the claim, directly citing Althusser, that:

> So far as we know, no class can maintain state power in a lasting form without exercising at the same time its hegemony over and within the State ideological apparatuses.[260]

Consequently, he maintains, this "capture" of the ideological state apparatuses will open the way to winning over the coercive apparatuses of the state and he holds out a vision of a modernised democratic army acting as "an intellectual educator of men skilled in protecting territory from outside attack"[261] rather than as an instrument of class rule. This does away with the need for insurrection and "the dictatorship of the proletariat" (workers' power and a workers' state) in favour of a "democratic", ie parliamentary and gradual road to socialism.

Nicos Poulantzas's *State, Power, Socialism* was published in 1978, a year after Carrillo's work. It begins with a critique of the proposition that Carrillo had called "a Marxist truth", namely that the state is an "instrument of the ruling class". Poulantzas states that, "There is certainly no general theory of the state to be found in the Marxist classics"[262] and rejects the "purely instrumental conception of the State" (which he also calls "the traditional mechanistic-economist conception")[263] which he describes as "bequeathed by Stalinist dogmatism".[264] Rather than seeing the state as an "instrument" he defines it as "the *specific material* condensation of a relation of class forces among classes and class fractions".[265]

However, this formulation, which at first appears more "sophisticated" and "advanced" than that of Carrillo (or Lenin), is deployed by Poulantzas to arrive at very much the same conclusions as Carrillo. The conception of the state as a condensation of class forces develops into the proposition that "*[t]he establishment of the State's policy must be seen a the result of class contradictions inscribed in the very structure of the State*" and the notion of "*contradictory relations enmeshed within the State*",[266] so that the state must also be grasped as "a strategic field and process of intersecting power networks".[267] This, in turn, leads to the notion that "the struggle of the dominated classes" is present "within the State" and that "popular struggles traverse the State from top to bottom".[268]

As a result, Poulantzas argues, the possibility exists that on the basis of a shift in the balance of class forces and major popular struggles it will be possible to "transform" the state rather than smash it. He writes of "a long stage during which the masses will act to conquer and transform the state apparatuses"[269] and that:

> For state power to be taken, a mass struggle must have unfolded in such a way as to modify the relationship of forces within the state apparatuses, themselves the strategic site of political struggle.[270]

Moreover, this strategy is directly counterposed to the Leninist strategy of dual power leading to the replacement of the old state machine by soviet power:

> For a dual power-type of strategy, however, the decisive shift in the relationship of forces takes place not within the State but between the State and the masses outside. In the democratic road to socialism, the long process of taking power essentially consists in the spreading, development, reinforcement, coordination and direction of those diffuse centres of resistance which the masses always possess within the state networks, in such a way that they become the real centres of power on the strategic terrain of the State.[271]

In response to these Eurocommunist perspectives the first thing to note is that nothing remotely approaching Carrillo's projected left hegemonic transformation of *any* of the "ideological state apparatuses" has occurred in the 40 years since they were advanced. Moreover, this cannot be attributed simply to unfavourable developments in the course of the struggle and the balance of political forces, for nothing approaching the establishment of left hegemony has *ever* occurred in these apparatuses under capitalism.

The unfortunate fact is that while such institutions as the education system or the mass media are subject to influence from below by popular struggles and are, indeed, quite adept at partially reflecting and absorbing such incursions, there are in all capitalist countries powerful structural factors which prevent their radical transformation or takeover.

Yes, certain radical teachers and professors will make progress and become influential and it may even be the case that certain faculties or university departments as a whole may go "Marxist" or left wing or whatever, especially in times of mass struggle and revolt, such as the late 1960s, but the commanding heights of the education system both at school and university level and in the administrative bureaucracy of the state will remain firmly out of reach. Yes, the bourgeois press will allow individual radical journalists a certain voice, the likes of John Pilger, Paul Foot and Eamonn McCann. And from time to time radical film makers like Ken Loach or Michael Moore or, in times past, Jean Luc Godard and Roberto Rossellini, or lefty comedians like Bill Hicks and Mark Steel will be permitted a niche presence. But the media as a whole—the multinational corporations that dominate the world news and enter-tainment market[272] and the state broadcasting companies dominant in individual countries—cannot possibly be captured or transformed by the left while capital and the capitalist state remain in place.[273]

If this is true of the ideological apparatuses, it is even more clearly true of the coercive state apparatuses and it is precisely these that have to be transformed if the Carrillo/Poulantzas strategy for transition to socialism is to be realised. Here it is only necessary to move from Poulantzas's highly "sophisticated" theoretical abstractions to examin-ing just a few actually existing coercive state institutions to see that this is a fantasy. Is it going to be possible, gradually or otherwise, to establish left hegemony in the CRS (the French riot police), the racist and mur-derous US police departments or the Golden Dawn-voting Greek police or the London Met? How? And what about the secret forces of the deep state, MI5 and MI6 or the French General Directorates for External and Internal Security or the FBI and the CIA?

And then there is the question of the most important of all the institutions of the state, the army or perhaps we should say the armed forces as a whole, which is the repository of decisive physical force in society. It is certainly true that the armed forces are not immune to popular pressure and that mass popular struggles will, as Poulantzas argues, have their effects "within" them. Indeed the fact that, in con-trast to the secret services and even more than the police, the armed forces are "mass" organisations whose rank and file are drawn over-whelmingly from the working class makes them the most susceptible of all state institutions to such "contamination". But, precisely for this reason, the armed forces are anything but democratic. On the contrary they are founded and constructed entirely on the principle of authority, discipline and following orders, orders issued by a high command which, as we have already shown, is completely tied to the ruling class and completely unsusceptible to left influence.

Consequently, in so far as the rank and file of the armed forces do start to be affected by popular struggles and to adopt radical ideas, they immediately face the problem, if they want to act on those ideas, of the orders they are receiving from their officers. To defy those orders is to engage in mutiny, a crime which has always been and remains subject to severe punishment and which by its nature threatens to "break up" or smash the state in true Leninist style. Short of this revolutionary action from below the generals, admirals and airforce commanders will retain the ability to use the military to suppress popular dissent and to obstruct radical change.

Clearly the only way in which it might be possible even to attempt to transform the character of such institutions would be through the election of a "left government" which would then pursue a policy of appointing its supporters to the head of such institutions. In other words the Eurocommunist strategy, for all its Marxist language, resolves itself in practice into a revived version of the old parliamentary road to socialism pursued, with no success, by the left wing of social democracy.

One of the most serious weaknesses in the schema of both Carrillo and Poulantzas is that not only do they underestimate these structural limitations to the transformability of the state apparatuses, they also more or less ignore the fact that their avowed enemy, the existing ruling class, will actively resist. Faced with a genuinely left government whose aim, as Carrillo and Poulantzas insist, is not to administer capitalism (á la mainstream social democracy) but to gradually transform it into socialism, there is zero chance that the ruling class will passively await its demise. On the contrary they will use all the many means at their disposal to prevent such an outcome and that will include forcing on the left government and the popular movement precisely the decisive physical confrontation the Eurocommunist strategy is designed to avoid. Given the imminent prospect of losing everything it has held dear for centuries, everything it believes in and identifies with the very basis of civilisation, why would the ruling class permit this to happen without provoking a real showdown?

Finally, it is a feature of both Carrillo's and Poulantzas's criticism of Leninism (and Marx) that they essentially accept and endorse the democratic claims and credentials of the Western parliamentary system. Carrillo is explicit:

As regards the political system established in Western Europe, based on representative political institutions—parliament, political and philosophical pluralism, the theory of the separation of powers, decentralisation, human rights, etc—that system is in essentials valid and it will be still more effective with a socialist, and not a capitalist, economic foundation.[274]

This is a position which I have to say is to the right of views that can be heard on any street corner or in any pub in the working class districts of Dublin since the crash of 2008, the bank bailout and the Troika-led imposition of austerity.

Poulantzas is less effusive and refers frequently (though vaguely) to the need for "a sweeping transformation of the state apparatus" but he, like Carrillo, speaks of his strategy as "the democratic road to socialism" and writes:

What is involved, through all the various transformations, is a real permanence and continuity of the institutions of representative democracy—not as unfortunate relics of the past to be tolerated as long as necessary, but as an essential condition of democratic socialism.[275]

Moreover, he argues that Lenin's insistence on the replacement of bourgeois parliamentarism by the "direct democracy" of the soviets was what prepared the ground for Stalinism:

Was it not this very line (sweeping substitution of rank-and-file democracy for representative democracy) which principally accounted for what happened in Lenin's lifetime in the Soviet Union, and which gave rise to the centralising and statist Lenin whose posterity is well enough known.[276]

In this way the positions of both Carrillo and Poulantzas are less advanced than and to the right of the instinctive revolt not only of the Irish working class in recent years but also of the Spanish masses in the Indignados movement of 2011 with its slogans of "They don't represent us!" and "Real democracy now!" and of the general spirit of the US and international Occupy movement.

The struggle today and tomorrow

So far I have argued that the core propositions of Lenin's *The State and Revolution* withstand all the many and varied critiques to which they have been subject. But any text written a hundred years ago is subject to the seemingly common sense objection that, "surely it must be out of date now". Actually ideas don't work like that. Pythagoras formulated his theorem more than 2,500 years ago; it still happens to be valid. Copernicus published his theory that the earth circles the sun, rather than the reverse, in 1543. We can fairly safely assume that when the 500th anniversary of this comes round it will still be the case. But of course the opposite is not true either, namely that all ideas that were once considered the case remain so. Copernicus also believed that the sun was the centre of the universe; this was an advance on thinking the earth was the centre but we now know it not to be so. In other words, these questions have to be judged on their merits and, as Marx pointed out in his second thesis on Feuerbach,[277] the ultimate test is human practice.

For this reason I want to conclude this chapter by examining the relevance of the Leninist theory of the state to some major contemporary struggles. I shall begin with the largest and most powerful revolutionary struggle of the 21st century so far, the Egyptian Revolution of 2011.

The Egyptian Revolution began on 25 January with a more or less spontaneous uprising. Of course the event had been called by various left and democratic organisations, but they thought they were calling a protest demonstration not an uprising. The starting point of the uprising was expressed in its main slogans: "Down! Down! Hosni Mubarak" and "The people want to bring down the regime!" But bringing down Mubarak and his regime involved confronting the Egyptian state or more precisely—and as we shall see the distinction is important—one section or one arm of the state: the police.

Mubarak's police were already widely hated by the population because of their daily interactions with the public, their systematic bullying, brutality and torture. When they attempted to drive the mass demonstration of 25 January off the streets, the people fought back and their ranks were swelled by hundreds of thousands more who poured out of the working class districts to join the revolt. Within days, 28 January was decisive, the police were defeated: it was they not the demonstrators who were driven off the streets and this occurred not only in Cairo but across Egypt, especially in the key cities of Suez and Alexandria. In the famous Battle of the Camel on 2 February, "the people" also defeated the regime's attempt to mobilize against them a counter-revolutionary army of thugs and criminal elements (*baltagiya*). The mass occupation of Tahrir Square was maintained. Then, as Mubarak clung to power, the Revolution on the streets started to spread to the workplaces in a mass strike wave. This decided matters and Mubarak resigned on 11 February.

Power now passed into the hands of the military in the form of the Supreme Council of the Armed Forces (SCAF). Significantly, the army had not been deployed against the people in the 18 days in which the Revolution was at its height. This enabled the propaganda claim that "the army and the people are one hand" to have a certain popular resonance and this was compounded by the fact that ever since the days of Nasser in the 1950s and 1960s the notion of the Egyptian army as a progressive force had considerable currency with sections of the Egyptian left—with Nasserites of course, but also with various left nationalists, Stalinists and Communists.

The assumption of power by SCAF by no means halted the development of the Egyptian Revolution and mass demonstrations continued, including with confrontations with the military police, but illusions in the neutrality and "patriotism" of the army, ie the core of the state, clearly slowed its momentum.

When the Presidential elections were held in May/June 2012, Mohammed Morsi of the Muslim Brotherhood very narrowly led in the first round with 25 percent versus 24 percent for Ahmed Shafiq, who was clearly the candidate of the military and of counter-revolution; the Nasserist leader, Hamdeen Sabahi, who was supported by much of the left, came third with 21 percent. In the second round Morsi defeated Shafiq by 51.7 percent to 48.3 percent. In other words, more than a year into the Revolution the candidate of the army could still command a mass vote.

This became even more important a year later. The Morsi government was a disaster for both the Egyptian people and for the Muslim Brotherhood itself. It did its very best to block any continuation of the Revolution, to demobilise protests on the streets and to collaborate with the military, but it satisfied nobody as the society spiralled into crisis. A huge popular revolt against the government swelled up spearheaded by a group called Tamarod (Rebellion). Tamarod presented itself as a progressive pro-revolution grassroots organisation, but it subsequently emerged that they always had links with the military.

On 30 June 2013 monster anti-Muslim Brotherhood government demonstrations took to the streets in Cairo and across Egypt. Maybe as many as 14 million mobilised and the next day a million people occupied Tahrir Square. Two days later the military, led by General al-Sisi, moved to arrest Morsi and other leaders and to depose the government. This was met with acclaim by many on the streets. The Brotherhood responded by insisting on the legitimacy of Morsi and his government and establishing two permanent protest sit-ins. On 14 August after six weeks of ongoing protest, the al-Sisi regime crushed these sit-ins by military force; a revolutionary military coup was now firmly established and sealed in blood. It remains in power today.

There has been widespread debate in Egypt and internationally about these events with debate focusing on what should have been, and should be, the attitude of the left to the Muslim Brotherhood. The Egyptian Revolutionary Socialists, for example, have been subject to much criticism for a) voting for Morsi against Shafiq in the second round in 2012 and b) for defending the Brotherhood against the repression they have been suffering since the coup. This debate has mainly been about the nature of Islamism and of the Muslim Brotherhood in particular, but the point I want to make here is that it should also have been about the nature of the state.

In reality, hostility to the Muslim Brotherhood, which was coloured by a good deal of Islamophobia, allowed many on the left to gloss over and turn a blind eye to the class nature and deeply reactionary character of the Egyptian state apparatus. In these circumstances a wider grasp of the Leninist theory of the state, which was held by the Revolutionary Socialists but by almost no other tendency on the Egyptian left, would have been of immense practical use. It would have made it much more possible to turn the anti-Morsi mobilisation in a progressive and revolutionary direction and much more difficult for al-Sisi to hegemonise that mobilisation.

The same issue resurfaced in relation to the attempted military coup in Turkey on 15 July 2016. Obviously history did not repeat itself in that the Turkish masses, overwhelmingly the Turkish working class, took to the streets to confront the tanks and prevent the coup. However, as in Egypt, it was clear that a substantial section of what is called "the nationalist left" were either entirely passive in their response to the coup or partially sympathetic to it on the grounds that the military might be a lesser evil than the "fascist" Islamist government of Erdogan and the AKP.

There are a number of reasons why the notion that the capitalist state and its military are in some way progressive or the ally of the working class (it has always been central to social democracy and labourism). But in many parts of the world, including Turkey and Egypt, it is due above all to the abandonment of Leninism, first in practice and then in words, by the official international communist movement.

In Greece, which has been the other decisive arena of struggle in the last few years, the question of the state has again been of great importance. The election of the Syriza government in January 2015 raised and focused the hopes of the left across Europe but, as the first electoral victory of a party with a Eurocommunist pedigree, it also promised to put to the test the Poulantzian strategy of "transforming" the capitalist state.[278] It seemed likely to be a severe test because of the notoriously reactionary and semi-fascist character of the Greek state apparatus that had ruled the country as a military dictatorship in 1967-1974 and whose police force were rumoured to vote 50 percent for the neo-Nazi Golden Dawn.[279] In the event, the test did not materialise for the simple reason that Syriza made no attempt to transform the Greek state (or to undermine or seriously modify Greek capitalism); instead, from the outset its leader, Alexis Tsipras, sought to placate and reassure the state apparatus, and the Greek ruling class as a whole, by appointing three "safe" right wingers—Nikos Kotzias, Panos Kammenos and Yiannis Panousis—to the Ministries of Foreign Affairs, Defence and Citizen Protection (the police) respectively.[280]

The most surprising, shocking even, of the appointments was that of Panos Kammenos, leader of the right wing and racist ANEL party. The claim was that this was necessary to establish a coalition with ANEL, which in turn was essential to enable Syriza to form a government, it being two seats short of an overall majority. In reality, this was neither a constitutional nor a political necessity; Syriza would have been in a very strong position to rule as a minority government, challenging the other parties to bring them down and precipitate an election (which Syriza would almost certainly have won). The assessment of the *Financial Times* is much more accurate: "Syriza's partnership with Mr Kammenos and his nationalist party is considered vital to maintaining the loyalty of the armed forces to a government led by former Communists".[281]

But if an all out confrontation between the Greek deep state and the Syriza government did not materialize because of Syriza's instant appeasement of the priorities of that state and its early abandonment of any kind of serious anti-capitalist strategy, such a confrontation never-theless did take place with the supra-national "institutions" of the EU and international capitalism, the so-called "Troika" of the European Central Bank, the EU Commission and the IMF.

Syriza came to power on the basis of its Thessaloniki Programme which pledged to end austerity by renegotiating the terms of Greece's crippling international debt and implementing a "National Reconstruction Plan" to confront Greece's immediate "humanitarian crisis" and "reverse the social and economic disintegration, to recon-struct the economy and exit from the crisis":[282]

> We demand immediate parliamentary elections and a strong negotia-tion mandate with the goal to:
> • Write-off the greater part of public debt's nominal value so that it becomes sustainable in the context of European Debt Conference. It happened for Germany in 1953. It can also happen for the South of Europe and Greece.
> • Include a "growth clause" in the repayment of the remaining part so that it is growth-financed and not budget-financed.
> • Include a significant grace period (moratorium) in debt servicing to save funds for growth.[283]

At the same time Syriza committed itself to remaining within the EU and the Eurozone. These radical anti-austerity aims were to be realised through negotiations with their "European partners". Alexis Tsipras, Yanis Varoufakis and other Syriza ministers consistently referred to the EU and its leaders as their "partners".

It is a feature of the political culture of the European left (outside of its "Leninist/Trotskyist" components) that it frequently combines hos-tility to its own national establishment and their political representatives (the likes of Merkel, Cameron, Blair, Sarkosy, Rajoy, Samaras, etc) and the police chiefs and generals of its own state, with a rose-tinted view of the representatives of those same establishments and states when they gather together internationally. As a result, there is a widespread notion that the EU and the United Nations (UN) are in some way progressive institutions embodying "left values" such as international cooperation and internationalism. In what can broadly be called the peace movement, it is common to find resolute opponents of almost all war, such as the late Tony Benn, who are equally resolute proponents of the UN. Moreover, this attitude seems to persist despite an abundance of evidence and experience to show that in all important matters the UN is nothing but an instrument of, and cover for, the interests of the major (imperialist) powers. As Perry Anderson has written:

> The UN is a political entity without any independent will. If we set aside its specialized agencies, most of which perform useful practical services of one sort or another, the core of the institution—that is, the General Assembly and Security Council—is a legitimating, not a policy-making, apparatus. Decisions reached by the organization are in essence embellishments of the relationships of power operative at any given time.[284]

Thus one often hears that Tony Blair's offence in 2003 was to embark on the invasion of Iraq without a second resolution from the UN as if sanctification by the UN would have made that invasion legitimate. At bottom this is the transfer of the reformist perspective on the existing state as an instrument to be harnessed for the transformation of society into the international arena. Obviously there are no quotations from Lenin about the EU or the UN but we do know that he and the Communist International in his day regularly referred to the League of Nations as a "thieves kitchen" and "league of imperialist bandits". Bukharin and Preobrazhensky in their *ABC of Communism*, which was a kind of Leninist revolutionary textbook, wrote:

> It is pure fable to say that the League of Nations has been founded to promote the cause of peace. In actual fact it has a twofold aim: the ruthless exploitation of the proletariat throughout the world, of all colonies and of the colonial slaves; and the crushing of the incipient world revolution.[285]

When Greek Finance Minister Yanis Varoufakis came to negotiate face to face with German Finance Minister Wolfgang Schauble and the Troika Eurocrats, he found their behaviour much more closely resembled that of imperialist bandits than that of partners. In an interview with the *New Statesman*, Varoufakis recorded how he was confronted with:

The complete lack of any democratic scruples, on behalf of the supposed defenders of Europe's democracy... To have very powerful figures look at you in the eye and say "You're right in what you're saying, but we're going to crunch you anyway."

[T]here was point blank refusal to engage in economic arguments. Point blank... You put forward an argument that you've really worked on—to make sure it's logically coherent—and you're just faced with blank stares. It is as if you haven't spoken. What you say is independent of what they say. You might as well have sung the Swedish national anthem—you'd have got the same reply.[286]

The reason the Eurocrats were not interested in Varoufakis's economic arguments was simple: the "negotiation" was not about the best economic policy for Greece and they were not "partners" of the Greek people; they were representatives of European capital and they had decided in advance that Syriza had to be forced to submit, publicly and humiliatingly, to draconian austerity in order to deter radical experiments or debt defiance anywhere else. And of course we know that despite the backing of a massive *Oxi* (No!) vote by the Greek people a few days earlier, the Syriza government on 8 July 2015 did just that—publicly submitted.

In short the whole episode was an object lesson in the simple truth that these institutions of the ruling class (the European Commission, the European Central Bank, the IMF, etc) cannot be "taken over" or "harnessed" or used to implement anti-capitalist policies or even policies that seriously conflict with the interests of the capitalist class. Had Syriza chosen the road of defiance and confrontation, there can be little doubt that the Greek state machine would have operated as an ally of the EU institutions against the Syriza government and against the working people of Greece. In those circumstances merely to end austerity, never mind achieve the transition to socialism, would have needed the revolutionary mobilization of the Greek working class to defeat and dismantle the authoritarian and reactionary Greek state apparatus.

Finally, there is the struggle unfolding as this book is being written around Jeremy Corbyn's leadership of the British Labour Party. When Corbyn was first elected leader in September 2015, David Cameron responded immediately saying: "The Labour Party is now a threat to national security". This was a double-edged barb. On the one hand, it challenged Corbyn to state, and prove, his loyalty to the British state and its main institutions (armed forces, police, security services, monarchy, etc) and was accompanied by concerted media attacks on him over symbolic issues like singing the national anthem and kissing the Queen's hand, clearly designed to cast doubt on this loyalty. On the other hand, it was a message to the British state and its military and security services to say that with Corbyn it was no longer business as usual. Within days an "unnamed" senior serving general had issued a warning in *The Sunday Times* of a possible "mutiny" against a Corbyn government:

> The Army just wouldn't stand for it. The general staff would not allow a prime minister to jeopardise the security of this country and I think people would use whatever means possible, fair or foul to prevent that. You can't put a maverick in charge of a country's security.
>
> There would be mass resignations at all levels and you would face the very real prospect of an event which would effectively be a mutiny.[287]

Since this episode, the lead role in the assault on Corbyn has passed to the Labour Party Blairites and the majority of MPs in the Parliamentary Labour Party, who have done their best to force him to resign and to oust him by means of a leadership challenge by Owen Smith. This spectacularly failed with Corbyn being re-elected on 24 September 2016 with a resounding 65 percent. Doubtless Corbyn's right wing Labour opponents (the Hilary Benns, Angela Eagles, Alasdair Campbells, and so on), who are far more loyal to the British state and ruling class than they are to the Labour Party, will do all in their power to ensure that their objection that Corbyn is unelectable becomes a self-fulfilling prophecy.

But should a Corbyn-led Labour Party, despite their best efforts and despite the media, nevertheless follow in the footsteps of Syriza and be elected, the question of the British state apparatus would come centre stage. It seems abundantly clear that far from collaborating or acquiescing in Corbyn's efforts at social transformation, that state apparatus, together with the power of British and international capital (and the EU and the US government, etc) will move to block, frustrate and undermine him at every turn, even to the point, if necessary, of unseating by force.

What these examples all demonstrate is that the analysis outlined a century ago in *The State and Revolution* that the existing state is an organ of class rule by the capitalist class and that it cannot be "taken over" by the working class but must be smashed and replaced by a new state based on workers' councils, retains all its relevance today. Indeed the more the level of struggle rises and intensifies the more important and central this analysis becomes.

4

The necessity of the party?

LENIN did not write a text on the party that is the equivalent of *The State and Revolution* or of *Imperialism: the Highest Stage of Capitalism*, a book or even pamphlet which sums up his main views on the question.[288] Nevertheless there is no concept so associated with Leninism as the idea of the party and this is perfectly reasonable and justifiable for several reasons. First, Lenin devoted his entire political life up to 1917 to building a party, the Bolshevik Party. Second, as soon as possible after the October Revolution, he along with the other Bolshevik leaders set about organising the Communist International, which was devoted to building and drawing together communist parties throughout the world. And third, it has been a hallmark of would-be Leninists of all tendencies (Stalinist, Trotskyists, Maoists and so on) that they have placed a premium on the construction of what they, in their different ways, saw as a Leninist-type party.

It is also the case that many on the left, who would see themselves as socialists, Marxists, even revolutionaries but would reject "Leninism", would cite the issue of "the Leninist Party" or "the Leninist model of the party" as their principle, or one of their principle reasons, for so doing. It is therefore obviously essential that a book examining the relevance of Lenin for today consider this question in some depth. To do this it is necessary to establish what are the core principles involved in the Leninist theory of the party and that in turn requires dealing with a couple of widespread misconceptions.

The first of these is that the Leninist party is an authoritarian structure dominated by an omnipotent, or would-be omniscient, leadership. Of course this was demonstrably the case in the Communist Party of the Soviet Union in the time of Stalin, when the word of the General Secretary was absolute and to express a different opinion—on anything—was literally to take one's life in one's hands. It was also true of the official Communist Parties of the Communist International in the Stalin era and beyond, albeit the punishment for disagreement was generally expulsion rather than extermination. However, it was emphatically not true of the Bolshevik Party in the days of Lenin.

In 1936 Leon Trotsky offered the following characterisation of the internal life of the Bolshevik Party:

> The inner regime of the Bolshevik party was characterized by the method of democratic centralism. The combination of these two concepts, democracy and centralism, is not in the least contradictory. The party took watchful care not only that its boundaries should always be strictly defined, but also that all those who entered these boundaries should enjoy the actual right to define the direction of the party policy. Freedom of criticism and intellectual struggle was an irrevocable content of the party democracy. The present doctrine that Bolshevism does not tolerate factions is a myth of epoch decline. In reality the history of Bolshevism is a history of the struggle of factions. And, indeed, how could a genuinely revolutionary organization, setting itself the task of overthrowing the world and uniting under its banner the most audacious iconoclasts, fighters and insurgents, live and develop without intellectual conflicts, without groupings and temporary factional formations?...
>
> The regime of the Bolshevik party, especially before it came to power, stood thus in complete contradiction to the regime of the present sections of the Communist International, with their "leaders" appointed from above, making complete changes of policy at a word of command, with their uncontrolled apparatus, haughty in its attitude to the rank and file, servile in its attitude to the Kremlin.[289]

Moreover the historical record clearly supports Trotsky's description. Not only was there regular dissent and debate in the party on everything from philosophy to tactics but Lenin was quite often outvoted; for example on participating in Duma elections in 1907, on unity with the Mensheviks in 1910, on boycotting the Democratic Conference in September 1917, and on postponing elections to the Constituent Assembly in December 1917. On a number of crucial occasions when Lenin did get his way, it was only after vigorous debate in which he succeeded in winning a majority to his point of view; for example over breaking with the Provisional Government and orienting on workers' power in April 1917, on launching the Insurrection in October 1917 and on signing the Brest-Litovsk Peace in January 1918. And in each of these cases Lenin's victory was not just a matter of his personal authority or the power of his arguments but the fact that over a period of time they were seen to correspond to the objective logic of events.

Yes, it is the case that internal party factions were banned in 1921 and that this was a retrograde and dangerous step, but it was conceived of as a temporary measure in a very extreme situation at the end of the Civil War and it testifies to the fact that factions were allowed up to that point. Moreover, the banning of organised factions did not signify the banning of debate, which continued. Only with the rise to power of Stalin from 1923 onwards did the real shut down of inner-party democracy occur and that did not become absolute until Stalin's complete victory in 1927-1928.

The second misconception is that to advocate the Leninist theory of the party is to advocate adopting or attempting to imitate "the organisational model" of the Bolshevik Party. I call this a misconception partly because no such fixed or formulated "model" actually existed and partly because copying or imitating the organisational practices of the Bolsheviks in any systematic or detailed way is not possible anywhere in Europe today or probably anywhere in the world. And I do not mean by this not desirable I mean, literally, not possible.

For example organisational forms developed under conditions of clandestinity cannot be replicated in conditions of legality and bourgeois democracy because even loyal activists will not accept them without the objective necessity created by the police threat. Operating under repression, in and of itself, creates a different attitude to and conception of discipline than operating under relative freedom. Any attempt to artificially impose such norms results only in reducing "the party" to a microscopically small sect of fanatics. Again the principle basis of Bolshevik organisation was the factory cell. This made sense in the Petrograd of the Putilov works and the Vyborg District, and perhaps it made sense in the Manchester of the 1960s and early 1970s (and possibly in the Pearl River Delta of contemporary China), but is clearly not viable in Britain today or in most of the countries of Western capitalism.

A note is in order here on the concept of "democratic centralism", often treated as the hallmark principle of Leninist organisation. Democratic centralism means the combination of democratic decision making and unity in action to implement those decisions. In fact every political party, short of a totally authoritarian fascist or Stalinist one, reformist and revolutionary alike, and pretty much every form of workers' organisation including trade unions, has to combine an element of democracy with an element of centralism. Without any democracy there are unlikely to be any members or membership dues. Without any centralism there is no organisation; the whole point of party or trade union organisation is to get large numbers of people to act together.

What can vary a lot is the degree and scope of both the democracy and the centralism and the relation between the two. The organisation of a trade union strike usually proceeds on the basis of a democratic vote on whether or not to strike followed by (ideally) unanimous implementation of the decision, with anyone crossing the picket being regarded as a scab. But a trade union would, quite rightly, not expect unanimous implementation of a decision to campaign or demonstrate against a war, even if the union voted to officially support that campaign. The Bolshevik Party clearly practised a more rigorous form of democratic centralism than this in terms of its level of democratic debate and the range of issues on which unity was expected.

Nevertheless, the history of the Bolshevik Party shows that its democratic centralism was far from being a fixed or absolute code. A few examples illustrate this. In 1905, during and after the 1905 Revolution, Lenin and the Bolsheviks argued for a boycott of the Tsarist Duma on the grounds that it was a sham. In 1906 some members of the Russian Social Democratic Labour Party (RSDLP) nevertheless ran for the Duma and were elected. Far from denouncing them Lenin supported them. Then at a Congress in April 1906, when the Mensheviks opposed the boycott, Lenin was the only Bolshevik delegate to vote with the Mensheviks (ignoring Bolshevik faction discipline). Formally, the Bolsheviks, after years of to-ing and fro-ing, finally broke with the Mensheviks and became a completely separate and independent party in 1912, but in many cases this was not implemented on the ground until well into 1917. As Trotsky records:

> In such workers' centres as Ekaterinburg, Perm, Tula, Nizhni-Novgorod, Sormovo, Kolomna, Yuzovka, the Bolsheviks separated from the Mensheviks at the end of May [1917]. In Odessa, Nikolaev,

Elisavetgrad, Poltava and other points in the Ukraine, the Bolsheviks did not have independent organisations even in the middle of June [1917]. In Baku, Zlatoust, Bezhetsk, Kostroma, the Bolsheviks divided from the Mensheviks only towards the end of June.[290]

Then there was the episode of the behaviour of Zinoviev and Kamenev in October 1917. Just a few days before the insurrection, they wrote of their opposition to the uprising in a non-party newspaper, thus also giving away that plans were afoot. Lenin denounced them furiously, calling them strike breakers and demanding their expulsion from the party. But in fact they were not expelled and remained part of the Bolshevik leadership.

What this shows is that it would be wrong to see democratic central-ism as the defining characteristic of Bolshevism or of the Leninist theory of the party. Nor, and this is particularly the case given the absence of any definitive or comprehensive text, can we base ourselves on individual quotations taken out of their historical context. Rather what we have to do is draw out from a consideration of Lenin's writing and practice as a whole the core principles underlying his attitude to the question of the party and on that basis assess the validity and relevance of those principles today. This approach is especially necessary because it is only these underlying principles and not specific organisational forms that can be generally applicable today. Fortunately the work needed to make possible such an overall assessment has, by and large, been done.[291]

Two core principles

The first core principle of the Leninist theory of the party is simply that it is necessary to build a revolutionary party. By revolutionary party I mean a party that is explicitly committed to socialist revolution, whose leadership and membership (in their overwhelming majority) unam-biguously accept revolution as their goal and by revolution I do not mean the metaphorical use of the word but an actual mass uprising.

Lenin's first-ever national political initiative was his campaign, along with Plekhanov, Martov and others, to draw together the various Social Democratic[292] circles scattered across Russia into a single nationwide revolutionary party. In 1897 he wrote:

The creation of a durable revolutionary organisation among the factory, urban workers is therefore the first and most urgent task confronting Social-Democracy...

> And so, to work, comrades! Let us not lose precious time! Russian Social-Democrats have much to do...to unite the workers' circles and Social-Democratic groups scattered all over Russia into a single Social Democratic Labour Party.[293]

Over the next six years Lenin pursued this goal relentlessly through the failure of the first attempt at a founding congress in 1898 (all the delegates were elected) to the Second Congress of the RSDLP in London in 1903. In the course of this campaign he vigorously insisted on his total opposition to the reformist tendency in Germany launched by Eduard Bernstein and on his opposition to any political or organisational compromise with this tendency in Russia:

> The notorious Bernsteinism...is an attempt to narrow the theory of Marxism, to convert the revolutionary workers' party into a reformist party. As was to be expected, this attempt has been strongly condemned by the majority of the German Social-Democrats. Opportunist trends have repeatedly manifested themselves in the ranks of German Social-Democracy, and on every occasion they have been repudiated by the Party, which loyally guards the principles of revolutionary international Social-Democracy. We are convinced that every attempt to transplant opportunist views to Russia will encounter equally determined resistance on the part of the overwhelming majority of Russian Social-Democrats.[294]

Bernstein's reformism received very little overt support in Russia, which is why we do not find Lenin writing the equivalent of Luxemburg's *Reform or Revolution*, a lengthy dissection of the reformist case. Much more widespread was the tendency known as "economism", which argued that the main task of Russian Marxists was simply to "assist" the economic struggle of the working class. It was partly because he thought that "economism" represented a Russian version of Bernsteinism, that Lenin polemicised so vehemently against it, above all in *What is To Be Done?* Lenin believed that any tendency to concentrate only on economic struggles and not raise political demands would leave the leadership of the political struggle against Tsarism to the liberal bourgeoisie who would betray it and wreck the revolution.

Another significant factor shaping Lenin's position was the reality of dealing with the Tsarist police. Lenin argued that in a police state it was a matter of practical necessity that the revolutionary organisation remain secret and relatively small, composed largely of "professional revolutionaries":

> [S]uch an organisation must consist chiefly of people professionally engaged in revolutionary activity; ...in an autocratic state, the more we *confine* the membership of such an organisation to people who are professionally engaged in revolutionary activity and who have been professionally trained in the art of combating the political police, the more difficult will it be to unearth the organisation.[295]

Operating under conditions of illegality clearly mitigated strongly against the development of a reformist wing to the party. The motive here may have been purely practical but the effect was the same.

What distinguished Lenin from many other leading figures in Russian Social Democracy at this time was not just his advocacy of revolution rather than reformism but his willingness to split organisationally over this question or indeed any tendency towards economism. When the Union of Social Democrats Abroad split over the economism issue in 1901 Lenin wrote:

> the principal cause (not pretext, but cause) of the split was a difference of opinion on principles, namely, a difference between revolutionary and opportunist Social Democracy.[296]

And he approvingly quoted Lassalle to the effect that:

> it is precisely internal Party struggles that lend a party strength and vitality; that the greatest proof of a party's weakness is its diffuseness and the blurring of clear demarcations; and that a party becomes stronger by purging itself".[297]

Having devoted the best part of six years to the project of a establishing an all-Russian Social Democratic Party and seeing it come together at the Second Congress in 1903 Lenin then faced a split among his own close collaborators, the board of *Iskra*. This proved to be the start of the permanent division in Russian Social Democracy between

Bolsheviks (majority) and Mensheviks (minority), which culminated in two parties on opposite sides of the barricades in October 1917.

At the time the seriousness of the split was probably not apparent to any of the participants. At issue was a difference about the definition of membership of the party—Lenin and the Bolsheviks were for a "hard" border based on participation in a party organisation; Martov and the Mensheviks wanted a "softer" looser definition—and a dispute about the composition of the Iskra editorial board, so to many people it seemed like just an argument about words and personalities. In the years that followed, especially during the revolutionary year of 1905, there were many attempts (often supported by Lenin) at reunification. Nevertheless, with hindsight it is clear that the heart of the 1903 split were different conceptions of the party, with Lenin for a strictly demarcated thoroughly revolutionary party and Martov for leaving the door open to softer, less defined elements and favouring a party more on the lines of western Social Democracy.[298]

Lenin's intransigence on the question of an independent revolutionary party also led him, in the years of reaction that followed 1905, into bitter conflict with "the liquidators" (who wanted to close down the underground activities of the party in favour of a broad legal workers' party) and with "the conciliators", such as Trotsky, who still hoped to bring all the factions of Russian Social Democracy together. Looking back at these disputes at a distance of over a century they cannot fail to seem, to anyone not a specialist or an obsessive, obscure to the point of impenetrability and conducted with labels (opportunists, recallists, boycotters, liquidators, conciliators, etc) which have little or no contemporary resonance.[299] Unsurprisingly the "standard" academic view of these disputes is that they were driven by Lenin's "factional" personality, his desire for uncontested personal power. But the upshot was that by the start of the First World War in 1914, Lenin had built an uncompromising revolutionary party with a serious base in the working class.

This party was fundamentally different from the other parties of the Second International (to which the Bolsheviks remained affiliated) in that unlike German Social Democracy or the Austrian, French, Italian and other Socialist Parties, Lenin's Bolshevik Party had no reformist wing. It is probably the case that up until 1914 Lenin did not fully realise that he was doing this and that, as Lars Lih has argued, he believed that essentially he was doing the same thing in Russia as Karl

Kautsky and the SPD had done in Germany. But in reality this was not the case. The collapse of the Second International, and especially German Social Democracy, into social patriotism (support for their "own" countries in the War) in August 1914 opened Lenin's eyes both to the reformist nature of Kautskyism and international social democracy and to the specific character of the Bolshevik Party:

> Typical of the socialist parties of the epoch of the Second International was one that tolerated in its midst an opportunism built up in decades of the "peaceful" period, an opportunism that kept itself secret, adapting itself to the revolutionary workers, *borrowing* their Marxist terminology, and evading any clear cleavage of principles. This type has outlived itself. If the war ends in 1915, will any thinking socialist be found willing to begin, in 1916, restoring the workers' parties *together* with the opportunists, *knowing from experience* that in any new crisis all of them to a man (plus many other spineless and muddle-headed people) will be for the bourgeoisie, who will of course find a pretext to ban any talk of class hatred and the class struggle?[300]

From this point on, Lenin was for a complete political break with social democracy and all strands of reformism, not only in Russia but internationally. He proposed dropping the name "Social Democrat" as irrevocably compromised and adopting Marx's old name Communist and declared in favour of a new Third International. When the new Communist International was actually formed in 1919, it was on the basis of an explicit commitment to proletarian revolution, destruction of the capitalist state and the dictatorship of the proletariat. In 1920 Lenin, fearing that the Comintern was becoming "fashionable" and attracting reformist and "centrist"[301] (semi-reformist) elements, drew up "21 Conditions" which had to be fulfilled by parties wishing to affiliate to the International and which were designed to exclude the reformists. These were wide ranging and severe, including the necessity of combining legal and illegal activity, conducting propaganda in the armed forces and supporting all national liberation movements, especially against the party's "own" bourgeoisie. On the question of reformists they stated:

> 2. Any organisation that wishes to join the Communist International must consistently and systematically dismiss reformists and "Centrists" from positions of any responsibility in the working-class movement...

7. It is the duty of parties wishing to belong to the Communist International to recognise the need for a complete and absolute break with reformism and "Centrist" policy, and to conduct propaganda among the party membership for that break. Without this, a consistent communist policy is impossible. The Communist International demands imperatively and uncompromisingly that this break be effected at the earliest possible date. It cannot tolerate a situation in which avowed reformists, such as Turati, Modigliani, Kautsky and others, are entitled to consider themselves members of the Third International. Such a state of affairs would lead to the Third International strongly resembling the defunct Second International.[302]

Up to the Social Democratic betrayal of 1914 Lenin applied this policy of breaking with and excluding reformists to some extent instinctively and only really in relation to Russia, but from August 1914 he applied it with full consciousness and internationally. In any event it is evident that this was a core principle of Lenin's approach to the question of the party throughout his political activity.

The second core principle is a dialectical complement to the first: it is that the revolutionary party can only be built on the basis of establishing the closest possible relationship with the mass of the working class through participation in its day-to-day struggles. I have already written in Chapter 1 above of Lenin's personal organic relationship with the workers but it was also something he *always*, from the earliest days through to the Communist International, fought for in the party. In the 1897 article (cited above) in which he first set out his plan for a revolutionary party Lenin also wrote:

Inseparably connected with propaganda is *agitation* among the workers, which naturally comes to the forefront in the present political conditions of Russia and at the present level of development of the masses of workers. Agitation among the workers means that the Social-Democrats take part in all the spontaneous manifestations of the working-class struggle, in all the conflicts between the workers and the capitalists over the working day, wages, working conditions, etc, etc. Our task is to merge our activities with the practical, everyday questions of working-class life, to help the workers understand these questions, to draw the workers' attention to the most important abuses, to help them formulate their demands to the employers more precisely and practically, to

develop among the workers consciousness of their solidarity, consciousness of the common interests and common cause of all the Russian
workers as a united working class that is part of the international army
of the proletariat.[303]

And when in *What Is To Be Done?* he spoke of confining party
membership to professional revolutionaries to evade the police, he
immediately, in the next sentence, added that in an autocratic state, "the
more we *confine* the membership...the *greater* will be the number of
people from the working class and from the other social classes who will
be able to join the movement and perform active work in it".[304]

He repeated the same idea in 1904 in *One Step Forward, Two Steps
Back*, his account of the split with the Mensheviks:

> The stronger our party organisations, consisting of real social-demo-
> crats, the less wavering and instability there is within the party, the
> broader, more varied, richer and more fruitful will be the party's influ-
> ence on the elements of working class masses surrounding it.[305]

What establishing the closest possible links with the masses meant
in practice was first and foremost building the party in the factories. In
1897 Lenin wrote:

> Our work is primarily and mainly directed to the factory, urban work-
> ers... The creation of a durable revolutionary organisation among the
> factory, urban workers is therefore the first and most urgent task con-
> fronting Social-Democracy, one from which it would be highly unwise
> to let ourselves be diverted at the present time.

And:

> Agitation among the workers means that the Social-Democrats take
> part in all the spontaneous manifestations of the working-class struggle,
> in all the conflicts between the workers and the capitalists over the
> working day, wages, working conditions, etc, etc. Our task is to merge
> our activities with the practical, everyday questions of working-class
> life, to help the workers understand these questions, to draw the work-
> ers' attention to the most important abuses, to help them formulate
> their demands to the employers more precisely and practically, to
> develop among the workers consciousness of their solidarity, conscious-
> ness of the common interests and common cause of all the Russian

workers as a united working class that is part of the international army of the proletariat.[306]

Then, at the time of *What Is To Be Done?* Lenin emphasised also the need to "go among all classes of the population"[307] and take up all cases of oppression and tyranny. This point about taking up all cases of oppression is extremely important and will be discussed fully in the next chapter.

In the 1905 Revolution it meant engaging even with the police-run Zubatov trade unions and Father Gapon (who was not only a priest but also a police agent); it meant combating the sectarian tendency inside the Bolshevik Party to reject the recently created Petersburg Soviet in the name of the Party's claimed right to lead; and it meant Lenin arguing to "open the gates of the party" to the workers and to greatly broaden out the party committees. In the period of reaction after the defeat of the 1905 Revolution it meant defending participation in the very restricted Tsarist Duma in order to retain some links to the masses. As the movement began to recover it meant relating to the student demonstrations of 1910 and then, with the mass strikes following the massacre at the Lena goldfields in 1912, it meant publishing *Pravda* a legal daily newspaper full of popular articles.

The ability of Lenin and the Bolshevik Party to relate to the mass of workers, soldiers and sailors in 1917 is something I have already stressed at length and need not be repeated here; the October Revolution would not have been possible without it. Moreover, the same dialectic of first establish the independence of the revolutionary party and then reach out to the masses reappears as a central theme in Lenin's leadership of the Communist International. At the Second Congress of the Comintern the "21 Conditions" already referred to were complemented by one of Lenin's most important books, *Left-Wing Communism—An Infantile Disorder*, written to combat the "ultra-left" tendency manifesting itself within the International as a result of the revolutionary wave of 1919 that brought many enthusiastic but inexperienced recruits to the revolutionary socialist cause. Lenin begins with a summary of the history of Bolshevism along the lines argued here and then focuses on the two main questions at issue in the debate with the lefts: the need to work in "reactionary" trade unions and to participate in bourgeois elections and parliaments.

On the question of working in the unions, Lenin argued with great vehemence.

> Yet it is this very absurdity that the German "Left" Communists perpetrate when, *because* of the reactionary and counter-revolutionary character of the trade union *top leadership*, they jump to the conclusion that...we must withdraw from the trade unions, refuse to work in them, and create new and *artificial* forms of labour organisation! This is so unpardonable a blunder that it is tantamount to the greatest service Communists could render the bourgeoisie...
>
> To refuse to work in the reactionary trade unions means leaving the insufficiently developed or backward masses of workers under the influence of the reactionary leaders, the agents of the bourgeoisie, the labour aristocrats, or "workers who have become completely bourgeois"...
>
> If you want to help the "masses" and win the sympathy and support of the "masses", you should not fear difficulties...but must absolutely *work wherever the masses are to be found.* [Lenin's emphasis] You must be capable of any sacrifice, of overcoming the greatest obstacles, in order to carry on agitation and propaganda systematically, perseveringly, persistently and patiently in those institutions, societies and associations—even the most reactionary—in which proletarian or semi-proletarian masses are to be found: the trade unions and the workers' co-operatives (the latter sometimes, at least).[308]

For the same reason, in order to relate to the masses, Lenin insisted on the necessity of participation in parliamentary elections. The Left Communists contended that parliamentarism had become politically obsolete and should no longer be engaged in. Lenin rejected this:

> Parliamentarianism is of course "politically obsolete" to the Communists in Germany; but—and that is the whole point—we must *not* regard what is obsolete *to us* as something obsolete *to a class, to the masses.* Here again we find that the "Lefts" do not know how to reason, do not know how to act as the party of a *class*, as the party of the *masses.* You must not sink to the level of the masses, to the level of the backward strata of the class. That is incontestable. You must tell them the bitter truth. You are in duty bound to call their bourgeois-democratic and parliamentary prejudices what they are—prejudices. But at the same time you must *soberly* follow the *actual* state of the

class-consciousness and preparedness of the entire class (not only of its communist vanguard), and of all the *working people* (not only of their advanced elements).[309]

Lenin argued that as long as a majority or even a significant minority of the working class and of the masses continued to have illusions in the parliamentary process and to follow the bourgeois or reformist parties it what was essential to use elections to reach those masses and help them to learn, through actual experience, the limitations of parliamentary politics. It was also necessary to use the platform of parliament in a revolutionary way:

"the struggle on the parliamentary rostrum is *obligatory* on the party of the revolutionary proletariat *specifically* for the purpose of educating the backward strata of *its own class*, and for the purpose of awakening and enlightening the undeveloped, downtrodden and ignorant rural *masses*".[310]

In 1921, as the revolutionary wave of 1919-1920 began to ebb, Lenin again took up the theme of the need to relate and win over the majority of the working people. He was particularly insistent on this in the aftermath of the March Action in Germany when the Communist Party artificially attempted to galvanise or instigate a revolution on the basis of minority support:

In Europe, where almost all the proletarians are organised, we must win the majority of the working class and anyone who fails to understand this is lost to the communist movement; he will never learn anything if he has failed to learn that much during the three years of the great revolution.[311]

The matter was summed up in the resolution "On Tactics" adopted at the Third Congress of the International in July 1921:

From the day of its foundation the Communist International has clearly and unambiguously stated that its task is not to establish small Communist sects aiming to influence the working masses purely through agitation and propaganda, but to participate directly in the struggle of the working masses, establish Communist leadership of the struggle, and in the course of the struggle create large, revolutionary, mass Communist Parties".[312]

Having outlined these two core principles—the independent organisation of the revolutionary party and the establishment of the closest relationship with the mass of working people—and shown how they both run like red threads through the entirety of Lenin's writing and political work, it remains to emphasize that *the key* to the Leninist party is precisely the ability to *combine* both principles or tasks. Achieving one or the other by itself is relatively easy. Almost any small group can set itself up as the "independent revolutionary party" with a "correct" revolutionary programme for the whole country or, indeed, the whole world—nationalise the banks and basic industries under workers control! Arm the workers! All power to the workers' councils! Workers of the world unite! And so on. Equally it is fairly straightforward to establish close relations with the class by joining and working in trade unions and community campaigns, but not raising political questions or the need to build a revolutionary party. It is doing both that is difficult but also essential. Moreover it is an art which revolutionaries have to learn not just from books, but in practice because it involves continually shifting the balance between agitation and propaganda, building the party and mass campaigning according to the concrete situation.

Is a revolutionary party still necessary today?

A century ago Lenin's argument for a revolutionary party, backed by the immense authority of the recently victorious Russian Revolution, carried the day with, first, hundreds of thousands and then millions of workers and revolutionaries globally. That is far from being the case today. Adherents of Leninism are now a small minority within the workers' movements of all countries and the recent mass radical movements of the streets. On the contrary in many of the most important struggles of the last few years there has been, especially in the initial stages, a distinct hostility to any and all political parties. There was an element of this in Tahrir Square in the Egyptian Revolution of 2011 and it was very strong in the Indignados movement in Spain, where all political parties and banners were banned. Similar sentiments existed in much of the Occupy movement internationally and were also present in parts of the anti-water charges movement in Ireland in 2014-2016. Much of this can be seen as resulting from disillusionment with the "mainstream" parties, particularly right wing social democracy which from PASOK in Greece to the Labour Party in Ireland is widely seen as having deceived "the people" and let them down. At the same time, there is clearly a specific suspicion of would-be revolutionary parties and a belief that they may be out just to use the mass movement to serve their own agenda.

Such attitudes also existed in Lenin's day but he did not devote much time to them:

> Erler's attempts to give the question more "profundity" and to proclaim that in general political parties are unnecessary and "bourgeois" are so supremely absurd that one can only shrug one's shoulders...
>
> Repudiation of the Party principle and of Party discipline...is tantamount to completely disarming the proletariat in *the interests of the bourgeoisie*. It all adds up to that petty-bourgeois diffuseness and instability, that incapacity for sustained effort, unity and organised action, which, if encouraged, must inevitably destroy any proletarian revolutionary movement.[313]

Today the question must be dealt with more carefully and more thoroughly. First let us grant, for the sake of argument, that all political parties have anti-democratic and oligarchical tendencies. But then the same is true of virtually every institution in this society: trade unions, hospitals, schools, universities, welfare departments, private businesses, state media corporations, police, the armed forces and so on. Indeed, with the exception of trade unions, political parties tend to be more democratic and less hierarchical than any of the institutions listed above which, generally speaking, contain no democratic or elective component whatsoever. So unless we attribute the hierarchical character of political parties to human nature, we are forced to the conclusion that their anti-democratic features derive from the hierarchical undemocratic and class structured character of the capitalist society within which they arise and operate. In any case these anti-democratic characteristics, in so far as they are widespread, cannot plausibly be attributed to the organisational form of the political party as such.

Second let us assume, again for the purpose of the argument, that it were possible actually—with the wave of a magic wand—to abolish all political parties so that all deputies, MPs, local councillors and other elected representatives were unaffiliated individuals, "independents' as they are usually called. Would this benefit the working class and the majority of people? No, it would not. On the contrary, in such circumstances it would the rich, the bourgeoisie, who would benefit enormously because they would be able to use their personal wealth and all their other advantages (connections, cultural capital, etc) to dominate politics even more than they do at present. Only through collective organization—be it in unions or in parties—are working people able to resist the power of capital and the domination of the bourgeoisie.

Nor is this just a question of elections. Even more important is the bourgeoisie's ideological hegemony. Marx wrote as far back as 1845 that:

> The ideas of the ruling class are in every epoch the ruling ideas, ie the class which is the ruling material force of society, is at the same time its ruling intellectual force. The class which has the means of material production at its disposal, has control at the same time over the means of mental production, so that thereby, generally speaking, the ideas of those who lack the means of mental production are subject to it.[314]

And if that was true in the middle of the 19th century, it remains true in the era of CNN, Fox News, Murdoch and Disney. This hegemony is not, of course, total or uncontested even spontaneously by individuals. Nevertheless the extent to which across the board resistance to bourgeois ideology—resistance that counters not only the ruling class's immediate day-to-day propaganda but its whole worldview, its philosophy, its economic theory, its theories of history and so on—can be sustained by *individuals* without organisation is decidedly minimal. The bourgeoisie is organised by means of its political parties and leaders, its innumerable media outlets, its think tanks, its control of the education system and numerous other institutions, to promote its ideology. The working class and socialists need *their* organisations to formulate, develop and promulgate their world outlook. Trade unions play a role in this but their "economic" character makes this very limited. Political parties, which draw together "intellectuals" and workers, which raise the intellectual level of their members and produce what Gramsci called "organic intellectuals", ie intellectuals inseparably connected to the working class, while also obliging the intellectuals to learn from the workers,[315] are crucial here. Lenin drew attention to this function of the socialist party in 1905:

We also have some organisational experience and an actual organisation, which has played an educational role and has undoubtedly borne fruit... The working class is instinctively, spontaneously Social-Democratic, and more than ten years of work put in by Social-Democracy has done a great deal to transform this spontaneity into consciousness.[316]

And Gramsci developed it:

One should stress the importance and significance which, in the modern world, political parties have in the elaboration and diffusion of conceptions of the world, because essentially what they do is to work out the ethics and politics corresponding to these conceptions.[317]

[It is necessary] to work incessantly to raise the intellectual level of ever-growing strata of the populace, in other words, to give a personality to the amorphous mass element. This means working to produce elites of intellectuals of a new type which arise directly out of the masses, but remain in contact with them to become, as it were, the whalebone in the corset. This...is what really modifies the "ideological panorama" of the age.[318]

Of course, no magic wand for disappearing parties exists and in reality the only way "all" political parties can be abolished is by repression carried out by a fascist or military dictatorship and this would be massively damaging to the interests of working people. The only other possible scenario remotely resembling the abolition of all political parties is one in which it is parties of the left or the working class that are abolished or reduced to insignificance. As we know this has been, for all practical purposes, the case in the United States for most of the last hundred years—hardly an example for the left to follow. Just as those who proclaim their "opposition on principle to all violence" only ever succeed in inducing oppositional movements to remain non-violent and never have the slightest hope of persuading capitalist states to renounce violence (disband their armies, police, etc) so there is no possibility of the capitalist class being persuaded to give up their parties—to dissolve the Tory Party in Britain, the Democrat and Republican Parties in the United States, the Christian Democrats in Germany and so on. The arguments against parties in general will have traction only on our side and especially among people who are newly radicalising or engaged in their first major struggle. This is why they do work, regardless of intentions, to, in Lenin's words, politically "disarm the proletariat in the interest of the bourgeoisie".

An error sometimes made by anarchists or autonomists, who oppose parties on principle, is that they mistake the ready response their position sometimes gets in spontaneous mass movements with mass radicalisation and the adoption of revolutionary sentiments when in reality it is a combination of political naiveté and anti-political lack of clarity or "conservatism" (with a small c) which can go in a number of different directions. An indication of the weakness and superficiality of these anti-all political parties sentiments is the rapidity with which, faced with the concrete reality of a [bourgeois] election, they can flip over into uncritical support for a reformist party provided it engages in a certain amount of radical rhetoric.

The most dramatic example of this is the transformation of the Indignados or 15M Movement in the Spanish state into support for Podemos. Angered by the severe effect of the 2008 crash on the Spanish economy, mass unemployment and severe problems of evictions and homelessness, the 15M movement launched a series of occupations of public squares in the run up to the 2011 Spanish elections. Clearly inspired by Tahrir Square and the Arab Spring, the movement expressed deep alienation from the established political system with its two-party oscillation between the right wing People's Party (PP) and the "moderate" socialists (PSOE). The central slogans were: "They don't represent us!" and "Real Democracy Now!" The initiators and core activists of the movement were relatively small groups of anarchists and autonomists, but it very rapidly attracted mass support. Between 20,000 and 50,000 joined the initial occupation of Puerta del Sol in Madrid. This increased when the police tried to remove occupiers from the squares. It is estimated that on 19 June, a million people demonstrated across the state and in the course of the movement as a whole, which lasted throughout the year, something like 6-8 million people took part in one or other of its occupations, assemblies or demonstrations.[319]

The movement did a lot of its business through mass popular assemblies which practised a version of direct democracy involving consensus decision making. It was marked by strong hostility to all political parties and trade unions. The authoritarianism involved in this ban on political parties, which was enforced by stewards, is a contradiction which the anarchists involved seemed not to notice but as a result revolutionary socialist organisations who wanted to be involved were obliged to leave their banners, placards and papers at home and participate, at least ostensibly, simply as individuals.[320]

I have critiqued the weaknesses of this method of decision making elsewhere,[321] but the point I want to stress here is that in January 2014 a large part of this movement, supposedly committed to direct democracy, horizontalism and opposition to all forms of conventional politics, threw in its lot behind a new political party, Podemos. Podemos' Political Secretary, Íñigo Erréjon, has stated that, "We are not the party of 15M—mainly because any party that claimed to be the party of 15M would be a fraud...given that it is a heterogeneous movement" and "Podemos is not the expression or electoral translation of 15M".[322] Nevertheless it is a fact, as Susan Watkins has noted, that when Pablo Iglesias put out a call for a new, anti-austerity platform for elections to the European Parliament, "nearly a thousand local circles began forming almost spontaneously, built by 15M and far left activists"[323] and it has to be the case that the bulk of the over 100,000 members and more than a million votes it immediately attracted were people who had participated in 15M. And particularly remarkable is the fact that Podemos was set up explicitly as an initiative from above by intellectuals, mainly from the Complutense University of Madrid "without", as Errejón recognises, "any previous consultation between movements, or between assemblies or among the indignados"[324] and around a preselected "charismatic leader", Pablo Iglesias.

Moreover, Podemos was indisputably a reformist party. Some confusion has existed about this because Podemos counterposed itself so emphatically to the PSOE as a party of the "political caste" and because there has been a tendency among some commentators to identify reformism entirely and exclusively with traditional social democracy so that Podemos, and Syriza, were seen as not being reformist. But in fact the project of the Podemos leadership was explicitly never more than to win a parliamentary majority and bring about a "transformation" of Spanish society, without even specifying a transformation into socialism. Iglesias, writing in *New Left Review*, refers to "the impossibility of socialism and revolution" and comments dismissively that "seen from the present, it is quite moving that there were political leaders in Spain who believed in the viability of these projects."[325]

The case of Podemos may be the most dramatic instance of this rapid transition from anti-politics to support for a party but it is by no means the only one. Something similar happened in the United States with the candidacy of Bernie Sanders. His campaign for the Democratic nomination in 2016 was very much fuelled by supporters of the Occupy movement, which had operated on similar anti-political party rules to 15M. Even in Greece, where the "old left" traditions were stronger, there was a similar switch from "autonomist" anti-austerity street demonstrations and rioting to voting for Syriza.

This pattern raises two issues: first, that for many people hostility to all political parties is probably not a thought through opposition to the existence of parties as such but an opposition to their presence in what are seen as "autonomous" or "grassroots" campaigns or movements; and second, the idea that the time of Leninist revolutionary parties is over and that the model for today, and for the future, is a "broad left party" such as Syriza, Podemos or the Corbynite British Labour Party. I will discuss these questions in turn,

Parties and campaigns: Leave your politics at the door!

Anyone with experience of community or national campaigns over single issues or groups of related issues or of trade union and workers' struggles over wages or jobs will have encountered this. "This issue is non-political" some campaigners will say, "It's just about our basic human rights", or "This is above politics, it's about justice and humanity". So you are welcome as individuals but "please leave your politics at the door". In this scenario, political parties are acknowledged as having a role to play in society but only in their "legitimate" sphere of parliament and parliamentary elections, not in this campaign or struggle for x, y or z.

There is much to be said about this attitude. It reflects and accepts the bourgeois (and the reformist) view of politics as the exclusive sphere of "professional politicians" and parliamentary representatives in contrast to the activities of ordinary people who are seen as non-political. And it is an illusion that *any* issue is, or can be, "above politics"; politics is about the struggle over how society is run and therefore, by its nature, involves issues of morality, of justice, of humanity and of life and death. But it also speaks to two important features of popular consciousness at the present time. The first is the idea that the presence of "left wing extremists" (ie revolutionary parties) will "put people off" and prevent the campaign gaining mass support. The second is the conviction or at least suspicion that political parties are only in it for themselves, are just trying to win votes and recruits and sell their papers, and therefore will try to distort or "hijack" the campaign. These, it seems to me, are real concerns that need to be addressed.

Let's begin by acknowledging that would-be revolutionary parties do want to get votes, recruits and paper sales. Any far left party that doesn't want these things, ie is not trying to grow, will not be long for this world. So does this put people off? The evidence suggests it does not. In the biggest political campaigns I have seen over the last half century—the Vietnam Solidarity Campaign of the late 1960s, the Anti-Nazi League of the late 1970s, CND in the early 1908s, the Anti-Poll Tax campaign of 1989-1990, the Stop the War Coalition movement against the Iraq War in 2003 (all in Britain) and the anti-water charges campaign of 2014-2015 (in Ireland)—left wing parties with their placards, banners and paper sellers were active and highly visible. It did not deter hundreds of thousands of people from taking to the streets. No one who seriously wants to resist fascism or stop an imperialist war or defeat a hated tax and is prepared to do something about it is going to say "I want to protest but I'm not going to in case I end up standing next to an SWP placard or someone tries to sell me a left wing newspaper". And in a number of these campaigns it was a would-be Leninist revolutionary party that was actually in the driving seat—this was clearly the case with the Anti-Nazi League where it was the Socialist Workers' Party (SWP), the Poll Tax (the Militant Tendency) and Stop the War, the SWP again.

But perhaps the intervention or leading role of a party may damage a campaign by diverting it from its purpose in the interests of the party or the party's ideology. Obviously this cannot be ruled out. There are times when revolutionaries and revolutionary parties behave badly or stupidly, but there are times when everyone behaves badly or stupidly. All campaigns have leadership of some kind and the leadership being reformist rather than revolutionary or supposedly "non-political" or not politically affiliated equally offers no guarantee against bad leadership. However, there are serious reasons why the involvement of organised revolutionary Marxists is likely to be a substantial advantage to a campaign, be it local or national.

First, in so far as they take their own ideology seriously (and they do) they will start from the view that as socialists "they have no interests separate or apart from those of the proletariat as a whole" (Marx) and will be doing their best to help the campaign win. Serious revolutionaries do actually fight for concrete reforms. Secondly, in so far as they hope to gain recruits from the campaign (which they will) it will be and has to be through being the best activists, both the most hard working and with the best ideas on how to win. Thirdly, membership of a revolutionary party will actually assist the activists in the campaign by enabling them to draw on the experience of other members and their knowledge of previous struggles, local, national and international. As Trotsky said, "the party is the memory of the class". I wrote recently about how this worked in relation to a specific struggle, the anti-water charges campaign in Ireland in 2014-2016:

> First, even in terms of an immediate struggle such as the anti-water charges movement having a revolutionary socialist party at its heart is a very *positive* thing—it helps the campaign to win.
>
> A revolutionary party brings together activists from Clondalkin and Ballyfermot, Artane and Dun Laoghaire, Cork and Sligo, Wicklow and Wexford. It also involves people who fought the household charges and the bin tax and some who resisted water charges the first time around. In the party these activists can pool their experience and form a coherent strategy.
>
> This was what happened and on that basis we argued that it was not enough just to resist the installation of water meters—important as that was—but we needed mass demonstrations. And mass demos were not enough—we needed a mass boycott. But the mass boycott also needed masses on the streets to sustain it. And that resistance to meters and the demos and the boycott needed to be accompanied by a challenge at the ballot box.
>
> And this strategy has been proven correct. But in fact each part of it was resisted at various times by elements in the movement. To win it we needed a coherent group of people—at the heart of the movement—patiently arguing for this strategy.[326]

The details are obviously specific but the essentials of the argument apply, I think, to a very wide range of campaigns and movements. Importantly, they apply also to trade union struggles and strikes but with a particular added dimension. The added dimension is that strikes and other industrial disputes are generally speaking led by union leaders and union officials, but union leaders and officials do not share the same interests as their members but form a distinct social layer standing between and mediating between the workers and the employers. As a social layer they are characterised by: 1) higher pay (in the case of top leaders, much higher) and better conditions than the workers they represent; 2) the relative detachment of their conditions from those of their members, for example a union official who gives away a tea break in negotiations does not thereby lose his/her tea break; 3) a working life which leads to spending more time talking to management than to the shop floor; and 4) a tendency to view disputes not as struggles to be won but as problems to be solved.

At the same time union officials remain ultimately dependent on the existence of the union and its membership to pay their wages and are therefore subject to pressure from below. If the union officials openly abandon all attempts to represent their members, the members will either remove the officials or leave the union; either way the officials will be out of a job. Their material interest, without bribery and regardless of ideology, is to maintain the balance between the employers and the workers. This objective social position produces in the trade union bureaucracy an equally objective tendency to vacillate between the classes.

This tendency to vacillate and therefore to sell out their members has been demonstrated by union leaders and officials again and again historically and internationally: examples range from the German trade union leaders who blocked strikes before the First World War, through the British TUC who betrayed the General Strike in 1926 and let down the Miners' Strike in 1984-1985, to the Irish trade union leaders who adopted social partnership with the government for 25 years, to the leadership of COSATU in South Africa, to virtually all the leaders of the US trade unions since the 1930s. It is reasonable to say that union leaders who remained uncompromising and principled, like Jim Larkin and Arthur Scargill, are the exception rather than the rule.

However, neither this analysis nor this history is known to most workers and when they go on strike, especially for the first time, they often feel they have no choice but to trust their union leaders, particularly when these leaders are promising support and making militant speeches (as they often do). But workers who are members of a revolutionary party are able, because the party is the memory of the class, to learn from the experience of others that trade union leaders should not be relied on. It is not a question of rejecting the unions (we have seen how insistent Lenin was on this) but of learning how to work within the unions, alongside the officials when they support their members' struggles but independently of them when they weaken or sell out. The collective experience and training provided by a revolutionary party is indispensable here and it will not be provided by reformist or left reformist parties, which are almost invariably linked to and dependent on sections of the trade union bureaucracy. Naturally the union officials will be hostile to this involvement as they will see it as undermining their authority with the workers and will doubtless warn their members against the influence of extremists/militants/troublemakers and so on.

Thus I have argued that, on balance, the participation of organised revolutionary socialists, ie of revolutionary groups and parties, is beneficial to the struggles of working people. But if at this stage we step back from these specific arguments about the role of parties in campaigns and strikes, we can see that at the heart of this whole debate is again the question of reformism. The view that the legitimate sphere for political parties is parliamentary elections, while community campaigns limit themselves to single issues and trade unions concentrate on wages and conditions in the workplace, is central to reformism and the nature of the role played by reformism, in the past and in the future, is central to the argument for a revolutionary party.

The role of reformist parties

The party "model" of choice for most left wing socialists and left activists today, at least in Europe, is not a revolutionary party but some kind of broad left party. Something along the lines of Syriza (before the Tsipras leadership capitulated to the EU), Podemos, Front de Gauche, the Corbyn Labour Party, the Portuguese Left Bloc, Die Linke in Germany, the Scottish Socialist Party (before its disastrous splits over its leader, Tommy Sheridan), the Danish Red-Green Alliance and so on.

The case for this kind of party rests on three main arguments: first, that they are the means, the only real means, of achieving left unity; second, that they are the only real means of achieving the size, the critical mass, necessary to mount any sort of serious challenge to capitalism as opposed to being a fringe irrelevance; and third, that they "transcend" the old debate between reform and revolution by bringing together both reformists and revolutionaries in a strategy of transformation of the system.

The first two arguments are very powerful, are very much interconnected and have a strong appeal: the first because the overwhelming majority of the left and of politically aware working class people understand the need for unity against the right and against the employers, and the second because the far left, the avowed revolutionaries, do seem to be an insignificant minority more or less everywhere. The third argument is much weaker. In reality these left parties mark a return to the kind of organisation—an alliance of reformists and revolutionaries—characteristic of the Second International, which then and now actually subordinates revolutionaries to a reformist perspective in that they are committed to a parliamentary transformation of society. Having argued at length (in Chapter 2 above) that this will not and cannot succeed because, among other things, of the nature of the capitalist state, I will not repeat the arguments here. However, it should be noted that for most people on the left the first two arguments are so immediate and compelling that they simply set the third argument aside or put it on the back burner. This does not mean, of course, as the fate of Syriza demonstrated, that the problem goes away.

But here it also needs to be said that the problems of reformism and reformist parties are by no means confined to their inability to deliver socialist or radical change when they assume office. In fact the problems begin long before the winning of any sort of parliamentary majority and they have very serious effects on the working class struggle in the here and now. Reformist parties, including the new left reformist parties are "electoralist"; overwhelmingly their main priority is the winning of elections and how they perform in elections is the main criterion by which they judge their success or failure. But electoralism has a logic to it and that logic is pretty implacable: to win elections you have to persuade, if not an outright majority, at least a plurality of the electorate to vote for you. But the consciousness of the majority of the population is dominated by the ideas of the ruling class, by bourgeois ideology. Not all by any means, but nevertheless a majority accept ideas such as that businesses have to make a profit, that (capitalist) law should be obeyed, that (excessive) immigration is a problem, that there is some kind of common national interest and that the national army should be supported in war. This means that a left party focused primarily on winning elections comes under immense pressure to modify and compromise any sort of radical programme it may have put forward, in order to win votes.

This scenario, which has been played out many times, is currently running in Britain with regard to Jeremy Corbyn and the Labour Party. Much to everyone's surprise, veteran left winger Jeremy Corbyn was elected leader of the Labour Party by a landslide in September 2015. From the moment of his victory, he was subject to intense attack by both national media and by other Labour MPs and former Labour leaders. He was denounced for holding views on war, immigration, Ireland, Palestine, the monarchy and much else that could be considered outside of the mainstream "consensus" and because of this was deemed "unelectable". In 2016 he was challenged for the leadership by a "moderate" MP, Owen Smith, but after a vigorous campaign involving extraordinarily well-attended and enthusiastic public rallies all over Britain, Corbyn was re-elected with an even larger majority.

Given that he received more support from Labour Party members than had been received by any previous leader, this second victory would normally have been accepted as conclusive and more or less everyone would have "rallied behind the leader". But this has not happened and the main reason cited by leading Labour figures is that Labour is a long way behind the Tories in opinion polls. In this situation even commentators like Owen Jones and Paul Mason with reputations as outspoken leftists have been issuing dire warnings and calling for Labour to "listen to the electorate" about immigration and drop its opposition to the Trident nuclear weapons system. Up to now Corbyn has proved pretty resistant to these pressures but there have also been some signs of his weakening. One instance was over the Brexit referendum on leaving the EU. Corbyn's position had been, like Tony Benn and most of the Labour Party far left in the past, to oppose the EU on anti-capitalist and democratic grounds. But in 2016 he reached an agreement with the Labour right and centre to support the Remain campaign in the referendum.[327] Another instance has been Corbyn's main ally and Shadow Chancellor, John McDonnell, supporting the £369 million refurbishment of Buckingham Palace as a "national monument"[328] and Corbyn's recent statements on migration have been growing more ambiguous.[329]

If, as is the case with the Labour Party, electoral success is seen as the primary and overriding objective, this kind of slippage is close to inevitable and it has very serious consequences for working class consciousness. For example, in so far as immigration is accepted as a problem by the Labour Party as well as the Tories, this not only accepts the mainstream consensus but actually reinforces it and simultaneously strengthens the argument of the racist right that since immigrants are a problem they should be sent home. And a similar dynamic applies with Trident and many other issues.

It is useful to consider here the difference between the reformist and revolutionary (Leninist) approach because there is more involved than revolutionaries simply being more "principled" and more intransigent. For the revolutionary Marxist, raising the consciousness of the working class is of the highest importance, more important than winning elections, because it is the working class itself that is the agent of social transformation with MPs playing only a subordinate role. In contrast, for reformists, even very left reformists, it is the parliamentary deputies and government ministers who are the key actors with the working class playing a supportive role.

Nor is the damage done by reformist electoralism confined to programmatic concessions and their impact on consciousness, it also extends to the working class struggle itself, especially mass strikes. It is a key component of the mainstream consensus, invariably endorsed by the media, that strikes are a) a bad thing, b) unpopular and c) that militant protests, especially where "violence" is involved, are even worse and even more unpopular. Consequently, just as there is pressure to moderate ideological and political positions, so there is pressure to dissociate from, or downplay, extra-parliamentary struggles. Moreover, this dovetails with the approach of trade union leaders who tend to be a mainstay of (and major source of funds for) all reformist parties and who likewise tend to see strikes as problems to be solved and kept out of the hands of hotheads and militants.

The experience

In his 1924 book *Lessons of October*, Leon Trotsky argued that "the principle lesson of the last decade" was that "without a party, apart from a party, over the head of a party, or with a substitute for a party, the proletarian revolution cannot conquer".[330] What he had in mind was the fact that between 1916 and 1923 Europe had witnessed numerous uprisings and working class challenges to capitalism (in Italy, Bulgaria, Spain, Hungary, Finland, Ireland, Britain and, above all, in Germany) but in only one case, Russia, had the revolution actually won. This victory, Trotsky believed, was due to the role played by the Bolshevik Party and its leadership. In all the other cases, especially Germany, the absence of such a party and of correct revolutionary leadership, brought about the failure of the revolution.

Naturally Trotsky's claim is disputed. Those who reject a revolutionary perspective for today tend, unsurprisingly, to deny the existence of revolutionary opportunities in these years. For example Eric Hobsbawm observed:

> My generation...was brought up on the story of the betrayal of the German Revolution of 1918 by the moderate Social Democratic leaders... For a few weeks or even months in 1918-19 a spread of the Russian Revolution to Germany could seem on the cards.
>
> But it wasn't. I think today there is historical consensus about this... I don't think Germany belonged to the revolutionary sector of Europe... A German October revolution, or anything like it, was not seriously on and therefore didn't have to be betrayed.[331]

Nevertheless, despite Hobsbawm's claim of "historical consensus", there are a number of detailed historical studies that support Trotsky's conclusions, most importantly, Chris Harman's *The Lost Revolution* and Pierre Broué's *The German Revolution 1917-23*.[332] That these years demonstrated the need for a revolutionary party, a "modern prince", was also a central part of the arguments advanced by Gramsci in the 1920s and in his *Prison Notebooks*.

But what of the experience since that time? In fact there have been many revolutionary upheavals or partial revolutions. China 1925-1927, Spain 1936, France 1936, Italy and Greece 1944-1945, Hungary 1956, France 1968, Chile 1970-1973, Portugal 1974-1975, Iran 1979, Poland 1980-1981, China 1989, Indonesia 1997-1998 and Egypt 2011 are examples.[333] Yet in none of these was a revolutionary party of any size or quality present and in none of them was a revolutionary breakthrough achieved. Of course to establish a causal link between the former absence and the latter failure concrete analysis is required.

This was provided by Trotsky in relation to France and Spain in 1936 and by various writers in relation to May '68, Chile, Portugal, Iran and Poland.[334]

There is no need to recapitulate all these studies here but I will present two examples: May 1968 in France, whose 50th anniversary is approaching, and the Egyptian Revolution of 2011.

France in 1968 did not experience a moment of revolutionary crisis equivalent to Russia in September-October 1917 or Germany in the summer and autumn of 1923; the army had not come over to the revolution, there was no insane inflation and there were no soviets or workers' councils. Nevertheless there was a general strike involving 10 million workers—probably the largest general strike in history at that point in time—there were numerous factory occupations and, of course, there was serious street fighting in Paris between the students and their allies and the riot police. That there was an exhilarating revolutionary atmosphere is attested to by almost everyone who took part.[335] There was certainly enough of a threat to throw the French government into disarray and to send the President, General de Gaulle, scurrying out of Paris to consult with his generals.

However, in terms of political leadership on the side of the insurgents there was huge weakness. The trade unions and the workers' movement were largely dominated by the very conservative and very Stalinist French Communist Party (PCF). Among the students there was a chaotic mélange of revolutionary ideas ranging from an amorphous anarchism or libertarian communism around charismatic individuals such as Daniel Cohn-Bendit to a number of very small groups, known as groupuscules, of Maoist and Trotskyist persuasion.[336]

To develop the movement in a revolutionary direction, to move it towards a French October, it was necessary to unite the revolutionary spirit of the students with the power and social weight of the working class and to advance a programme of demands which could focus the workers' strikes and occupations (these had begun spontaneously and lacked coherent demands). The PCF, which dominated the factories, was opposed to both these tasks. It had originally denounced the student revolt as "pseudo-revolutionaries [who] serve the interests of the Gaullist government and the big capitalist monopolies"[337] and used its stewards to keep students and workers apart on the demonstrations and repel the students when they sent delegations to the factories. As far as the strikes were concerned, it wanted, and worked to bring about, a settlement and an early return to work.

The anarchist, Maoist and Trotskyist groupuscules would have liked to have overcome these divisions but they lacked any serious base in the workplaces or unions and so were largely powerless. Clearly what was required, and was missing, was a revolutionary party with roots among both the workers and the students built in advance of the May explosion. This would not have made the victory of the revolution in any way guaranteed but it would have given it a chance. In the event the PCF was able, despite worker resistance, to close down the strikes and occupations on the basis of limited economic concessions and this allowed General de Gaulle to restore order and win the subsequent general election.[338]

The form taken by the Egyptian Revolution of 2011 was different from that of the May Events. Emerging out of 30 years of the Mubarak dictatorship the left and the labour movement as a whole were much weaker than in France. Egyptian communism had both compromised itself and nearly been destroyed by its entanglement with Nasserism and there was no equivalent to the CGT, the Communist dominated trade union federation in France. Egyptian "trade unions" were state controlled bodies, not really unions at all.

On the other hand the street confrontations in Egypt, beginning on 25 January and coming to a head on 28 January and in "the Battle of the Camel" on 2 February, were much larger, not in any way confined to students or to Cairo, and more violent, producing over 800 martyrs. They were also far more successful in that both the police, on 28 January, and the counter-revolutionary lumpen proletariat or "baltagiya" in the Battle of the Camel[339] were smashed off the streets and hundreds of police stations, vehicles and ruling party buildings were set on fire nationwide. There was no equivalent to the 10 million-strong general strike but strikes, especially by the Malhalla textile workers, did play a key role in preparing the way for the uprising and in forcing Mubarak out on 10-11 February.

The existence of a significant revolutionary party in January 2016 would have strengthened and deepened the revolution, but it is not plausible to suggest that it would or could have led, there and then, to the establishment of workers' power; illusions in both the army and the Muslim Brotherhood were far too prevalent at that point in time.

Where the absence of a large, rooted revolutionary party made a real difference was in 2013.

The victory of the revolution over Mubarak secured the holding of democratic elections which were won by the Muslim Brotherhood. But the Muslim Brotherhood government was a disaster. It displayed all the worst features of moderate passive reformism and thoroughly alienated the mass of the population through its mishandling of the economy and general incompetence while at the same time antagonising the Egyptian ruling class and the army. In this situation, a mass movement arose, again of immense proportions but lacking all political clarity. It developed around an anti-government petition launched by a youth movement called Tamarod (Rebellion). Judged by many of its leading personnel, Tamarod appeared to have emerged out of the anti-Mubarak revolution, but it later became clear that elements of Tamarod had links with the military. The anti-Muslim Brotherhood petition attracted huge support and on 30 June 2013 Tamarod and an assortment of other political forces (including groups linked to the old regime) called a demonstration demanding the fall of the government. The turnout on the day was truly enormous possibly as big as anything in the great mobilisations of 2011.

But within these demonstrations were both revolutionaries hoping to overthrow the Muslim Brotherhood government from the left and pro-military elements hoping for the overthrow of the government by the generals. It was the latter that had the initiative and on 3 July when the military, led by General al-Sisi, struck, arresting Mohammed Morsi, the Muslim Brotherhood president, and launching a coup which rapidly turned into an all-out counter-revolution. The Brotherhood responded by insisting on the "legitimacy" of the Morsi presidency and their government and by organizing their own continuous street protests. They established two street sit-ins, one near Cairo University in Giza and a larger one at Rab'aa in Nasr City. After nearly six weeks of ongoing protest, on 14 August the al-Sisi regime dispersed the sit-ins by means of brutal massacres killing at the very least, by their own admission, 638 Muslim Brotherhood supporters and injuring and arresting thousands more.[340] The counter-revolutionary coup was now firmly in place and sealed in blood and it has returned Egypt to military rule every bit as brutal as the rule of Mubarak.

Throughout this period there did exist in the embryo of a serious revolutionary party, the Egyptian Revolutionary Socialists (RS). The RS were, and still are, an excellent organisation but, emerging out of clandestinity and the wreckage of the Middle Eastern left, it was, through no fault of its own, very small and inexperienced. In an absolutely necessary attempt to grow and establish mass roots they recruited large numbers of young revolutionaries inspired by the 18 revolutionary days. Inevitably, these young recruits were full of the infantile ultra-leftism described by Lenin and this led to various mistakes. But before they had time fully to resolve these problems, they were confronted by an exceptionally difficult situation, the politically ambiguous Tamarod movement and mass mobilisation of 30 June, which it was ill equipped to deal with. And it also lacked the size to significantly influence the course of events when millions of people were in motion.

Could or would the existence of a battle-hardened revolutionary party of the size and experience of the Bolsheviks in February or June 1917 have been able to avert the disaster of June-August 2013? No one can say for certain, but it would have had a real chance. A mass party with worker militants in the factories and communities and some presence in the villages could have advanced a programme capable of directing anti-Brotherhood anger to the left rather than the right. With the vast numbers involved this would have opened up new and exceptionally favourable revolutionary possibilities.[341]

Finally there is the situation in Europe and elsewhere today. There is clearly not any sort of revolutionary conjuncture; nevertheless there is a developing polarisation between the far left and the far right with the centre under threat everywhere. Again this places a premium on political organisation. Where the left can focus the anger of the masses at the neoliberal austerity imposed since the 2008 crash, the whole society can radicalise, as has occurred in Greece, Spain and Ireland. Where the left is unable to provide this focus, the radical racist right and outright fascists are able to take advantage as is the case France, Austria, the Netherlands, Britain and, of course, Trump.

What this experience shows is that the hundred years since 1917 have, despite major economic, social and political changes, in no way diminished the need for a revolutionary party. This is because the fundamental features of the class struggle from which the necessity of a revolutionary party derives—the hegemony of bourgeois ideology, the uneven development of political consciousness and confidence among the mass of the working class, the centralised power of the capitalist state and the damaging and treacherous role of reformism—are still in place and will continue to operate for the foreseeable future.

Conclusion

It follows from all this experience and from the political arguments I have advanced that the core principles and key characteristics of the Leninist party, outlined earlier in this chapter, provide also the starting point for how the necessary revolutionary party should be built. It must begin with the establishment of a core unequivocally committed to international socialist revolution and then on the basis of and around that core build the closest possible relationship with the day-to-day struggles of the working class in its workplaces and communities.

How this combination is actually to be achieved will, of course, vary from country to country and from concrete situation to concrete situation and can be determined only in practice. As Gramsci noted, "in reality one can 'scientifically' foresee only the struggle, but not the concrete moments of the struggle". I will return to this question in the final chapter. But it is evident, as Lenin so clearly understood, that the fate of the revolution, and thus of humanity, depends on it.

5

Lenin and the fight against oppression

ANY overview of the last 50 or so years of class and political struggle internationally must recognise the major role that has been played by a multitude of movements, campaigns and struggles directed against various forms of oppression and disadvantage, alongside of, but by no means confined to, the basic economic and political struggle of the working class.

The list of such movements is a long one and I will mention here only some of the most obvious: the struggle against colonialism and apartheid, the Black movement in the US (through its various phases: civil rights, Black Power down to Black Lives Matter); the women's liberation movement or second-wave feminism (also going through many phases); the Gay liberation movement beginning with Stonewall and evolving into the LGBT movement and to LGBTQ or LGBT+); the Latino movement; the international student revolt of the late 1960s; the disability movement; the environmental movement; the peace or anti-war movement; Palestine solidarity and so on. The range of issues raised and tackled is even wider. For example the fight against racism has expanded to include the defence of immigrants, asylum seekers and refugees, combating the rise of Islamophobia, and anti-fascism, with also numerous nationally specific variants such as the question of Native Americans in the United States and Indigenous Peoples in South America, Australia, New Zealand and elsewhere, Hindu chauvinism in India, Han chauvinism in China, anti-Copt prejudice in Egypt, Sunni-Shia sectarianism in the Middle East, anti-Roma racism in Europe, anti-Traveller racism in Ireland and anti-Kurdish and anti-Armenian racism in Turkey. Again the list is infinite. It is also evident that the range of concerns of sexual politics has undergone considerable extension especially with the massive, though still of course incomplete, transformation of attitudes towards homosexuality and the emergence of the trans issue.

The dominant ideological/political banner under which the majority of these battles have been conducted in this period has been, and remains, "liberal equality" and/or liberal democracy; the claim that in a democracy all citizens should be treated as equals, regardless of "race", religion, national origin, gender, sexual orientation, etc, and the belief that this can be achieved without challenging the economic basis of capitalist society. But along with the liberal position, sometimes under its umbrella and sometimes in competition with it, we have also seen numerous campaigns waged under the banners of separatism (as in Black nationalism or feminist separatism), identity politics of one kind or another and, more recently, of privilege theory and intersectionality.

Socialist and Marxist opposition to oppression has also always been an element, albeit often a minority one, within all these struggles. But it is now manifestly the case that no progressive or left party or movement, never mind a revolutionary socialist one, can operate without a more or less comprehensive view on these questions. In this chapter I will argue that although many of these movements mostly developed 40 to 50 years after his death, Lenin, nonetheless, has important things to contribute to the ongoing debate on these issues.

The tribune of the people

I want to begin making this argument by quoting extensively from one of Lenin's most famous texts, *What is to be Done?* Written in the last months of 1901, *What is to be Done?* was a vigorous polemic against the so-called Economist trend in Russian Social Democracy at this time. It is worth reminding the reader that at that time (and until the First World War) the term Social Democracy was used by Lenin and by Marxists internationally to refer to the Marxist socialist movement and that when Lenin speaks of a Social Democrat he has in mind what today would be called a revolutionary socialist. The "Economists" were a tendency in the Russian movement who maintained that the main task of Social Democrats was to focus, almost exclusively, on the economic struggle of the working class against the capitalists in the factories and workplaces.

Lenin was vehemently opposed to this idea and this trend because, although he had done a good deal of economic agitation himself, he saw it as connected to Eduard Bernstein's reformism (or revisionism) then developing in Germany and because he believed that its consequence in Russia would be to leave the leadership of the struggle against the Tsarist autocracy to the liberal bourgeoisie (who would betray it). In contrast he insisted that socialists should work to raise the political consciousness of the working class and the working class should take the lead in the struggle for democracy (the bourgeois democratic revolution).

In the course of his polemic with Economism, Lenin developed an argument about the need to expose and challenge all forms of oppression in the Tsarist state. This aspect of *What is to be Done?* has received little attention because of the overwhelming focus on Lenin's comments about "introducing socialism into the working class from the outside" which have been seized on as evidence of his allegedly condescending view of the working class, but his points about taking up the struggle against oppression are both central to *What is to be Done?* and of lasting importance:

> [N]ot only must Social-Democrats not confine themselves exclusively to the economic struggle, but...they must not allow the organisation of economic exposures to become the predominant part of their activities. We must take up actively the political education of the working class and the development of its political consciousness...
>
> The question arises, what should political education consist in? Can it be confined to the propaganda of working-class hostility to the autocracy? Of course not... Agitation must be conducted with regard to every concrete example of *this* oppression (as we have begun to carry on agitation round concrete examples of economic oppression). Inasmuch as this oppression affects the most diverse classes of society, inasmuch as it manifests itself in the most varied spheres of life and activity— vocational, civic, personal, family, religious, scientific, etc, etc—is it not evident that *we shall not be fulfilling our task* of developing the political consciousness of the workers if we do not *undertake* the organisation of the *political exposure* of the autocracy in *all its aspects?* In order to carry on agitation round concrete instances of oppression, these instances must be exposed (as it is necessary to expose factory abuses in order to carry on economic agitation).[342]

As was often the case with Lenin, he repeats the same point again and again to drive it home. I won't quote all Lenin's statements but a number of examples are helpful:

Is it true that, in general, the economic struggle "is the most widely applicable means" of drawing the masses into the political struggle? It is entirely untrue. *Any and every* manifestation of police tyranny and autocratic outrage, not only in connection with the economic struggle, is not one whit less "widely applicable" as a means of "drawing in" the masses. The rural superintendents and the flogging of peasants, the corruption of the officials and the police treatment of the "common people" in the cities, the fight against the famine-stricken and the suppression of the popular striving towards enlightenment and knowledge, the extortion of taxes and the persecution of the religious sects, the humiliating treatment of soldiers and the barrack methods in the treatment of the students and liberal intellectuals—do all these and a thousand other similar manifestations of tyranny, though not directly connected with the "economic" struggle, represent, in general, *less* "widely applicable" means and occasions for political agitation and for drawing the masses into the political struggle? The very opposite is true.[343]

And

Working-class consciousness cannot be genuine political consciousness unless the workers are trained to respond to *all* cases of tyranny, oppression, violence, and abuse, no matter *what class* is affected.[344]

And again

In a word, every trade union secretary conducts and helps to conduct "the economic struggle against the employers and the government". It cannot be too strongly maintained that *this is still not* Social-Democracy, that the Social-Democrat's ideal should not be the trade union secretary, but *the tribune of the people*, who is able to react to every manifestation of tyranny and oppression, no matter where it appears, no matter what stratum or class of the people it affects.[345]

Going back to Marx and Engels, one finds that they held progressive views, especially by the standards of the day, on women's emancipation, on national oppression (particularly of Ireland and Poland) and that in the American Civil War they unambiguously supported the anti-slavery North.[346] However, one does not find in their writings this kind of programmatic statement, this insistence on the absolute necessity for a socialist and a socialist party to take up and actively contest *all* issues of oppression. Nor would such a stance have been typical of any of the other parties of the Second International. Lenin's position in this regard was new and genuinely pioneering and it is worth noting that among the groups he mentions as meriting solidarity are both students and "religious sects". Moreover, in contrast to the way he later distanced himself from some of the formulations in *What is to be Done?*, referring to how he had "bent-the-stick" in his struggle against the Economists, [347] the theme of combating all forms of oppression was one he returned to again and again throughout his political career.

The main form of racism in Tsarist Russia was anti-Semitism, so this can serve as a useful example. For Lenin, as for all the Russian revolutionaries, total opposition to anti-Semitism was a point of principle from the earliest days of the movement and as Lenin noted "the Jews provided a particularly high percentage (compared to the total of the Jewish population) of leaders of the revolutionary movement". The principal anti-Semitic organisation and the main organisers of pogroms were the pro-Tsarist, ultra-nationalist Black Hundreds. Lenin's writings from first to last use the term "Black Hundreds" as a by-word for extreme reaction in much the way that fascism came to be used by the left later in the 20th century. In a lecture on the 1905 Revolution in Zurich Lenin says:

> Tsarism knew perfectly well how to play up to the most despicable prejudices of the most ignorant strata of the population against the Jews, in order to organise, if not to lead directly, the pogroms—those atrocious massacres of peaceful Jews, their wives and children, which have roused such disgust throughout the whole civilised world. [348]

In March 1914 Lenin records with pride how the Bolshevik fraction in the Duma proposed a bill "to remove all limitations of rights placed upon the Jews, and all limitations whatsoever connected with descent from or membership of any particular nationality". He comments:

> To the agitation of the Black Hundreds, which endeavour to turn the workers' attention to the persecution of non-Russians, the worker must present his conviction of the necessity for complete equality, for complete and final renunciation of any special privileges, for any particular nation.
>
> The Black Hundreds are conducting a particularly hateful agitation against the Jews. The Purishkeviches try to make the Jewish people a scapegoat for all their own sins. The Russian Social-Democratic

Workers' Fraction have therefore rightly given pride of place in their Bill to the position of the Jews.

The schools, the Press, the Parliamentary tribune—everything and anything is being utilised in order to sow ignorant, evil and savage hatred against the Jews.

In this black, blackguardly business there engage not only the scum of the Black Hundreds, but also reactionary professors, scientists, journalists, deputies, etc. Millions, even milliards, of roubles are spent in order to poison the mind of the people.

It must be a point of honour for the *Russian* workers that the Bill against national oppression should be reinforced by tens of thousands of proletarian signatures and declarations.[349]

In 1919, at the height of the Civil War, when Petlyura and other Whites were carrying out the most terrible massacres in the Ukraine and elsewhere, Lenin made a recording of a short speech on anti-Jewish pogroms which can still be listened to (with English subtitles) on YouTube.* It remains an exemplary demonstration of socialist popular anti-racist propaganda.[350]

As I mentioned, passages in *What is to be Done?* referred to the defence against persecution of religious sects. Lenin was a staunch atheist but he was a no less staunch defender of religious freedom and he was keen that socialist propaganda should not give offence to people's religious feelings.[351] It is interesting in this context to look at the Bolsheviks' relations with Islam and with Muslims in the early years of the Revolution. David Crouch, in an outstanding article on this subject, sets the scene.

Muslims had suffered massively at the hands of Russian imperialism. The anger came to the surface after the introduction of conscription in Central Asia during the First World War, when the mass rebellion in summer 1916 saw 2,500 Russian colonialists lose their lives. The revolt was followed by ferocious repression: the Russians massacred some 83,000 people. The crisis of Tsarism in 1917, therefore, radicalised millions of Muslims, who demanded religious freedom and national rights denied them by the empire. On 1 May 1917, the First All-Russian Congress of Muslims took place in Moscow. Of 1,000 delegates, 200

---

* At https://www.youtube.com/watch?v=ioljxQsgUM4. It can also be found simply by googling Lenin on anti-Semitism.

were women. After heated debates the congress voted for an eight-hour working day, the abolition of private landed property, confiscation without indemnity of large properties, equality of political rights for women and an end to polygamy and purdah. The congress meant that Russia's Muslims were the first in the world to free women from the restrictions typical of Islamic societies of that period.[352]

Crouch goes onto show that after the Bolsheviks came to power they "aimed, as far as possible, to make amends for the crimes of Tsarism against national minorities and their religions". On 24 November the new Soviet government issued the following declaration "To all the Muslim workers of Russia and the East":

> Muslims of Russia…all you whose mosques and prayer houses have been destroyed, whose beliefs and customs have been trampled upon by the Tsars and oppressors of Russia: your beliefs and practices, your national and cultural institutions are forever free and inviolate. Know that your rights, like those of all the peoples of Russia, are under the mighty protection of the revolution.[353]

This was followed by a programme of affirmative action ending the domination of the Russian language, returning native languages to schools and government business and promoting Indigenous people to leading positions. In addition:

> Sacred Islamic monuments, books and objects looted by the Tsars were returned to the mosques: the Sacred Koran of Osman was ceremoniously handed over to a Muslim Congress in Petrograd in December 1917. Friday, the day of Muslim religious celebration, was declared the legal day of rest throughout Central Asia.[354]

All of this, which stood in the starkest contrast to the later anti-Islamic campaigns under Stalin, proved very successful in winning over many Muslims to the side of the Revolution. There is also no doubt it reflected the ideas and attitudes of Lenin.

It is anything but accidental that one of the issues, probably the most important issue, which led to Lenin, shortly before his death, breaking off relations with Stalin and calling for his removal as General Secretary was the question of the latter's lack of respect for the national rights of the Georgians.[355] Lenin's passion on this matter was extreme. When Stalin accused him of "national liberalism", Lenin replied on 6 October 1922:

I declare war to the death on dominant nation chauvinism. I shall eat it with all my healthy teeth as soon as I get rid of this accursed bad tooth.

It must be *absolutely* insisted that the Union Central Executive Committee should be *presided over* in turn by a:

Russian,

Ukrainian,

Georgian, etc.

Absolutely![356]

When the Central Committee of the Georgian Communist Party resigned in protest at Stalin's plan to force Georgia into an all Caucasian Federation and Ordzhonikidze, Stalin's agent, responded with personal threats and violence, Lenin (who was just recovering from another stroke) wrote on 30 December:

I suppose I have been very remiss with respect to the workers of Russia for not having intervened energetically and decisively enough in the notorious question of autonomisation, which, it appears, is officially called the question of the Soviet socialist republics...

If matters had come to such a pass that Orjonikidze could go to the extreme of applying physical violence, as Comrade Dzerzhinsky informed me, we can imagine what a mess we have got ourselves into. Obviously the whole business of "autonomisation" was radically wrong and badly timed.

It is said that a united apparatus was needed. Where did that assurance come from? Did it not come from that same Russian apparatus which, as I pointed out in one of the preceding sections of my diary, we took over from Tsarism and slightly anointed with Soviet oil?...

It is quite natural that in such circumstances the "freedom to secede from the union" by which we justify ourselves will be a mere scrap of paper, unable to defend the non-Russians from the onslaught of that really Russian man, the Great-Russian chauvinist, in substance a rascal and a tyrant, such as the typical Russian bureaucrat is. There is no doubt that the infinitesimal percentage of Soviet and sovietised workers will drown in that tide of chauvinistic Great-Russian riffraff like a fly in milk.

Here we have an important question of principle: how is internationalism to be understood?

The next day he returned to the subject:

In my writings on the national question I have already said that an abstract presentation of the question of nationalism in general is of no use at all. A distinction must necessarily be made between the nationalism of an oppressor nation and that of an oppressed nation, the nationalism of a big nation and that of a small nation.

In respect of the second kind of nationalism we, nationals of a big nation, have nearly always been guilty, in historic practice, of an infinite number of cases of violence; furthermore, we commit violence and insult an infinite number of times without noticing it. It is sufficient to recall my Volga reminiscences of how non-Russians are treated; how the Poles are not called by any other name than Polyachiska, how the Tatar is nicknamed Prince, how the Ukrainians are always Khokhols and the Georgians and other Caucasian nationals always Kapkasians.

That is why internationalism on the part of oppressors or "great" nations, as they are called (though they are great only in their violence, only great as bullies), must consist not only in the observance of the formal equality of nations but even in an inequality of the oppressor nation, the great nation, that must make up for the inequality which obtains in actual practice. Anybody who does not understand this has not grasped the real proletarian attitude to the national question, he is still essentially petty bourgeois in his point of view and is, therefore, sure to descend to the bourgeois point of view.

...In one way or another, by one's attitude or by concessions, it is necessary to compensate the non-Russian for the lack of trust, for the suspicion and the insults to which the government of the "dominant" nation subjected them in the past.

The Georgian [*Stalin*] who is neglectful of this aspect of the question, or who carelessly flings about accusations of "nationalist-socialism" (whereas he himself is a real and true "nationalist-socialist", and even a vulgar Great-Russian bully), violates, in substance, the interests of proletarian class solidarity, for nothing holds up the development and strengthening of proletarian class solidarity so much as national injustice.[357]

Thus, for Lenin, opposition to all oppression was such a feature of his politics from first to last that it can, and should, be added as a third core principle of the Leninist Party to the two discussed in the last chapter (the independent organisation of revolutionaries and relating to the working class).

The standpoint of the proletariat

However, this is still not the whole story of Lenin's position. The quotation from *What is to be Done?* which I cited earlier "Working-class consciousness cannot be genuine political consciousness unless the workers are trained to respond to all cases of tyranny, oppression, violence, and abuse, no matter *what class* is affected"[358] continued immediately, "unless they are trained, moreover, to respond from a Social-Democratic point of view and no other."

What does "from a Social-Democratic point of view" mean here? Clearly "Marxist" and also "the standpoint of the working class or proletariat"—an expression Lenin used a lot. That in turn signified a number of things for Lenin.

First, that the demand for equality, regardless of race, nationality, religion and gender, was a democratic demand and one which, like other democratic demands, the proletariat and its party should take the lead in championing. Lenin believed that the proletariat would be far more consistent in fighting for (bourgeois) democratic demands than would be the bourgeois liberals.

Second, that the proletariat as the "advanced class" (another frequent Lenin expression) would lead all the oppressed masses in the revolution. In Russia this meant primarily the peasantry, of course, but it included all sections of the oppressed, including many of the petty bourgeoisie and the oppressed nationalities. Leadership here did not mean giving orders but taking the lead in the struggle, and he assigned this role to the proletariat not because of its supposed moral superiority or messianic mission but on the basis of its objective economic and social position.

Third, one of main reasons for combating oppression was precisely to make unity possible—unity between women and men, Jew and gentile, etc. This applied even, or you could say particularly, in the case of national oppression where Lenin insisted that in order to unite the workers of the oppressor nation with the workers of the oppressed nation, the working class of the oppressor nation had to defend the right of the oppressed nation to secede but the ultimate aim of this was to bring about international unity and the free merger of all nation states.

Fourth, at the level of the Party there should be a single united organisation, not separate organisations for women or Jews (or Blacks, etc).

Ultimately, and this was partially realised in the Communist International, there should be one united world party. This principle led to a sharp conflict with the Jewish Bund in 1903. The Bund was a Jewish socialist workers organisation which was affiliated to the Russian Social Democratic Labour Party (RSDLP) but which wanted not only to preserve its autonomy but also demanded the exclusive right to represent and organise Jewish workers in Russia and Poland. The RSDLP, both Bolsheviks and Mensheviks, rejected this demand at its Second Congress in 1903 and as a consequence the Bund walked out and went its own way.[359]

Fifth, the struggle against oppression—for racial, religious, national and gender equality—could not be brought to a successful conclusion under capitalism. It required socialist revolution. Thus after the Revolution, Lenin repeatedly pointed out that centuries after their bourgeois revolutions and despite all their declarations in favour of equality none of the capitalist democracies had delivered even formal legal equality for women. Here, almost in its entirety, is the speech he made on International Women's Day in 1920. It gives a condensed and clear expression of his position:

> Capitalism combines formal equality with economic and, consequently, social inequality. This is one of the principal distinguishing features of capitalism, one that is mendaciously screened by the supporters of the bourgeoisie, the liberals, and that is not understood by the petty-bourgeois democrats... But capitalism *cannot* be consistent even with regard to formal equality (equality before the law, "equality" between the well-fed and the hungry, between the property-owner and the property-less). And one of the most flagrant manifestations of this inconsistency is the *inferior position* of woman compared with man. Not a single bourgeois state, not even the most progressive, republican democratic state, has brought about complete equality of rights.

> But the Soviet Republic of Russia promptly wiped out, *without any exception,* every trace of inequality in the legal status of women, and secured her complete equality in its laws.

> It is said that the level of culture is best characterised by the legal status of woman. There is a grain of profound truth in this saying. From this point of view, only the dictatorship of the proletariat, only the socialist state, could achieve and did achieve a higher level of culture.

Therefore, the foundation (and consolidation) of the first Soviet Republic—and alongside and in connection with this, the Communist International—inevitably lends a new, unparalleled, powerful impetus to the working women's movement.

For, when we speak of those who, under capitalism, were directly or indirectly, wholly or partially oppressed, it is precisely the Soviet system, and the Soviet system only, that secures democracy. This is clearly demonstrated by the position of the working class and the poor peasants. It is clearly demonstrated by the position of women.

But the Soviet system represents the final decisive conflict for the *abolition of classes,* for economic and social equality. *For us,* democracy, even democracy for those who were oppressed under capitalism, including democracy for the oppressed sex, *is inadequate.*

The working women's movement has for its objective the fight for the economic and social, and not merely formal, equality of woman. The main task is to draw the women into socially productive labour, extricate them from "domestic slavery", free them of their stultifying and humiliating resignation to the perpetual and exclusive atmosphere of the kitchen and nursery.

It is a long struggle, requiring a radical remaking both of social technique and of customs. But this struggle will end with the complete triumph of communism.[360]

The Leninist view that to defeat and eradicate the oppression of women or racism, etc it is necessary to overthrow capitalism has very frequently been taken to mean that women or people of colour, etc, should "wait" until the revolution or alternatively that with the revolution sexism and racism will disappear "automatically". Neither of these things is the case. Neither Lenin nor any serious Leninist ever suggested that women, or anyone else, should "wait" for the revolution. On the contrary struggles against all forms of oppression begin, and must begin, under capitalism and these struggles are an important element in the revolution. It is simply that achieving complete equality is not possible without socialist revolution. Moreover, the revolution may be a necessary condition for full emancipation but it is not in itself a sufficient one. As the quotation above makes clear "the fight for the economic and social, and not merely formal, equality of woman" will be "a long struggle".

Applicability today

The contemporary relevance of Lenin's insistence on the need for socialists to combat all oppression is obvious. At the start of this chapter I referred to the role played by a multitude of movements over the last 50 years or so. Now as I write these lines in February 2017, we see huge anti-Trump demonstrations across America and, to some extent, round the world. The main *focus* of these demonstrations (though they also express general opposition to Trump) has been first his dreadful misogyny, hence the vast Women's March on Washington and solidarity marches elsewhere, and second his overt racism, with the wave of protests against his Muslim travel ban and his refusal of refugees. So far, it has not been economic issues that have brought people out on the streets.

It is also the case that the *principle* of opposing all oppression has now generally been won in most of the labour and trade union movements and most left or "progressive" movements, internationally. This is not, of course, absolute and will not be,[361] but compared to the situation in, say, the 1950s and after when it was quite common to find trade unions taking reactionary and really backward positions on racism, women's equality, gay rights, etc, there has been a huge progressive change. Consequently Lenin's opposition to all oppression, which was pioneering in 1901, is no longer controversial on the serious left. The same cannot be said for his view that oppression should be fought from "the standpoint of the working class". On the contrary, this idea would seem "strange", almost "outlandish" and certainly "dogmatic" to many of the contemporary advocates of "equality". Moreover, theoretically, it stands in a critical relation to the various ideological strands—liberal, separatist, identity politics, privilege theory, and intersectionality— which have hegemonised anti-oppression struggles in recent decades. So I shall focus on this point here.

The liberal view that holds that the struggle for "equality" ("legal equality", "equality of opportunity", etc) can be pursued successfully separately from the struggle for economic equality and the class struggle has many "advantages" in terms of popularity. It is the least threatening to the ruling class and the media and therefore seems to offer the best prospects of winning over the middle ground and thus achieving practical change. This seems like "common sense" to many campaigners and so they are often willing to go along with it and defer to it even when their personal or private inclinations would be for something more radical. Nevertheless the facts of history tell heavily against it. In 1921 Lenin wrote:

> Take religion, or the denial of rights to women, or the oppression and inequality of the non-Russian nationalities. These are all problems of the bourgeois-democratic revolution. The vulgar petty-bourgeois democrats talked about them for eight months. In not a *single* one of the most advanced countries in the world have these questions been *completely* settled on *bourgeois-democratic* lines. In our country they have been settled completely by the legislation of the October Revolution.[362]

In 2017 this remains true. The United States is naturally the most important example. Founded on the principle that "all men are created equal", 240 years on it is awash with racism and sexism. Its electoral law still prevents large numbers of black and poor people from voting. Its justice system incarcerates a higher percentage of its population than any other country on the planet and these are disproportionately black people. Its police force regularly shoots people, especially black people, with impunity. It is still far from establishing a universal right to free, safe and legal abortion (which the Russian Revolution did in 1920) or to same-sex marriage and it has elected a President[363] who made his sexism overt in his election campaign and has boasted of molesting women. But what is true of the United States is also true throughout the bourgeois democratic world. I live in the Republic of Ireland and here there is still a constitutional bar on abortion and still an education system dominated by one religious denomination, Catholicism.[364] In France, the land of the great French Revolution and the birthplace of modern democracy, there is massive racism and discriminatory legislation against Muslims, while Marine le Pen of the fascist Front National reached the second round for the French Presidency in May 2017. In several other countries, notably Hungary, Austria and the Netherlands, we see a rise in fascist and far right forces. In short, liberal democracy is failing miserably, even its own terms, to deal with these problems of "equality". Everywhere there is a gender gap between the average pay of men and women.

There are deep structural reasons for this failure. A society based on economic inequality, as capitalism is, ie inequality between those who own and control the means of production and those who do not, cannot deliver "equality of opportunity". There is not, and cannot be, equality of opportunity between the child of a billionaire and the child of a poor family. Regardless of the law, the billionaire's child will have a thousand advantages when it comes to health, education, housing, culture, job opportunities, connections and everything else that shapes a child's opportunities in life.

Then there is the fact that a system characterised by major inequality is sustained by, and benefits from (or to be more precise its ruling classes benefit from) a multitude of other hierarchies and inequalities. The more every area of society is organised hierarchically and unequally—schools, hospitals, universities, offices, factories, social services, the military, etc—the more the ruling class is able to enforce its will in and through these institutions, the more it is able to mask the fundamental inequality and division between the capitalist class and the working class and present this inequality as an inevitable consequence of human nature. In so far as it can maintain one category of people, say migrant workers, as less entitled to basic rights than others, this helps turn this category into cheap labour who can more readily be exploited. In so far as it can present women as "basically mothers and housewives" and the family as the foundation of society, it can both obtain large amounts of domestic labour and child rearing for free and gain from using women as a cheaper and more vulnerable source of labour in the workplace.

In addition, those presiding over a system of class division and extreme economic inequality will find it greatly to their advantage to stir up antagonisms among those whom they exploit. Marx offered a brilliant analysis of how this worked in relation to Irish workers in Britain in the 19th century:

> Every industrial and commercial centre in England now possesses a working class divided into two *hostile* camps, English proletarians and Irish proletarians. The ordinary English worker hates the Irish worker as a competitor who lowers his standard of life. In relation to the Irish worker he regards himself as a member of the *ruling* nation and consequently he becomes a tool of the English aristocrats and capitalists against Ireland, thus strengthening their domination *over himself*. He cherishes religious, social, and national prejudices against the Irish

worker. His attitude towards him is much the same as that of the "poor whites" to the Negroes in the former slave states of the USA. The Irishman pays him back with interest in his own money. He sees in the English worker both the accomplice and the stupid tool of the *English rulers in Ireland*.

This antagonism is artificially kept alive and intensified by the press, the pulpit, the comic papers, in short, by all the means at the disposal of the ruling classes. *This antagonism* is the secret of the *impotence of the English working class*, despite its organisation. It is the secret by which the capitalist class maintains its power. And the latter is quite aware of this.[365]

The mechanism of divide and rule explained here is a feature of imperialism and capitalism everywhere, whether it is the antagonism between Protestant and Catholic workers in Northern Ireland or Hindu and Muslim in India or Sunni and Shia in the Middle East. In addition to the need for divide and rule, there is the usefulness of scapegoats. Why is there a housing shortage? It's because the single mothers/refugees/foreigners/gypsies are getting them all. Why is there an economic crisis? Because of the bankers, financial speculators and capitalists? No! Because of the *Jewish* bankers, financiers and capitalists, because of the Rothschilds and George Soros.

There is a counter tendency at work here that needs to be taken into account. In normal times the capitalist class wants hierarchies and sources of cheap labour, but it also wants a measure of social stability and it does actually need immigrants and "foreigners". It is not in the interests of the US ruling class, most of the time, to drive its black population into open revolt or for the British bourgeoisie to alienate all its Asian population (and the Asian bourgeoisie along with it, which now includes the powerful Chinese and Indian bourgeoisies). The same applies to women and other oppressed groups. So alongside their need for racism and sexism, etc, they also benefit from their declarations of anti-racism and "formal equality". They need, therefore, to maintain a *balance* or a *tension* between such public declarations and the mechanisms of divide and rule which need to be kept bubbling away at a safe level for use when needed. Politicians and the media have become expert at riding these two horses. But when the system goes into serious economic crisis as in the 1930s and in 2007-2008, the need for scapegoats increases and, invariably, political adventurers and in some cases outright fascist movements come forward to ramp up the hatred, as Trump, Farage, Le Pen, Wilders, etc, are doing at the moment.

None of this is a smooth or mechanical process. Within the ruling class there is both a certain division of labour (David Cameron and Boris Johnson, *The Daily Express*, *The Times* and the *Guardian*) and many conflicts and quarrels, as can be seen at present in the US over Trump and his travel ban. But overall there is zero chance of capitalist "liberal" democracy really fulfilling its promises to overcome bigotry, racism, gender oppression and so on. Only uprooting the system will do that.

On the face of it separatism seems much more radical than liberalism. Separatism has taken various forms at various times, as the above example of the Jewish Bund shows, but its main incarnations in recent times were in the Black Movement and then in the Women's Movement in the 1960s and 1970s, beginning in the United States and then being imitated or taken up elsewhere. In the spirit of the times, the separatists deployed very radical language declaring for the Black Revolution or the Women's or Feminist Revolution.[366]

It is easy to understand why separatism developed at this time. In the case of the Black Movement it was a product of a) the long and very intense racial oppression of black people in the United States including the legacy of slavery, lynching and Jim Crow; b) the failure of a liberal, integrationist, non-violent strategy to defeat racism, either in the South or the North, and the violent response of, as they saw it, white society to the peaceful Civil Rights Movement; c) the growing impatience and anger of a new generation of Blacks radicalised by the experience of that movement, epitomised by someone like Stokely Carmichael of the Student Nonviolent Coordinating Committee (SNCC); and d) the general passivity, and sometimes complicity, of the US labour movement on the question of racism.[367]

In the case of the US Women's Liberation Movement, the separatist trend largely grew out of the experience of radical women organising in the Civil Rights movement, the Anti-Vietnam War movement and the student movement, and was strongly shaped by the highly sexist atmosphere in those movements at the time; witness the infamous reply by Stokely Carmichael to a question about the position of women in the Black Movement: "The position of women in our movement is prone". The prevalence of sexist attitudes and behaviour in these movements of the 1960s was itself a product of a number of factors but one of them was the historic weakness of the US left and the near total eclipse of the earlier socialist tradition on women's emancipation.

But however understandable it may have been, separatism as a strategy suffered from fundamental flaws. In the case of Black separatism, the simple fact was that African-Americans constituted a small minority of US society, about 14 percent. Even if every single African-American signed up for the struggle, and this was never going to happen, a Black revolution to overthrow "white" rule or "white capitalist rule" was simply impossible. In reality a separatist strategy for Black revolution could only be a recipe for defeat at the hands of the American capitalist state. And this, of course, was what happened. Some Black revolutionaries hoped that a separate Black revolutionary organisation would be able to lead a (majority) multi-racial revolution, from the outside, or above, as it were. But this was, and is, very unrealistic. Such a separate organisation would lack the politics, the cadres and the roots to establish a real relationship with the non-black working class majority in either its communities or its workplaces. As it happens, there is a parallel here with the Bolsheviks and the Bund. In 1903 the Bund had a much larger membership, both relative to the Jewish working class and in absolute terms, than the entire RSDLP. But when it came to leading the actual Russian Revolution in either 1905 or 1917, the Bund was not even a contender. Jewish revolutionaries, like Trotsky, Kamenev, Zinoviev and Sverdlov, played key leadership roles—in Trotsky's case a decisive one—but as members of the Bolshevik Party, not the Bund.

Where women were concerned the mathematical impossibility of a separate women's revolution against the rule of men was not so obvious, women being more than 50 percent of the population, but it was still, and is still, not a real possibility. A revolution pits the unarmed and economically weak masses against a ruling class with immense economic and military resources. The masses can only win because they constitute the immense majority. Even as a large majority they cannot be victorious in a set piece confrontation with the forces of the state unless they have the capacity to win over or neutralise those state forces. A 51 percent women's revolution against 49 percent of men in which the men have the overwhelming preponderance of economic, political and military power was and is a non-starter, even if "all" women could be united on a cross-class, cross-politics basis, which they cannot be. This last point is proved by an abundance of historical experience stretching from the Paris Commune[368] to Margaret Thatcher, Angela Merkel, Theresa May and Marine Le Pen.

These stark realities could be masked by radical rhetoric and there was plenty of that around for a period. But in time the absence of any viable or realistic revolutionary perspective meant that revolutionary separatism evolved into reformist separatism. But even in terms of winning immediate and limited reforms, separatism was not an effective strategy. It meant, in any concrete campaign, setting a limit on the campaign's mobilising capacity rather than expanding it to the maximum.

Moreover, the logic of separatism had further fragmentation, further self-limitation built into it. If African-Americans should organise separately from whites because of white racism and women should organise separately from men because of male sexism, how should black women organise? Clearly they should be separate again. And among black women might there not also be homophobia calling for the separate organisation of lesbian black women. And so on ad infinitum.

The combination of the collapse of revolutionary separatism into reformist separatism and the logic of fragmentation resulted in "identity politics". Identity politics by and large abandoned the idea of completely separate organisation in favour of operating within integrated organisations—reformist and left parties, trade unions, NGOs, and even the education system and other institutions of the state—but on the basis of one's "identity" as African-American, a woman, a black woman, an LGBT woman, an LGBT woman of colour, etc.

Identity politics was a practice that emerged rather than a theory as such. In so far as it had theoretical roots, they probably lay in Max Weber's argument that "status" or social prestige were more important than class as bases for social action,[369] transmitted via innumerable university sociology courses; in the Nietzschean idea of history as an endless play of power struggles mediated via Foucault (as discussed in Chapter 3); and in the postmodernist rejection of the Marxist grand narrative of class struggle in favour of "personal stories".[370]

As a political practice this involved individuals making the *foundation* of their activity and their view of the world not their theoretical or political affiliation, but their personal circumstances and origin defined in terms of their ethnicity, gender, sexual orientation, etc: that is, particularly in terms of the oppression or oppressions from which they suffered. This could be seen by the way contributions at meetings or conferences would be prefaced by "speaking as a working class lesbian" or "as an Irish-American". In the language of identity politics, and identity politics put a huge emphasis on language, Rosa Luxemburg would be seen, and have seen herself, as first and foremost, not a Marxist and revolutionary socialist but as a Polish Jewish disabled woman.

As its strategy for combating oppression, identity politics came more and more to focus not on overthrowing capitalism, but on securing fair representation for each oppressed group within both the structures of the system (its parliaments, councils, academic faculties, hospital boards, police departments, etc) and the structures of the left (trade union committees, demonstration platforms, meeting line-ups, party councils and so on). This was indeed a just and progressive cause. It was right that there should be more women MPs and speakers at meetings, more black professors and doctors and so on. But as a strategy it was also extremely limited, a kind of minimalist reformism, and it tended to dovetail with and merge into the career strategy of individuals, especially in the academic world.

This raises an important question: to what extent does the election of black mayors and women MPs and the appointment of "minority" professors or people of colour as police chiefs actually improve the circumstances or lessen the oppression of the mass of "ordinary" ie working class, women, black or LGBTQ people? It is not possible to say it has no positive effect, but the historical experience demonstrates very clearly that the effect is minimal and very easily outweighed by other factors, such as worsening economic conditions. The most obvious example of this is the election of Barack Obama as the first black US President and the lack of impact of this on rates of black poverty, incarceration and death at the hands of the police. The election of Margaret Thatcher (and now Theresa May) as British Prime Minister tells the same story where working class women are concerned. And the same is true with appointments lower down the state and social apparatuses. The key contrast here is with the real gains made by oppressed groups through mass collective struggle—by the Civil Rights Movement, the women's movement, the disability movement, the Gay Liberation and then the LGBT movement. The latter, while still limited, have been far more substantial.

Privilege theory and intersectionality are developments of, and stand on the same ground as, identity politics. At one level privilege theory, with its focus on a multiplicity of "unearned" advantages held by white people, straight people, unincarcerated people, etc, is a reasonable description of reality as experienced by oppressed people in capitalist society. A black worker in a supermarket cannot fail to be aware that his white colleague, doing the same job, has a better chance of being promoted, is less likely to be abused at the checkout, is less likely to be arrested and in the event they were both arrested is less likely to be imprisoned. Similarly a woman worker in the same supermarket will know that she has less chance of promotion and more chance of being sexually harassed than a male worker; while an LGBTQ teenager is liable to be "queer bashed" and bullied in a way that is not true for straight teenagers and also be more prone to suicide. Whether "privilege" is the best word to describe these relative advantages is certainly debateable but the reality of different experience is undeniable.

But as analysis and strategy, privilege theory has serious weaknesses. 1) While it describes the various advantages and privileges that exist it fails to understand their structural and material roots. 2) It lacks an adequate sense of the distinction between relatively minor advantages that can divide people and the fundamental divisions in society. 3) In order to defeat oppression it is over reliant on appealing to the oppressor's individual consciousness and conscience, as in the injunction to "check your privilege!" This may possibly have some effect inside left wing campaigns and on college campuses but will be entirely ineffective when deployed with serious oppressors such as corporate executives, state officials, police chiefs and army generals. 4) The "check your privilege" mantra is also open to abuse precisely in the context of left campaigns and campuses where it can be used as a substitute for political debate so that a good argument from a "privileged" person can be dismissed in favour of a weak argument from an "oppressed person". 5) The emphasis on individual privilege can focus on the divisions *between* oppressed and exploited people just when unity and solidarity is what is needed.

The example of the black and white and male and female and straight and gay supermarket workers given above illustrates a lot of these points. It is true, as noted above, that there will be many differences in degrees of "privilege" between these workers (and many that I haven't mentioned such as disability, age, body size and so on). It is also true that many of the differences may hinder unity between these workers and that it would be the job of a socialist worker in this supermarket to counter any prejudices or oppressive behaviour based on these advantages. Nevertheless the *aim* of all this activity would be to unite all the supermarket workers against the supermarket bosses because if that unity is not achieved, those bosses would be able to ride roughshod over *all* the workers, black, white, men, women, straight, LGBTQ and disabled alike.

The concept of intersectionality was put forward in 1989 by the black feminist scholar, Kimberlé Williams Crenshaw. Mainly concerned in the first place with the situation of black women, it looked at how different identities and systems of oppression, in this case racism and sexism, intersected and overlapped to produce a distinct identity (the black woman). Originally advanced within a legal and academic context as a new "mindset" or theoretical framework, intersectionality lay fallow for a long period but in recent years has "gone public" as it were and started to reach a much wider audience, especially on the left. Clearly its scope is not restricted to the overlapping of racism and sexism but can be applied to the full range of social oppressions. Equally clearly, like privilege theory, it relates to and describes a verifiable empirical reality. To be a gay disabled Asian man, a lesbian black woman, or a working class Latino trans woman is in each case to be subject to multiple reinforcing oppressions. Moreover, compared to separatism and other versions of identity politics and privilege theory, intersectionality is much more facilitating of solidarity. It can be used to say, "We all, black, white, women, LGBTQ, disabled, etc, suffer from intersecting oppressions and should all stand together. This kind of spirit could be clearly seen in the massive mobilisations around the inauguration of Donald Trump.[371]

In this way, intersectionality moves towards, or can move towards, a socialist position, but there remains a significant difference between this and the Leninist approach. For intersectionality theory (like other forms of identity theory) social class oppression, while not denied, is just one form of oppression and one aspect of identity among many. For Lenin, as for Marx, class was the "master" category[372] and, as we have seen, the working class standpoint provided the ground from which all oppression was to be opposed. To the advocate of identity politics this is to falsely "privilege" the working class.[373]

To explore this we need to note that there are certain basic conceptual differences between the category of class and the other categories we are dealing with: race, gender, gender identity and sexual orientation, disability, etc. The category of class as used by Marx (and Lenin) derives directly and necessarily from the existence of *exploitative* social relations of production, from the way the core activity of any human society is organised. As Geoffrey de Ste. Croix put it, "Class (essentially a relationship) is the collective social expression of the fact of exploitation".[374] Consequently, it is impossible to speak or think of class equality in the way one can speak of or demand gender equality or racial equality or LGBTQ equality. Social class as a concept and as a reality presupposes an unequal and antagonistic relationship with other classes, so that "equality between classes" is a contradiction in terms.

From this relationship to exploitation it follows that the category working class *includes* where the other categories *exclude* and *excludes* where they *include*. Thus the category working class, especially when considered internationally, includes black workers, Asian workers, women workers, black women workers LGBTQ workers, etc, in all combinations but excludes black capitalists, women capitalists, etc. In contrast the category black or women includes black, women capitalists but excludes white workers, men and women, etc. Certainly these different conceptual exclusions don't necessarily correspond to the physical exclusion of people from campaigns or movements but they do make a strategic difference. A working class perspective tends to unify, through struggle, those whom identity politics tends to divide and identity politics tries to unify those whom class politics tries to divide.

The question is which strategic orientation is more realistic and more effective both for the immediate struggle against particular oppressions and for wider social change? The central argument for the working class perspective, ie for Lenin's view, is that it offers the maximum potential in terms of numbers and social power: for example, it offers the possibility of mass strikes or a general strike and widespread workplace occupations. The argument against this is that it is purely an abstract potential and that in reality the working class is so permeated by racism, sexism, homophobia and narrow economistic self-interest that there is no reasonable prospect of this potential being realised, especially in the cause of the oppressed. As a consequence, and in the meantime, each oppressed group has no alternative but to focus on organising itself and tending to its own business.

To this it can be replied that it is certainly true that there is racism, sexism and all kinds of bigotry to be found in the working class; it couldn't be otherwise with a class that is downtrodden, exploited, alienated, bombarded by the capitalist media and generally under bourgeois ideological hegemony. But the extent to which this is the case should not be exaggerated. There is much historical and contemporary evidence to show that bigotry in its various forms is less prevalent in the working class than in the middle and ruling class, particularly when we talk about the organised working class.

To illustrate this, let us look briefly at the history of the labour movement in Britain in relationship to racism. It has been a fundamental fact of British politics over many decades that trade unions have been the largest mass organisations of the British working class, that they have been the main organisational and financial backers of the Labour Party and that a majority of working class people tend to vote Labour. In contrast, the Conservative Party receives most of its funding from big business and is supported by the majority of the upper middle class and the ruling class. Now from a socialist point of view both the trade unions and the Labour Party have frequently sinned grievously, by both commission and omission, on questions of racism, but it is indisputable that, overall, they have been more progressive than the Tories. It is the Tory Party that has consistently harboured within its ranks an overtly racist right wing (such as Enoch Powell, the Monday Club and later Ukip supporters, and open supporters of racist Rhodesia and South African Apartheid). Labour, on the other hand, has been the home of strong anti-racists such as Bernie Grant, Diane Abbott and Jeremy Corbyn. Similarly, the trade union movement has frequently lent its support to anti-racist campaigns and sometimes actively mobilised against racism. These facts reflect the differential extent of racism in their respective class bases.

This contrast applies also to other issues of oppression. It was a Labour government that legalised homosexuality in 1967 and the Tories who brought in the homophobic Clause 28 in 1988. It was Labour who legalised abortion in 1967 and the main pressure to restrict it has come from the Tories. It is the TUC who, alongside women's groups, has frequently defended a woman's right to choose. I have given British examples here, but they are replicated in other countries. In Ireland, for example, it was Dunnes Stores shopworkers and their union that led the boycott of South African goods in 1984 and in the successful Marriage Equality referendum in 2015 which legalised same-sex marriage, it was working class areas that generally returned the highest yes votes.

However, the most important point is that it is in the course of struggle, above all struggle in its highest form, revolution, that bigotry and prejudice within the working class is most overcome and this is greatly assisted, as Lenin stressed, the more there exists within the struggle conscious socialists and revolutionaries actively arguing against the bigotry and prejudice. It was the mass revolutionary workers' movement, the Chartists, which elected the mixed-race son of a slave, William Cuffay, to its National Executive in 1842. It was working class Battersea which elected the Indian Communist revolutionary, Shapurji Saklatvala, as its MP in 1922. It was in revolutionary Russia that the workers' Petrograd Soviet twice (in 1905 and 1917) elected a Jew, Leon Trotsky, as its President and it was the Russian Revolution that decriminalised homosexuality and legalised abortion.[375] It was in May '68 that hundreds of thousands took to the streets chanting "We are all German Jews" after the revolutionary student leader, Daniel Cohn Bendit was attacked by the right for his "foreign" origins. It was at the height of the Egyptian Revolution in 2011 that Muslims and Coptic Christians united and physically defended each other's right to pray in Tahrir Square. It is also the case that it is in the course of an overall rise in struggle that the struggles of oppressed groups on their own behalf most tend to develop. It was in the Easter Rising of 1916 and the Irish Revolution that women, including lesbian women, came to the fore.[376] It was the general radicalisation in the United States and internationally in the 1960s that gave birth to the women's liberation and gay liberation movements.

In contrast, the often heard idea that first we will get our own people together, that first we will unite ourselves as blacks, women, etc, and then we will make alliances, may sound reasonable but is in fact utopian. It will never happen that Colin Powell and Condoleeza Rice or Hilary Clinton and Michelle Obama link arms with the Black Panthers or join the Stonewall rioters; they may attend the anniversary commemorations, but that is a different matter. In reality all oppressed communities and sectors, like the working class as a whole, radicalise and unite in an uneven and incomplete form. There is always unity in action between the more advanced and radicalised sections in demonstrations, on picket lines and on the barricades, before there is ever "complete" unity of any one group or community.

The historical experience, therefore, vindicates Lenin.* His core strategy for the fight against oppression, about which he was so insistent, though formulated over a century ago, is in important respects in advance of the modern liberal, separatist and identity politics strategies so prevalent today. Saying that, however, should emphatically not be taken to mean that there is nothing much to learn from the many struggles of the oppressed over the decades, that it is sufficient simply to repeat what Lenin said. Nothing could be further from the truth and nothing so alien to the spirit of Lenin himself who was always learning from life, from the struggle and from the working class.

The need to learn

Lenin's writings on women's emancipation show that while he was a consistent advocate of equality his analysis and understanding of women's oppression was decidedly limited. He tended to see women's oppression as a survival or remnant of serfdom and feudalism, which the bourgeoisie had failed to eradicate,[377] and he lacked a developed analysis of the role of the family in modern capitalism. Yes, the Russian Revolution decriminalised homosexuality in 1917, but there is no analysis of gay oppression, let alone LGBTQ oppression to be found in Lenin. When he writes about sex and sexuality, as he did to Inessa Armand in January 1915, he sounds puritanical and slightly embarrassing to modern ears, with talk about "dirty" and "clean" "fleeting kisses and passion", etc.[378] The same is true of some of the comments on sex attributed to him by the German revolutionary, Clara Zetkin.[379] Any

---

* There is a final argument often put from the standpoint of identity politics which I have not discussed here. This is that the inadequacy of workers' revolution or socialism as a strategy for ending oppression is demonstrated by the continued oppression of women, LGBTQ people and the persistence of racism in all the so-called "Communist" or socialist countries from the Soviet Union to Eastern Europe to North Korea and even to Cuba. I shall discuss this issue more fully in the next two chapters. Here I will simply say, that if these countries are really examples of socialism and not, as this author believes, of state capitalism, then not only is the Leninist strategy for fighting oppression invalidated but so is the whole of Leninism and the whole of Marxism because these Stalinist regimes not only failed to deal with racism and sexism, they also failed to emancipate the working class.

would-be contemporary Leninist who wrote or spoke in similar vein today would invite ridicule. Again there is no mention in Lenin of disability and the struggle for disability rights and the issues that this raises. Similarly, the great struggles against racism, particularly but not exclusively in the United States, have served to deepen and broaden the understanding of Marxists and revolutionaries on this vital question.

But, of course, neither Lenin nor anyone else is able to escape totally from the experience and attitudes of their time or fully anticipate the results of struggles yet to emerge. This simply reinforces the need, which Lenin would have been the first to acknowledge, to develop Marxism in dialectical interaction with the struggle.

6

Does Leninism lead to Stalinism?

The nightmare of Stalinism

Joseph Stalin ruled the Soviet Union as its absolute dictator from 1928 to his death in 1953. There can be no equivocation about this: the Stalinist regime was an utter nightmare.

In terms of human rights it was, as everyone knows, an extreme tyranny. Democracy of any kind was non-existent; it was a one-party state in which all elections were ruthlessly rigged so that the ruling Communist Party candidates always won with close to 100 percent of the vote. No political, intellectual or cultural criticism or opposition was permitted. There were a series of purges and show trials in which past oppositionists or possible future oppositionists were accused of fantastic crimes and conspiracies, invariably convicted and either executed or sent to the gulag archipelago in Siberia, close to a death sentence. The whole social life of the country was held in an iron totalitarian grip by the party/state and the secret police and intellectual life in general assumed a Kafkaesque character in which history was continually being rewritten, a scientist could be required to endorse scientific theories he or she knew to be bogus and a composer could be condemned because their music was not in the approved style.

Nor can it plausibly be claimed that even if life was intolerable for "intellectuals" at least it was reasonably good for ordinary working people who kept their heads down. On the contrary, the living standards of the working class were forced down to fund industrialisation in the Five Year Plan and held at a low level. Housing conditions were appalling. Work discipline was intense and trade union rights and the right to strike were non-existent. Trade unions existed, of course, but they were completely controlled from above by the party/state, which also constituted the management of industry. And it was "ordinary people", workers and peasants, who made up the vast majority of those sent to the camps and used as forced labour on a huge scale. In addition there was the scourge of famine, with several million people dying in the famine of 1932-1933, mainly in the Ukraine but also in other parts of the Soviet Union, such as Kazakhstan and at least tens, perhaps hundreds of thousands in a smaller famine in 1946-1947 which struck the Ukraine again and also Moldova.[380]

The only serious counter to this indictment is to cite the prodigious economic development and growth achieved first in the 1930s[381] and then in the 1950s, which transformed backward Russia into a major industrial and military power. But there are three major objections to this defence: a) the growth and industrialisation was achieved at the expense of Russia's working people; b) in historical perspective it was not greater than was achieved at the same or other times by capitalist societies such as the United States, Japan and, in recent decades, China; and c) in time the economic growth started to slow and then virtually ground to a halt thus precipitating the collapse of the regime in 1989-1991.

Stalinism was also a reactionary disaster for women, LGBT+ people and for national minorities. As we have seen in Chapter 5, the Revolution in Lenin's time was hugely progressive in all these areas but Stalinism reversed all the gains that were made. The Russian Revolution proclaimed its commitment to complete legal and social equality for women and in 1920 the Soviet Union was the first country in the world to make abortion completely legal and free. Stalinist Russia recriminalised abortion in 1935[382] and introduced medals for motherhood (having numerous children). One of the earliest acts of the Bolshevik government in late 1917 was the decriminalisation of homosexuality and there were openly gay members of the government such as Georgy Chicherin who served as Commissar for Foreign Affairs from May 1918 until 1930. In 1933 homosexuality was again made illegal and remained so until 1993. Under Stalin, there was a general policy of Russification and many of Russia's national minorities suffered severe oppression, with the dissolution of a number of the Soviet Union's national republics and the forced deportation of their *entire* populations: for example, the Volga-German Republic in 1941, the Kalmyks in 1943, and the Chechens and the Crimean Tatars in 1946. The Stalinist regime also cynically exploited and encouraged anti-Semitism.[383]

For all these reasons and many others (I have given here only the briefest summary), to characterise Stalinist Russia (or post-Stalin Russia or the replica regimes it spawned along its borders) as socialist or communist is to damn socialism and communism, as many who insist on this designation are well aware. Similarly to assert continuity between Lenin and Stalin or that it was the nature of Leninism that created or caused Stalinism, to hold what I will call "the continuity thesis", is to damn Lenin and Leninism.

The debate on this question has raged since at least the 1930s but it has never been anything like an equal debate. On the continuity side stand a) the entire Western establishment and more or less all of its media; b) the vast majority of the academic world across all its disciplines, beginning with history and Soviet or Russian studies; c) the majority of international social democracy; d) in a mirror image of the bourgeois establishment view, the Stalinist regimes themselves and the vast majority of the international communist movement; e) anarchism, including its most influential spokesperson, Noam Chomsky.

On the discontinuity side, arguing that there was a fundamental break between Leninism and Stalinism, stand only Leon Trotsky and the Trotskyists (including "dissident" Trotskyists like Tony Cliff, Raya Dunayevskaya, C L R James, Hal Draper, Chris Harman, Alex Callinicos, etc) and a few other independent Marxist intellectuals such as Ralph Miliband, Lars Lih and Marcel Liebman, with Isaac Deutscher occupying an intermediate position. So in quantitative terms it has been no contest; the continuity thesis has been so overwhelmingly dominant as to constitute what could be called "a consensus" and, by those so inclined, simply asserted as fact.

Moreover the continuity position has the considerable advantage of corresponding to surface appearances. Chronologically Leninism did lead to Stalinism and there was apparent continuity in the regime and in its language and in the claims it made about itself, at least if you do not look too closely. But, as Marx said, "all science would be superfluous if the outward appearance and the essence of things directly coincided"[384] and the sun appears to go round the earth but in reality, as we all now know, it is the other way round. So what are the actual arguments for and against the continuity thesis?

The continuity thesis

We should begin by noting that the continuity thesis rests on and is reinforced by a key idea in bourgeois ideology, which is also widely accepted as common sense. This is that capitalism is "natural" or corresponds to "human nature", whereas socialism is contrary to human nature and therefore can only be imposed on society by force and dictatorship. According to this way of thinking, only free-market capitalism, in which the existence of private ownership of the means of production limits the power of the state, is compatible with freedom and democracy.

This is further strengthened by two notions that are even more deeply engraved in our collective thinking: namely that there always has been and always will be social and political hierarchy—human nature again—and that the mass of ordinary people are congenitally incapable of running society. Consequently the concept of an equal or classless society is utopian and revolution which stirs up the masses, especially revolution made in the name of workers' power and socialism, is dangerous and doomed to fail; it is also an inherently deceptive process in which naïve or unscrupulous leaders "use" the masses for their own ends to make the revolution only to put them back in their place afterwards. The continuity between Lenin and Stalin, between the October Revolution and the Stalinist police state of the 1930s is thus seen as a particularly virulent example of this general pattern. This scenario is also paralleled by the Nietzsche/Foucault view of history as a process driven by the will to power so that the sequence Tsar-Lenin-Stalin is viewed as merely one more example of the endless play of power struggles.

Regarding the human nature/capitalism equals freedom, socialism is dictatorship/all revolutions lead to tyranny arguments, there is a sense in which the whole of Marxism is a reply to these bourgeois apologetics. I have written quite extensively on these issues in the past[385] and will not go over this ground now, except to say that the existence of many thousands of years of egalitarian foraging societies constitutes an empirical refutation of the idea that hierarchy and class division are inevitable and that socialism is incompatible with human nature. But generally speaking, the Lenin-Stalin continuity thesis is presented without explicit mention of this ideological framework. Rather it is simply asserted as historical fact (which enables it to be accepted by those, such as Chomsky, who might recoil from these conservative assumptions). However, the existence of the framework in the background is important because its "common sense" status greatly assists the uncritical acceptance of the continuity narrative. This narrative runs as follows:

1. Lenin was, from the outset, a deeply authoritarian personality with dictatorial or even totalitarian ambitions.

2. The Bolshevik Party was largely Lenin's creation and it was constructed in his own image as the instrument of these ambitions.

3. In 1917 the Bolsheviks, at Lenin's prompting, took advantage of the crisis and chaos in Russia and its weak government to seize power in an opportunistic coup and impose their rule on Russian society.

4. This rule led more or less inexorably to the totalitarian police state of the 1930s (and of the period up to the fall of Communism in 1989-1991) which exhibited an intensification of the levels of repression but not a fundamental or qualitative change.

5. The essential continuity between this coup and the later Stalinist dictatorship is proved, above all, by the authoritarian behaviour of Lenin and the Bolsheviks in the early years of their rule.

6. Further proof is supplied by the fact that in every case where declared Leninists have taken power, the outcome has been essentially the same, single party rule in a police state: witness Eastern Europe, China, North Korea, Cuba and Vietnam.

7. Let us consider the last, most general, point first. What it relies on is taking the self-declaration of the political leaderships concerned at face value. In reality, in all of these cases (with the exception of Cuba), the political leadership was already thoroughly Stalinised and in none of them did the political strategy pursued remotely resemble that of the historical Lenin (or that advocated in this book). In Eastern Europe "Communist" power was conquered not through workers' revolution from below but by means of Red Army occupation at the end of the Second World War. As Chris Harman has written:

> The Russian army had ensured the police and secret police were in the hands of its appointees. Now a series of moves were used to destroy resistance to Russian dictates. First, non-Communist ministers were forced out of office; the social democratic parties were forced to merge with Communist parties regardless of the feelings of their members;

then Communist Party leaders who might show any sign of independence from Stalin...were put on trial, imprisoned and often executed. Kostov in Bulgaria, Rajk in Hungary, and Slansky in Czechoslovakia were all executed. Gomulka in Poland and Kadar in Hungary were merely thrown into prison.[386]

This was not a case of Leninism leading to Stalinism but of Stalinism leading to Stalinism.

In both China and Cuba the revolution was carried through by guerrilla armies, based in the countryside on the peasantry with a middle class leadership.[387] To say these revolutions were not Leninist is not to engage in pedantry or to adopt some narrow or dogmatic definition according to which the Leninist label is denied to those who differ on some point of doctrine or secondary question. The difference is on the issue that for Marxism (and for Lenin himself) is absolutely fundamental—the class nature of the revolution and the class basis of its political leadership.

For Marx and Lenin, as we have seen, the revolutionary struggle and the social basis of the revolutionary movement and party was first and foremost the working class and *not* the peasantry. This was because the working class, concentrated in modern industry and in great cities, had the potential power to defeat capitalism and the ability, once it had conquered state power, to be both the producing class and the ruling class at the same time, thus paving the way for a classless communist society. In contrast the peasantry, while it had an important role to play in the revolution as an ally of the proletariat, lacked the capacity to emancipate itself or lead the construction of socialism.

In China and Cuba the peasants were able to form the rank and file of the revolutionary guerrilla army and defeat the greatly weakened Kuomintang and Batista regimes, but what they could not do, because of their social position rooted in farming in the countryside, was take control of the main forces of production, which were located in the cities, and thus themselves run the economy and the state. Instead they had to hand over the running of society to their leaders who became the embryo of a new, state capitalist, ruling class. So it is quite wrong to attribute the anti-democratic character of either the Chinese or the Cuban regimes to the application of Leninist doctrine.[388]

Regarding points 1-3 of the above narrative, I have already discussed them in Chapter 1. To summarize: the notion of Lenin's power-seeking motives is psychologically implausible and unhistorical as an explanation of his embarking on a political course involving imprisonment, exile and isolation; the Bolshevik faction and party was never a Lenin dictatorship, but was very democratic and very much a workers' party; the October Revolution succeeded precisely because it was not a coup or putsch but because it had overwhelming working class support.

To these factual considerations I would add a methodological one. The idea that an event of world significance such as the Russian Revolution and its historical development over 80 years including the emergence of a major new society can be explained or understood as primarily, or mainly, a consequence of the ideas or actions of one individual or one small organisation, rather than mass social forces is a particularly blatant example of "the great man" theory of history. It is akin to saying that the structure of 18th century English capitalism was determined by the personal character of Oliver Cromwell or the organisation of the New Model Army or that the regime of Italian fascism was mainly shaped by the dictatorial personality of Mussolini. In other words, it is not serious history. A serious analysis of the rise and causes of Stalinism must begin with the objective material conditions prevailing in Russia and internationally in the years following the Revolution and it must examine how these conditions impacted on Russia's social structure and shaped the balance of class forces.

To say this is not to espouse a mechanical determinism or deny the role of ideology, or politics or even individuals.[389] It is not even to deny that at certain moments these can be decisive in tipping the balance between contending forces. But it is to insist that they take their place as only the final links in the chain of explanation and not as prime movers. However, this leaves open the possibility of arguing that even if objective factors, such as Russia's economic backwardness, were primary the ideology and the organisational practices of Leninism/ Bolshevism nevertheless played an important role in facilitating the emergence of Stalinism. Here the question of the behaviour of Lenin and the Bolsheviks in the period between October 1917 and 1922 is crucial and it is on this ground that the arguments of a number of anti-Stalinist Marxists, such as Samuel Farber and Robin Blackburn,[390] have sometimes converged with those of conservative, liberal or anarchist anti-Marxists.

The charge sheet, the list of claimed offences, which can be laid at Lenin's door, is formidable. First, that from the outset he rejected a "broad" coalition with other "socialists" such as the Right SRs (Socialist Revolutionaries) and the Mensheviks, in favour of a narrow government with only the Left SRs and with a clear Bolshevik majority. Thus, it is said, Lenin set off on a course away from pluralist soviet democracy in the direction of party dictatorship.

Second that, despite the Bolsheviks having ceaselessly demanded the calling of the Constituent Assembly, Lenin opposed holding elections for the Assembly in autumn 1917 and then, when they were held and produced a large anti-Bolshevik majority, he dissolved the Assembly by force in January 1918, so taking a further step in the direction of single-party dictatorship.

Third, that Lenin launched, in December 1917, the Cheka (All-Russian Emergency Commission for Combating Counter-Revolution and Sabotage) which was responsible for the Red Terror during the Civil War and later evolved into the secret police, the GPU, the NKVD and the "Great Terror" of Stalin's purges in the 1930s.

Fourth, that Lenin, from 1918 onwards, imposed a policy of one-man management of industry in place of the initial workers' control.

Fifth, that beginning with the banning of the Cadets in December 1917, Lenin moved step by step to the outlawing of all other political parties by May 1919 and the establishment of a one-party state.

Sixth, that Lenin and the Bolshevik government bloodily suppressed the revolt of the Kronstadt sailors in March 1921 and accompanied this by banning factions within the Party, thus driving a further nail into the coffin of free debate.

The continuity thesis assessed

Any discussion of the merits of this indictment must begin with an acknowledgement that all the charges in this list are based on indisputable historical fact. The Bolshevik government did dissolve the Constituent Assembly, establish a political monopoly, etc, and rule in an increasingly authoritarian fashion in the years in which it was headed by Lenin. These facts are what make this component in the continuity thesis the strongest part of this whole argument.

At the same time it must also be acknowledged that in relation to each of these charges there is another side of the story. Thus it can be argued, from a Marxist and Leninist point of view, that the dispersal of the Constituent Assembly was justified because the Soviets represented a higher form of democracy, specifically working class democracy, than the Assembly, which was a form of bourgeois parliament. While the suppression of Kronstadt, bitter as it was, can be justified on the grounds that mutiny of the naval garrison, strategically located at the entrance to Petrograd, threatened to reopen the just concluded Civil War and so, regardless of the subjective intentions of the soldiers, play into the hands of the counter-revolution. But rather than launch into the very detailed historical argument necessary to make an assessment of each charge, I want first to pose a basic question: why did Lenin and the Bolsheviks behave in this increasingly authoritarian manner?

To answer that it was a result of Lenin's authoritarian personality takes us back to ground we have already covered and rejected and is also open to the powerful objection that if it were really a matter of Lenin's personal psychology, he would have been blocked (or even removed) by others around him. Remember it is a matter of demonstrable fact that in the early years of the revolution there was no automatic deferral to Lenin.[391] At the very least we would need to be talking about a collective authoritarian mentality on the part of all or most of the leading Bolsheviks. Not only is there a lack of evidence for this, there is much evidence to the contrary. For example in Moscow, where the October Insurrection did not pass off smoothly as it did in Petrograd, and there were six days of serious street fighting, there was the following episode recounted here by Victor Serge:

> On the 29th [October] in the evening, after a terrible day in which the headquarters of the insurrection nearly fell, a twenty-four hours' truce was signed: it was quickly broken by the arrival of a shock battalion to join the Whites. The Reds on their side were reinforced by artillery. Gun batteries went into action on the squares, and the Whites retreated to the Kremlin. After long vacillations, due to their desire to avoid damage to historic monuments, the MRC [Military Revolutionary Committee] decided to order the bombardment of the Kremlin. The Whites surrendered at 4 pm on 2 November. "The Committee of Public Safety is dissolved. The White Guard surrenders its arms and is disbanded. The officers may keep the sidearms that distinguish their

rank. Only such weapons as are necessary for practice may be kept in the military academies... The MRC guarantees the liberty and inviolability of all." Such were the principal clauses of the armistice signed between Reds and Whites. The fighters of the counter-revolution, butchers of the Kremlin, who in victory would have shown no quarter whatever to the Reds—we have seen proof—*went free.*[392]

Serge comments:

Foolish clemency! These very Junkers, these officers, these students, these socialists of counter-revolution, dispersed themselves throughout the length and breadth of Russia and there organized the Civil War. The revolution was to meet them again, at Yaroslavl, on the Don, at Kazan, in the Crimea, in Siberia and in every conspiracy nearer home.[393]

Then there was the question of the death penalty. On the very first day after the insurrection, on the initiative of Kamenev, the death penalty was abolished. Lenin thought this was a mistake and that it would be impossible to defend the revolution without firing squads,[394] but this was hardly the action of a group of authoritarian leaders set on establishing their personal dictatorship. Victor Serge, a revolutionary with deeply libertarian and humanistic instincts, offered the following assessment of the general character of the Bolsheviks:

The October Revolution offers us an almost perfect model of the proletarian party. Relatively few as they may be, its militants live with the masses and among them. Long and testing years—a revolution, then illegality, exile, prison, endless ideological battles—have given it excellent activists and real leaders, whose parallel thinking was strengthened in collective action. Personal initiative and the panache of strong personalities were balanced by intelligent centralization, voluntary discipline and respect for recognized mentors. Despite the efficiency of its organizational apparatus, the party suffered not the slightest bureaucratic deformation. No fetishism of organizational forms can be observed in it; it is free of decadent and even of dubious traditions.[395]

An alternative explanation is that the authoritarianism was a consequence of Bolshevik ideology. But this does not fit the facts at all. First, because Bolshevik/ Leninist ideology as it evolved from 1903 to the beginning of 1917 did not envisage the immediate conquest of power by the proletariat in Russia at all; they did not believe the Russian Revolution would move beyond the limits of radical bourgeois democracy and capitalist property relations. Second, because in so far as they did form theoretical conceptions regarding the nature of Soviet power and the dictatorship of the proletariat, it did not include the notion of one party rule. Rather their idea was that, just as in capitalist democracies with bourgeois parliaments, the government would be formed by the party with a parliamentary majority so in the Soviet state, state power would reside in the Congress of Soviets and the government would be formed by the party with a majority in the Soviets. As Lenin expressed it in November 1917 in a statement "'To all Party Members and to all the Working Classes of Russia":

> It is a matter of common knowledge that the majority at the Second All-Russia Congress of Soviets of Workers' and Soldiers' Deputies were delegates belonging to the Bolshevik Party.
>
> This fact is fundamental for a proper understanding of the victorious revolution that has just taken place in Petrograd, Moscow and the whole of Russia. Yet that fact is constantly forgotten and ignored by all the supporters of the capitalists and their unwitting *aides*, who are undermining the fundamental principle of the new revolution, namely, *all power to the Soviets*. There must be no government in Russia other than the *Soviet Government*. Soviet power has been won in Russia, *and the transfer of government from one Soviet party to another is guaranteed without any revolution, simply by a decision of the Soviets; simply by new elections of deputies to the Soviets* [my emphasis]. The majority at the Second All-Russia Congress of Soviets belonged to the Bolshevik Party. Therefore the only Soviet Government is the one formed by that Party.[396]

What any conscientious reading of Russian history or of Lenin's writings in the years 1917-1921 shows is that overwhelmingly the main factor determining the actions of Lenin and the Bolshevik government was the force of circumstances. Even the first step of forming a Bolshevik government, which as we have just seen Lenin was prepared to defend on principle, involved an element of necessity. The SRs and Mensheviks had walked out of Soviets as the Insurrection was taking place. Nevertheless, at the insistence of the Bolshevik right (Zinoviev, Kamenev, Rykov, etc), who had opposed the October Revolution, negotiations for a coalition were undertaken. But the Right SRs and Mensheviks demanded both a majority for themselves and the exclusion of Lenin and Trotsky; in other words they would only join a coalition that would undo the October Revolution. In the end a coalition was formed with the Left SRs on 18 November. But the coalition broke down over the signing of the Brest-Litovsk peace (itself determined by necessity) and the SRs took to arms to oppose the government; they attempted to assassinate Count Mirbach, the German Ambassador, to provoke a war with Germany and then launched an uprising on the streets of Moscow.

Similarly with the dispersal of the Constituent Assembly the principle of Soviet rule was articulated by Lenin in combination with considerations of necessity. Thus Lenin's "Theses on the Constituent Assembly" of December 1917 began:

> 1. The demand for the convocation of a Constituent Assembly was a perfectly legitimate part of the programme of revolutionary Social-Democracy, because in a bourgeois republic the Constituent Assembly represents the highest form of democracy and because, in setting up a Pre-parliament, the imperialist republic headed by Kerensky was preparing to rig the elections and violate democracy in a number of ways.
>
> 2. While demanding the convocation of a Constituent Assembly, revolutionary Social-Democracy has ever since the beginning of the Revolution of 1917 repeatedly emphasised that a republic of Soviets is a higher form of democracy than the usual bourgeois republic with a Constituent Assembly.
>
> 3. For the transition from the bourgeois to the socialist system, for the dictatorship of the proletariat, the Republic of Soviets (of Workers', Soldiers' and Peasants' Deputies) is not only a higher type of democratic institution (as compared with the usual bourgeois republic crowned by a Constituent Assembly), but is the only form capable of securing the most painless transition to socialism.

But went on to say:

> 13. Lastly, the civil war which was started by the Cadet-Kaledin counter-revolutionary revolt against the Soviet authorities, against the workers' and peasants' government, has finally brought the class struggle to a head and has destroyed every chance of setting in a formally democratic way the very acute problems with which history has confronted the peoples of Russia, and in the first place her working class and peasants.

14. Only the complete victory of the workers and peasants over the bourgeois and landowner revolt (as expressed in the Cadet-Kaledin movement), only the ruthless military suppression of this revolt of the slave-owners can really safeguard the proletarian-peasant revolution. The course of events and the development of the class struggle in the revolution have resulted in the slogan "All Power to the Constituent Assembly!"—which disregards the gains of the workers' and peasants' revolution, which disregards Soviet power, which disregards the decisions of the Second All-Russia Congress of Soviets of Workers' and Soldiers' Deputies, of the Second All-Russia Congress of Peasants' Deputies, etc *becoming in fact* the slogan of the Cadets and the Kaledinites and of their helpers. The entire people are now fully aware that the Constituent Assembly, if it parted ways with Soviet power, would inevitably be doomed to political extinction.[397]

In short, we *must* disperse the Constituent Assembly because if we don't it will become a rallying point for the counter-revolution.

The element of necessity and pressure to introduce ever harsher measures grows as the circumstances of the Revolution became more desperate, as they rapidly did. The main driver of this was the intensifying civil war and its accompanying White Terror. In one sense the counter-revolutionary civil war began before October with the attempt of late August and it continued immediately after the insurrection. On the night of 28 October, Junkers (cadets from the military colleges) surrounded and captured the Kremlin in Moscow which had been occupied by the Bolsheviks. The workers in the Kremlin who had surrendered were promptly lined up in the courtyard and mowed down by machine gun fire. Serge comments:

> This massacre was not an isolated act. Practically everywhere the Whites conducted arrests followed by massacres... Let us remember these facts. They show the firm intention of the defenders of the Provisional Government to drown the revolution in blood.[398]

This, of course, is how counter-revolutions behave as is shown by many historical examples from the Paris Commune to Franco in Spain, Pinochet in Chile or al-Sisi in Egypt in 2013. In early 1918 the Bolsheviks were provided with a vivid object lesson as to what their fate would be should they lose: the White Terror in Finland which followed the defeat of the workers' uprising there. More than 8,000 "reds" were executed and 80,000 taken prisoner, of whom over 11,000 were allowed to starve to death. As John Rees says, "In all, the Finnish White Terror claimed the lives of 23,000 Reds. It was a fate which must have burnt itself into the minds of the Bolsheviks and steeled their hearts during the civil war."[399]

Even so it was not until these counter-revolutionary attempts escalated into full-scale war combined with major foreign intervention in mid-1918 that the Red Terror developed on an extensive scale. And this was in circumstances where the White armies behaved with the utmost savagery and sadism, including anti-Semitic pogroms that pre-figured the Nazis. In 1919 in the Ukraine 150,000 Jews were slaughtered, that is one in 13 of the Ukrainian Jewish population.[400] Moreover in the darkest days of this war the Bolsheviks lost control of by far the largest part of Russia. They were assailed on all sides, very nearly lost Petrograd and were reduced to an area around Moscow, approximately the size of the old Muscovy Principality. That the Revolution and the Bolsheviks were fighting for their lives is true in the most literal sense; that they responded with harshness and brutality is hardly surprising.

But the sheer ferocity of the Civil War was by no means the only factor in this situation. Another was the conduct of the other political parties: the Cadets, SRs and Mensheviks. To simply say that Lenin and the Bolsheviks banned all other parties, including the other "socialist" parties, and established a one-party state makes it sound as if this was done out of ideological intolerance. In reality it was a response to the fact that to a greater or lesser extent all these parties either supported the Whites or half supported them and engaged in armed actions against the Soviet government. This was first and most clearly the case with the Cadet party, which had already collaborated with Kornilov and Kaledin (leader of the Don Cossack white rebellion in late 1917). But it applied also to the Right SRs after the dissolution of the Constituent Assembly. They gave full support to the rebellion of the Czechoslovak Legion in May 1918 and when the Legion occupied Samara the SRs formed an anti-Bolshevik government there. The same thing happened involving various combinations of Cadets, Right SRs, "populist" socialists and Mensheviks, in a number of regions where the Czechoslovak Legion or other White forces took control.

In addition to this there were conspiracies and terrorist attacks within Bolshevik-controlled areas. I have already referred to the Left SR assassination of Count Mirbach, but there was also the assassination by a Right SR of the Bolshevik leader Volodarsky on 20 June 1918 and on 30 August an attempt on Lenin's life by the SR Fanya Kaplan[401] and on the same day a successful murder of Cheka head, Uritsky, also by an SR. It was in response to these and similar events that the Bolsheviks banned the other parties.

In addition to the military consequences of the Civil War and also of immense significance, were its terrible economic and social consequences. Even before the Revolution or the Civil War Russia was already suffering from the effects of three years of devastating war which claimed over 1.7 million lives and ruined the economy. To this must be added the disruptive effects of the revolution itself and the severe losses of population, territory and industry occasioned by the Treaty of Brest-Litovsk, and a total Allied Blockade from April 1918:

> By 1918 Russia was producing just 12 percent of the steel it had produced in 1913. More or less the same story emerged from every industry: iron ore had slumped to 12.3 percent of its 1913 figure; tobacco to 19 percent; sugar to 24 percent; coal to 42 percent; linen to 75 percent. The country was producing just one fortieth of the railway track it had manufactured in 1913. And by January 1918 some 48 percent of the locomotives in the country were out of action.
>
> Factories closed, leaving Petrograd with just a third of its former workforce by autumn 1918. Hyperinflation raged at levels only later matched in the Weimar Republic. The amount of workers' income that came from sources other than wages rose from 3.5 percent in 1913 to 38 percent in 1918. In many cases desperation drove workers to simple theft. The workers' state was as destitute as the workers: the state budget for 1918 showed income at less than half of expenditure.[402]

Inevitably this meant famine and disease. The urban population collapsed as workers fled to the countryside in search of food and epidemics of typhus and cholera raged:

> Deaths from typhus alone in the years 1918-20 numbered 1.6 million, and typhoid, dysentery and cholera caused another 700,000... Suffering was indescribable. Numerous cases of cannibalism occurred. A quarter of Russia's population—35 million—suffered from continuous acute hunger.[403]

It is hardly surprising that in these dreadful circumstances the Bolsheviks were forced to resort to harsh and dictatorial measures. In order to deal with the famine and prevent mass starvation in the cities it was necessary to send armed detachments of workers to the countryside to forcibly requisition grain, but this stretched to breaking point the relationship with the peasantry which was so essential to the revolution in an overwhelmingly peasant country. It also aggravated relations with those political forces, like the SRs, whose social base was middle peasants. This further accentuated the need for authoritarian rule.

To read Lenin's writings during this period is to read someone totally aware of the disaster facing the country. Again and again he refers in speeches and letters to the workers to "the extremely difficult situation", the "desperate situation" "this exhausted and ravaged country", etc. Here are a couple of examples:

> Comrades, the other day your delegate, a Party comrade, a worker in the Putilov Works, called on me. This comrade drew a detailed and extremely harrowing picture of the famine in Petrograd. We all know that the food situation is just as acute in many of the industrial *gubernias*, that famine is knocking just as cruelly at the door of the workers and the poor generally...
>
> We are faced by disaster, it is very near. An intolerably difficult May will be followed by a still more difficult June, July and August... The situation of the country is desperate in the extreme.[404]
>
> The first six months of 1919 will be more difficult than the preceding.
>
> The food shortage is growing more and more acute. Typhus is becoming an extremely serious menace. Heroic efforts are required, but what we are doing is far from enough.[405]

However, every time Lenin speaks of the catastrophe facing the country he combines this with an unflinching determination to resist, to do everything possible to defend the Revolution and to hold out till the arrival of aid from the international revolution. The passage quoted immediately above continues:

> Can we save the situation?
>
> Certainly. The capture of Ufa and Orenburg, our victories in the

South and the success of the Soviet uprising in the Ukraine open up very favourable prospects.

We are now in a position to procure far more grain than is required for semi-starvation food rations...

Not only can we now obviate famine, but we can even fully satisfy the starving population of non-agricultural Russia.

The whole trouble lies in the bad state of transport and the tremendous shortage of food workers.

Every effort must be made and we must stir the mass of workers into action... We must pull ourselves together. We must set about the *revolutionary mobilisation* of people for food and transport work. We must *not confine ourselves* to "current" work, but go beyond its bounds and discover new methods of securing additional forces...

Of course, the hungry masses are exhausted, and that exhaustion is at times more than human strength can endure. But there is a way out, and renewed energy is undoubtedly possible, all the more since the growth of the proletarian revolution all over the world is becoming increasingly apparent and promises a radical improvement in our foreign as well as our home affairs.[406]

This passage, in tone and content, is typical of numerous articles, letters and speeches by Lenin in that period. So too is the reference to the international revolution which Lenin invokes again and again. Holding out until the arrival of the international revolution was central to the whole Bolshevik perspective, and long before the dark days of the Civil War. It was the expectation that the Russian socialist revolution would spark the spread of the revolution across Europe, above all to Germany, that justified not only the harsh measures of the Civil War but also the October insurrection itself. Until Stalin began to promulgate the doctrine of "socialism in one country" in late 1924, it was common ground among all Russian Marxists that it would not be possible to build socialism in Russia alone and Lenin repeatedly stated that "there would doubtlessly be no hope of the ultimate victory of our revolution if it were to remain alone"[407] and at the Seventh Party Congress in March 1918 the following resolution was formally passed:

The Congress considers the only reliable guarantee of consolidation of the socialist revolution that has been victorious in Russia to be its conversion into a world working-class revolution.[408]

The emphasis I have placed on the horrors of the Civil War and its accompanying economic catastrophe as the main determinant of Bolshevik behaviour in these years—as opposed to aspirations to totalitarianism—is open to the objection that the end of the Civil War saw not a relaxation of the Bolshevik dictatorship but its reinforcement. After all, two on the list of charges against Lenin that I listed earlier, the suppression of Kronstadt and the banning of factions within the Party, date from after the Civil War is over. The fact is, however, that the pressures on the Bolshevik government were if anything intensified rather than eased following the victory of the Red Army over the Whites.

This was because while hostilities continued, the peasantry had to choose between on the one side the Bolsheviks and their forced food requisitions (which they deeply resented) and on the other the White armies who treated them at least as harshly and whose victory, they knew with certainty, meant the return of the landlords and the loss of their principal gain from the revolution, the land. Faced with this choice the peasantry, in their majority, opted for the Bolsheviks/Communists which, in the final analysis, is why they won the Civil War.[409] But the moment the Civil War was over, and the threat of landlord restoration receded, peasant anger turned against the Bolsheviks. Now, in their eyes, there was no justification whatsoever for hated food requisitions and they rose in revolt against the regime. Tony Cliff summarises what happened:

> Now that the civil war had ended, waves of peasant uprisings swept rural Russia. The most serious outbreaks occurred in Tambov province, the middle Volga area, the Ukraine, northern Caucasus and Western Siberia... In February 1921 alone the Cheka reported 118 separate peasant uprisings in various parts of the country.[410]

Rebellion in the countryside rapidly found a resonance with workers in the town. Many of the urban workers had until recently been peasants or had returned to their villages in search of food during the famine, so links between town and country were strong. Anti-Bolshevik strikes broke out in the Petrograd district and the revolt of the Kronstadt sailors was part of this same process. And this revolt by peasants-workers-sailors was reflected in terms of tensions and splits inside the Bolshevik Party, including its top leadership. In the four months leading up to the Tenth Party Congress in March 1921 there was a huge debate inside the Party on the relationship between the state and the trade unions, with Trotsky, Bukharin and others (eight members of the Central Committee in all) arguing for the state to take control of the unions; Shliapnikov, Kollontai and the Workers' Opposition arguing for trade union control of production; and Lenin, Zinoviev and others (the "Platform of the Ten") taking an intermediate position which would leave the state and the party in control of industry but allow the unions the right to defend the workers against the state, which Lenin said had become a "workers' state with a bureaucratic twist to it".[411]

The dispute was intense and bitter. Lenin became convinced a) that the Party was on the verge of a split; b) that with sections of the population in revolt such a split could destroy the Revolution and open the door to the Whites; and c) that the root of the problem was the economic regime of War Communism, essentially the forced requisitioning of grain. His answer to the crisis was therefore to retreat on the economic front by introducing the New Economic Policy (NEP), which allowed a free market in grain so as to gain a breathing space, but combined this with strengthening the power and unity of the Party; hence the continuation of the ban on other parties and the introduction of the ban on factions. In other words, the devastation brought by the Civil War and the economic collapse continued to impose itself on Lenin and Bolsheviks even after the War was over.

The argument I have presented so far that the harsh measures of the Lenin-led government were the product of the situation it faced rather than its pre-ordained authoritarian inclinations raises two other issues. Even if this point is broadly accepted, does it follow from this that the actions and policy of the revolutionary government, designed to ensure its survival, were, as a whole, justified? And if they were justified overall, does this involve claiming that each and every one of Lenin's or the regime's actions were correct or justified?

On the last point the answer is clearly no. For example Victor Serge and Ernest Mandel, both partisans of the October Revolution, regard the establishment of the Cheka as a major mistake. Serge writes:

> I believe that the formation of the Cheka was one of the gravest and most impermissible errors that the Bolshevik leaders committed in 1918, when plots, blockades, and interventions made them lose their heads. All evidence indicates that revolutionary tribunals, functioning in the

light of day (without excluding secret sessions in particular cases) and admitting the right of defence, would have attained the same efficiency with far less abuse and depravity.[412]

The Red Army's march on Warsaw in August 1920, in a misguided attempt to stimulate or provoke a Polish revolution, was clearly both a major defeat and a serious political mistake with very damaging consequences, as Lenin himself admitted.[413] Making the ban on other parties permanent after 1921 and erecting it into a point of principle was also mistake.[414]

Unfortunately it would take a whole book, or several books, to go through all the actions of Lenin and the Bolsheviks during these years assessing the correctness or otherwise of each of them. The truth is neither Lenin nor the Bolsheviks as a whole, nor anyone else, could have gone through those years, defending the Revolution against overwhelming odds and in the most difficult of circumstances, without committing numerous mistakes and even crimes. The real historical issue is whether or not their overall strategy of trying to hold out until the international revolution came to their aid, with the harshness that necessarily entailed, was right and that in turn depends on whether there was an alternative.

Clearly there was one alternative: the alternative of defeat and a victory of the counter-revolution. But was there a "third way", some kind of social democratic or liberal middle ground? Lenin thought not:

> Either the advanced and class-conscious workers triumph and unite the poor peasant masses around themselves, establish rigorous order, a mercilessly severe rule, a genuine dictatorship of the proletariat—either they compel the kulak to submit, and institute a proper distribution of food and fuel on a national scale; or the bourgeoisie, with the help of the kulaks, and with the indirect support of the spineless and muddle-headed (the anarchists and the Left Socialist-Revolutionaries), will overthrow Soviet power and set up a Russo-German or a Russo-Japanese Kornilov, who will present the people with a sixteen-hour working day, an ounce of bread per week, mass shooting of workers and torture in dungeons, as has been the case in Finland and the Ukraine.
>
> Either—or.
>
> There is no middle course. The situation of the country is desperate in the extreme.[415]

Victor Serge agreed:

> If the Bolshevik dictatorship fell, it was only a short step to chaos, and through chaos to a peasant rising, the massacre of Communists, the return of the émigrés, and in the end, through the sheer force of events, another dictatorship, this time anti-proletarian.[416]

What was tragically not possible in those terrible circumstances was a model non-bureaucratic socialist democracy as envisaged in *The State and Revolution* or by Marx in *The Civil War in France*, still less an anarchist "Third Revolution" leading directly to a stateless communist society, what Serge called "infantile illusions".[417]

However, rejecting the idea that the Bolshevik regime in the early years was a product of Leninist totalitarianism and accepting that it was in the broad sense a necessity to prevent a White victory and some sort of Russian fascism still does not in itself refute the continuity thesis. It is also necessary to present an alternative, and superior, analysis of the rise of Stalinism and its relationship to Leninism.

Stalinism as counter-revolution

The key to such an analysis is understanding that the rise of the Stalinist bureaucracy was a product of the interaction of two major *objective* social factors—the weakness and exhaustion of the Russian proletariat and the isolation of the Russian Revolution.

On the eve of the First World War, Russia was still one of the most economically backward regions in Europe with a working class that constituted only a small minority in an overwhelmingly peasant country—for which reason it was generally assumed by Russian Marxists, including Lenin, that Russia was not yet ready for socialist revolution. The war itself further damaged the economy, though it also partially proletarianised millions of peasants by conscripting them into the armed forces. Then came the Revolution, Brest-Litovsk and the Civil War, whose catastrophic effects we have already alluded to.

Even at this stage the economic backwardness and the international situation were interacting and reinforcing each other. Had the Revolution spread to Germany in late 1917 or early 1918, there would have been no Brest-Litovsk and, almost certainly, no Civil War, which only really got going with imperialist aid. If the German Revolution had succeeded in late 1918 or early 1919 the Civil War would have ended much earlier. If Russia had been a more developed, more urbanised society, the Civil War would have had a very different character. The Revolution could have been defended by city and industry-based workers' militia (as was originally proposed in socialist theory) rather than creating a "standing" (in reality mobile) army, as was forced on them by the nature of the White armies.

The Russian economy emerged from the Civil War utterly devastated. Gross industrial production stood at only 31 percent of its 1913 level and production of steel at only 4.7 percent, while the transport system was in ruins. The total of industrial workers fell from about 3 million in 1917 to 1.25 million in 1921. And politically the condition of the Russian proletariat was worse even than these grim statistics suggest. A considerable proportion of the most militant and politically conscious workers, the vanguard of the class, had gone into the Red Army and many of them had perished. Others, again it tended to be the more politically engaged, had been drawn into administration and were no longer workers as such. The class was further weakened by its dispersal into the countryside in search of food during the famine and by sheer physical and political exhaustion.

As a result the Russian working class, which in 1917 had reached the highest level of consciousness and struggle, was now the merest shadow of its former self. By 1921 the class that made the Revolution had to all intents and purposes disappeared:

> [The] industrial proletariat...in our country, owing to the war and to the desperate poverty and ruin has become declassed, ie dislodged from its class groove and has ceased to exist as a proletariat.[418]

The role of the working class as the agents of socialist transformation and initiators of the transition to a classless society, as articulated in Marxist theory, is based not on the incorruptibility of revolutionary leaders but on the ability of the mass of workers to run society themselves and to exercise democratic control over such leaders as are indispensable in the transition period.[419] The Russian working class of 1921 lacked the capacity either to run society or control its leaders. The matter was compounded by the large number of former Tsarist officials who had been taken over and, out of necessity, incorporated into the state apparatus and by the fact that there had been an influx of careerists into the Party.[420] By this stage the socialist character of the regime was determined by the will of its Old Bolshevik leadership who constituted a small minority of its total membership. Lenin was acutely conscious of this:

> If we do not close our eyes to reality we must admit that at the present time the proletarian policy of the party is not determined by the character of the membership, but by the enormous undivided prestige enjoyed by the small group which might be called the old guard of the party.[421]

This was not sustainable for any length of time. In the end social being determines social consciousness as Marx said. In these circumstances the bureaucratisation of the party and state elite was an objective social process which gained a momentum of its own and operated not so much independently of as on and against that elite's intentions. Very near the end of his life, Lenin, deeply concerned at the situation he could see developing before his eyes, thrashed around rather desperately searching for organisational devices to slow or reverse the trend. He proposed various reforms to the Workers' and Peasants' Inspectorate (Rabkrin), which had been established in 1920 to combat encroaching bureaucratism. In December 1922 he suggested enlarging the Central Committee with new workers, then expanding the Central Control Commission and merging it with Rabkrin and finally removing Stalin as General Secretary.[422] Nothing substantial came of any of this, nor could it in the absence of pressure or mobilization from below. Day by day, month by month the growing caste of state and party officials, freed from popular control, became more entrenched in their power, more attached to the privileges, more detached from the working class and less and less interested in international revolution.

Given the exhaustion of the Russian working class the only thing that could have halted the process of bureaucratic degeneration was the victory of the revolution elsewhere, but this did not materialise. It was not that international revolution was a pipedream; on the contrary there was, as Lenin and Trotsky anticipated, a revolutionary wave across Europe including in Hungary, Italy, Ireland, Bulgaria and Germany. In March 1919, the British Prime Minister Lloyd George wrote to his French counterpart, Clemenceau:

The whole of Europe is filled with the spirit of revolution. There is a deep sense not only of discontent but of anger and revolt amongst the workmen against pre-war conditions. The whole existing order in its political, social and economic aspects is questioned by the mass of the population from one end of Europe to the other.[423]

But everywhere the revolution was beaten back. The decisive defeat was in Germany in the autumn of 1923 when the German Communist Party failed to act in an exceptionally revolutionary situation and the moment was lost. It is clear that the bureaucratisation in Russia was already a significant contributing factor to this defeat in that in 1923 the Party leadership of Zinoviev, Kamenev and Stalin refused Trotsky's offer to go to Germany to assist the German Revolution,[424] and also advised the leadership of German Communist Party against action at the crucial moment.[425]

In the final analysis Stalin, as a dominant figure in the Party, was the product rather than the producer of this situation: the bureaucracy "selected" him as their leader. But of course the moment he found himself in charge of the apparatus (he became General Secretary in 1922) and then a top Party leader (from 1923), he used his position to promote his supporters and build a machine loyal to himself. When, in autumn 1924, Stalin promulgated the idea of "socialism in one country" it contradicted the whole Marxist tradition since 1845 and indeed what he himself had written earlier in the year.[426] But as a slogan very much fitted the mood and needs of the apparatus. It appealed to their desire to put the perils and dangers of the "heroic" period of the Revolution behind them and get down to routine business without the risk of entanglements in risky foreign adventures.

"Socialism in one country" served as a banner under which Stalin and his supporters could wage their struggle against opposition in the Party, first that of Trotsky and then that of Zinoviev and Kamenev; they could be attacked as lacking faith in the Russian Revolution by virtue of their insistence on the need for international revolution. Stalin won this struggle decisively in 1927. The slogan also fitted well with the regime's economic policy of the mid-1920s which was the more or less indefinite prolongation of the NEP, the rejection of the accelerated industrialisation proposed by Trotsky and the Left

Opposition, and the perspective of moving towards socialism "at a snail's pace" as Stalin's ally Bukharin put it.[427]

However, the strategy of socialism in one country combined with the NEP contained fundamental contradictions. The NEP, with its free market in grain, had undoubtedly served its purpose of helping the Soviet economy and also people's living standards recover from their catastrophic state in 1921, but the more successful it was the more it encouraged the growth of a kulak (rich peasant) class in the countryside and, allied to them, of NEP men (merchants and traders) in the towns. The longer NEP continued, the more this class would develop as a threat to the state-owned economy controlled by the Communist Party. This tendency burst into the open in late 1927 and early 1928 with a mass refusal by the peasantry to sell their grain to the cities.

Socialism in one country was based on the premise that the Soviet Union could evolve into "complete socialism" provided it was not subject to military intervention by the West, but that was by no means guaranteed. Moreover, as well as direct military intervention, or rather prior to it, there was the pressure of economic competition from the rest of the capitalist world which, as Lenin had repeatedly stressed, remained far stronger and far more productive than the Soviet Union. How were that competition and the pressure it exerted to be resisted? Before "socialism in one country" the answer to this question was that it would be resisted and, in the last instance, could *only* be resisted by spreading the revolution. After that perspective was abandoned the answer had to be that it would be resisted by building up Russia's military strength, which in turn meant building up its economic strength.

Stalin, as he later made clear, had a serious grasp of this problem:

No comrades...the pace must not be slackened! On the contrary, we must quicken it as much as is within our powers and possibilities.

To slacken the pace would mean to lag behind; and those who lag behind are beaten. We do not want to be beaten. No, we don't want to. The history of old... Russia...she was ceaselessly beaten for her backwardness... For military backwardness, for cultural backwardness, for political backwardness, for industrial backwardness, for agricultural backwardness...

We are fifty or a hundred years behind the advanced countries. We must make good this lag in ten years. Either we do it or they crush us.[428]

These problems converged and came to a head in 1928 and Stalin's response was to abandon the NEP in a massive change of course. Having decisively defeated the Left and United Oppositions in 1927, he was now able to turn on Bukharin and the pro-peasant right making himself the unchallenged leader of the Party and dictator of Russia in the process. He launched a campaign to forcibly requisition more grain from the countryside and in mid-1928 introduced the First Five Year Plan which put Russia on the road to rapid industrialisation setting growth targets far in excess of anything advocated by the Opposition. Then, when the grain requisitions failed to deliver results, Stalin embarked on the forced collectivisation of agriculture.

The coming together of these three things—Stalin's establishment of absolute power, the herding of the peasants into state farms and the dramatic drive to industrialise—was called by Isaac Deutscher "the great change"[429] and by many others "the third revolution"[430] and the "revolution from above". In reality this was a profound counter-revolution. What made them a counter-revolution was that they constituted a transformation in basic socio-economic relations (in Marxist terms, the social relations of production): the bureaucracy's transformation of itself into a new ruling class, and the change from an economy essentially concerned with production for the needs of its people (ie "consumption") to one that was driven by competitive accumulation of capital, which is to say the central dynamic of capitalism.

Under the NEP, control of industrial production was vested in a combination of the Party cell, the trade union plant committee and the technical manager (known as the Troika). With the drive to industrialisation, the Troika was dispensed with in favour of unfettered control by the manager. Under the NEP living standards rose roughly in line with the (moderate) growth of the economy. In contrast, between 1928 and 1932, the years of the Five Year Plan, the economy grew very rapidly but living standards fell catastrophically. Alec Nove writes, "1933 was the culmination of the most precipitous peacetime decline in living standards known in recorded history."[431] And Michael Haynes and Rumy Hasan's study of mortality in Russia suggests that life expectancy at birth fell from 38.9 years in 1928 to 32.8 years in 1932.[432] In his book *State Capitalism in Russia*, Tony Cliff presents a mass of empirical evidence to demonstrate the reversal that occurred at this time. Here are two telling examples:

"Food baskets" per monthly wage[433]

	Number	Index
1913	3.7	100
1928	5.6	151.4
1932	4.8	129.7
1935	1.9	51.4

Division of gross output of industry into means of production and means of consumption (in percentages)[434]

	1913	1927-8	1932	1937	1940
Means of Production	44.3	32.8	53.3	57.8	61.0
Means of Consumption	55.7	67.2	46.7	42.2	39.0

The significance of these figures should be apparent when we recall the fundamental statement in *The Communist Manifesto* that:

In bourgeois society, living labour is but a means to increase accumulated labour. In Communist society, accumulated labour is but a means to widen, to enrich, to promote the existence of the labourer.

With the First Five Year Plan the Soviet Union embarked, under the pressure of world capitalism, on a process of "production for production's sake, accumulation for accumulation's sake" [Marx, *Capital*] on the basis of the most ruthless exploitation of wage labour. The social agent of this exploitation was the Stalinist bureaucracy, thereby undertaking the historical mission of the bourgeoisie and turning itself into a state capitalist ruling class, which, like every other ruling class, proceeded to help itself to numerous perks and privileges.

It is this economic transformation that fundamentally defines Stalin's "revolution from above" as a counter-revolution: the final defeat of the workers' Revolution of 1917 and the restoration of capitalism in a new state bureaucratic form. But the counter-revolutionary character of the process is indicated and confirmed by many other facts: by the fact that Stalin was only able to consolidate his rule by imprisoning and murdering millions of workers and peasants and virtually every old Bolshevik leader who had any connection with the Revolution and with Lenin;[435] by the extensive use of slave labour in the notorious gulags; by the abandonment of the party "maximum" which limited the wages of party members and an official campaign against "egalitarianism" as a bourgeois concept; by the restoration of bourgeois norms in daily life ranging from the language used to subordinates to the huge privileges accorded to army officers to the return on a large scale of prostitution; and by the draconian criminal penal code which included long prison sentences and the death penalty for juveniles.[436]

Indeed, there was hardly any aspect of social and political life in which Stalinism did not more or less trample on the policies and legacy of Lenin and of the early years of the Revolution. Far from being a continuation of Leninism or its fulfilment, Stalinism was its counter-revolutionary negation. And in the wider scheme of things it can be seen to be part of an international process of counter-revolution which included Mussolini and the triumph of fascism in Italy, the defeat of the British workers' movement culminating in the General Strike of 1926, the defeat of the Irish Revolution in 1923, the crushing of the Chinese Revolution in 1927 and, above all, the victory of Hitler in 1933.

Will it happen again?

It is possible to accept, at least in broad outline, the arguments presented here about the role of objective conditions in shaping the rise of Stalinism and yet return to the objection that nevertheless Leninist ideology played a certain role in facilitating the process. This is the position taken by Samuel Farber in his book *Before Leninism* which defends this view as follows:

> [M]ost of the undemocratic practices of "Leninism in power" developed in the context of a massively devastating civil war and in fact cannot be understood outside such a context. But while this is a very necessary part of the explanation for the decline and disappearance of soviet democracy, it is by no means sufficient.[437]

In addition, he argues, a significant role was played by what he calls Lenin's "quasi-Jacobin"[438] conception of revolution and revolutionary leadership. Similarly Simon Pirani claims:

> The Bolsheviks' vanguardism and statism made them blind to the creative potential of democratic workers' organisations, intolerant of other working class political forces and ruthless in silencing dissent.

He adds, "perhaps different choices in 1921 would have made possible different types of resistance to the reimposition of exploitative class relations".[439]

The problem with these arguments is that they can go on for ever without there being any clear criterion of proof. "But, surely, Leninist ideology played some part?" How much of a part? 30 percent? 10 percent? 5 percent? And so on ad infinitum.[440] But what really matters is not forming an exact estimation of the degree of responsibility of Lenin and the Bolsheviks for later Stalinism, but whether or not building a Leninist revolutionary party today invites a repetition of the Stalinist nightmare, should that party succeed in leading a successful revolution.

The analysis presented above which starts, as Marxist analyses should, from material conditions and the balance of class forces and sees the rise and victory of Stalinism as fundamentally a process of class struggle (rather than a product of ideology or psychology) suggests very strongly that workers' revolution today would not degenerate into a new version of Stalinism.

First, the hundred years since 1917 have seen an immense global development of the forces of production and a huge accumulation of wealth, which in a revolution would be expropriated by the working class. Any revolution in any major country today would begin on a much higher economic foundation than the Russian Revolution did. Second, and this is the most important thing, the working class internationally and in almost every individual country is an enormously larger and stronger force than it was in Russia. (I have provided the figures for this in Chapter 1.) It would be far harder to dissolve and atomise it than was the case in 1918-1921 and the counter-revolutionary forces would not have the base in the countryside that was the case then. Third, the global integration of the world economy is also far, far more advanced and this would greatly improve the possibility of spreading any successful revolution internationally. The revolution in transport and communications would massively facilitate this. In 1917 it took John Reed months to reach Petrograd and it was a couple of years after the revolution before Western socialists like Gramsci got to read much Lenin. Today, as we saw with the Arab Spring, the revolution would be live streamed on the internet and revolutionary leaders and ordinary workers alike would be able to appeal directly to the workers of the world to rise up in solidarity. It would be highly effective.

Let us make for a moment the worst assumptions (assumptions that I believe are false) about the intentions and ideology of the leaders of the revolutionary party that led the revolution in China or Brazil, Egypt, Spain or Ireland. Let us assume that the party leadership immediately sets about trying to undermine the workers' power and workers' democracy established in the process of the revolution and to appropriate power for itself. Why would the victorious working class allow this to happen? Why would working people who had liberated themselves in the most dramatic and heroic fashion permit their revolution victory to be usurped in this way, especially with the example of what occurred in Stalinist Russia to go on?

The Russian working class allowed it because they were devastated and destroyed by unbelievably horrific conditions. To believe that a future working class, in the absence of those conditions, would permit a repetition of the Russian scenario is to take an extremely dim view of the capacities of the working class and fall back into the crudest stereotypes of the conservative "human nature" theory which, of course, rules out socialism and human emancipation in general.

If, as I have maintained, an essentially Leninist revolutionary party is necessary for the victory of the revolution, then fear of a Stalinist-type outcome is no reason to refrain from building it.

7

Leninism today

To be a Leninist today is to be a revolutionary and a champion of the working class. Those who believe it is possible to be a Marxist or a Leninist without being a fighter for international workers' revolution are using the terms "Marxist" and "Leninist" in very different ways from the way they are used here,[441] for this was the core of all Marx and Lenin's theory and practice. However, to be an effective revolutionary socialist today also involves the three central pillars of Lenin's politics— his theory of imperialism, his theory of the state and his theory of the party, which together underpinned the Russian Revolution. This has been the main argument of this book. But since Lenin's time, life has also thrown up a number of problems whose resolution was and is a prerequisite for serious socialist practice.

Fascism and Stalinism

In the 1920s and 1930s the two most important new issues to present themselves were the rise of fascism and of Stalinism. The problem of understanding the nature of fascism and developing a strategy to fight it was a matter of life and death for the entire international labour movement in the 1930s and it has returned, albeit so far with less intensity, on many occasions up to and including the present. Faced with the challenge of Hitler and Franco "the left" (ie the Social Democrats and the Communists) failed lamentably, first failing to form a united front against the Nazis and so going down to defeat without a serious fight, then, in the Popular Front, subordinating the struggle of the working class to an alliance with the "democratic" bourgeoisie and so, no less damagingly, undermining and paralysing resistance to Franco.

The main theoretical work on this was done, and done at the time, by Leon Trotsky. In a series of brilliant articles, written while in exile in

Turkey in 1929-1933, Trotsky produced what remains to this day the most compelling analysis of the class nature of the fascist movement and mapped out a strategy, the workers' united front, which had it been applied in time could have prevented Hitler coming to power. As we face the threat of fascism in Europe today, socialists obviously need up-to-date concrete analyses, but the theoretical point of departure for those analyses should remain the work done by Trotsky.

For the international left the question of Stalinism proved more intractable and, theoretically, more damaging. The large majority of the international movement (ie of the Communist International and its fellow travellers and a significant layer of left social democrats) remained more or less uncritically loyal to Stalin and to the Soviet Union. The loyalty to Stalin persisted at least until Khrushchev's denunciation of Stalin's crimes in 1956 and to the Soviet Union, with diminishing intensity, a lot longer. This had calamitous consequences. In the short run it perverted the Comintern and its parties, turning them, at least partially, into instruments of Soviet foreign policy, rather socialist struggle. In the longer run it discredited socialism and alienated large swathes of working class people, as well as leading to the return of Communist Parties to reformism. But even among those Marxists and revolutionary socialists who opposed Stalinism and broke with it, there was theoretical confusion as to the nature of the Stalinist regimes, first in the Soviet Union and later elsewhere, and to the role of Stalinism in the international movement.

The main source of this confusion was that the Stalinist regime rested on state property, the nationalisation of the major means of production. In the minds of many socialists (and the bourgeois mainstream and right) capitalism was seen as basically defined by private ownership and state ownership was seen as the basis of a socialist economy.[442] Thus, confronted with the reality of Stalinism in 1956, the international communist movement by and large took refuge in the formula that Stalinism was a problem of the superstructure, or even of the "cult of personality" of the individual leader, arising on a socialist base. Even Leon Trotsky, who fought Stalin and Stalinism to the bitter end and grasped its counter-revolutionary character, nevertheless stumbled over the question of state property, which for him remained the defining characteristic of a workers' state.

This led Trotsky to the contradictory position that the Soviet state, which he recognised was not in any way under the control of the working class, nevertheless remained a workers' state, albeit a degenerated one. This in turn led to the mistaken prediction, in 1938-1939, that a regime embodying such contradictions could not survive the shock of war and that it would very soon collapse. When Stalinism emerged victorious from the Second World War and, far from collapsing, extended its control to the whole of Eastern Europe as well as China in 1949, many of Trotsky's supporters accepted the idea of socialist transformation of society without active working class self-emancipation and slowly but surely moved back towards Stalinism (sometimes in its Maoist or Castroite forms).

Another strand on the anti-Stalinist left rejected the equation of state property with workers' state but accepted the equation of capitalism with private property. This produced the theory that the Stalinist regime(s) were neither capitalist nor socialist but some new form of class or exploitative society. Politically, this left open the option (an option taken by most adherents of this view) that this new form of society was, by virtue of its totalitarian character, *more* reactionary than Western capitalism and that the West had to be supported in the Cold War. Theoretically, for those holding this view from a Marxist background, it raised the problem that the analysis of this "new" mode of production relied on categories not drawn from historical materialism and was lacking in a political economic foundation of the kind provided by Marx in *Capital*. In short, theoretically, it was an inconsistent mess.

Only when the fetish of state property was broken by the theory of state capitalism was this confusion resolved. The idea that Russia under Stalinism was state capitalist had a long and complex history, but it was developed in its most coherent form by Tony Cliff in the late 1940s and subsequently published as *Russia: A Marxist Analysis* and *State Capitalism in Russia*. In Cliff's hands the theory of state capitalism took as its point of departure not the form of property but the real relations of production and this made possible a theoretical analysis of Stalinism that was compatible with a) the empirical reality of the Soviet regime; b) the core Marxist principle of working class self-emancipation; and c) the classical Marxist analysis of historical development and the laws of motion of capitalism. This was also a theorisation that could be, and was, further developed by Cliff and others to apply to China, Vietnam, Cuba and so on.[443]

It could be said that with the "collapse of communism" this question has lost its significance and, for the moment, it is certainly less central than it was in 1950 or 1970. Nevertheless it remains relevant because a number of Stalinist or semi-Stalinist regimes still survive (in North Korea, Vietnam, Cuba and China); because the legacy of Stalinism, particularly in its Eurocommunist form, is still a substantial influence on wide sections of the international left and trade union movement; and because it is impossible to make an intellectually coherent case for socialism without a convincing explanation of Stalinism. There are also occasions, and they are not that rare, of conflict between the West and Russia (for example, over Ukraine and in Syria) when just as right wing labourites and social democrats invariably side with Washington there are others on the left whose knee-jerk reaction is still to side with Moscow.

Obviously there are a multitude of nationally or temporally specific issues which revolutionary socialists have to engage with on a daily basis, but I think it is possible to identify four key areas which it is currently essential for socialists and socialist organisations to address as a precondition of revolutionary practice, an answer to which can not be "looked up" in Lenin (or for that matter, Trotsky).

Current issues

The first is the political economy of modern capitalism: a theoretical analysis that encompasses the post-war boom, its breakdown in the 1970s, the neo-liberal response, the crash of 2007-2008 and the ongoing situation today. There is, of course, a vast Marxist literature on this, far too large to even summarise here, and ranging from figures such as Baran and Sweezy and Mike Kidron in the past, through to Robert Brenner, David McNally, Anwar Shaikh, Andrew Kliman, David Harvey, Joseph Choonara, Guiglielmo Carchedi and many others today. However, out of this wide and rich field I would mention particularly the work of Chris Harman, Alex Callinicos and Michael Roberts. What unifies these three is their common deployment of the theory of the tendency of the rate of profit to decline (an aspect of Marx never focused on by Lenin or the other Marxists of Lenin's generation) as the root cause of capitalist crisis.[444]

To put the matter as briefly as possible the argument can be made that the decline in the rate of profit was offset after the Second World War by massive arms spending which slowed the rise in the organic composition of capital. This, however, generated its own contradictions as the United States faced increased competition from Japan and Germany and with this came the return of the problem of falling profitability and the crises of the mid-1970s and early 1980s. Capitalism responded to these with the neo-liberal offensive spearheaded by Reagan and Thatcher. This was designed precisely to restore the rate of profit by shifting the share of total wealth from labour to capital internationally. But despite substantial success in redistributing wealth and income upwards, neo liberalism did not succeed in overcoming the underlying crisis of profitability—hence the collapse of 2007-2008, and the great recession that followed. Hence also the exceptionally sluggish recovery and the real possibility of further slowdown and another recession in the next couple of years.

Politically what is most important about this analysis is that it leads to a perspective of continuing economic instability, intensifying class conflict and increasing political polarisation—a set of circumstances in which it is possible for revolutionary politics, Leninist politics, to gain serious traction internationally. I will return to this vital question shortly.

A second issue with immense implications for practice is the contemporary shape and structure of the working class. This is partly a matter of responding to challenges to the Marxist theory of the working class, such as Hardt and Negri's theory of "the multitude" or Guy Standing's "precariat". But if the working class is, as I have argued throughout this book, the primary agent of revolution then questions such as what are the dimensions of the working class today, where it is concentrated and where it is likely to be strongest are very important. While good work has been done on these questions, there is as yet no comprehensive analysis.[445]

Third, there is the matter of combating oppression. As we have seen in Chapter 5, Lenin attached great importance to this and so must socialists today. What is clear though is that the range of oppressions that have to be taken up has changed and widened. Lenin always fought racism, especially anti-Semitism, but a number of major historical developments (the Nazis and the holocaust, the Civil Rights and Black movements in the United States, the numerous anti-colonial struggles, the anti-Apartheid struggle, the phenomenon of mass migration, the rise of Islamophobia and the refugee crisis and the rise of the far right using racism as their main ideological weapon) have combined to make the fight against racism of crucial importance internationally in a way that is qualitatively different from Lenin's day. This applies particularly to the question of Islamophobia, which, over the last 20 years or so, has become the main form of contemporary racism on a global scale. In Chapter 5 we saw the Bolsheviks' principled stand in defence of Muslim rights in Russia, but it is clear that this issue has caused much confusion on the far left, especially in France, even on the basic right of Muslim women to wear the hijab.[446]

Equally expanded is the struggle against sexism and for sexual liberation. Again Lenin was a principled supporter of women's emancipation and the Russian Revolution decriminalised homosexuality, but first "gay liberation" and now the LGBTQ struggle have assumed a significance that was not the case for Lenin. No revolutionary movement or party worthy of its name can fail to respond to these issues and others such as disability and mental health. New struggles, as yet unforeseen, may well arise. For revolutionary socialists in the Leninist tradition who aspire to be "tribunes of the people" the key is listening, learning and engaging while not losing sight of the core principle—the centrality of the working class. Important in this is understanding that the modern working class *is* female and male, black and white, multi-cultural, LGBTQ and straight and so on. Any mass united working class movement, say over health or housing or the minimum wage, will have to deal with all these questions within its own ranks or see itself broken into a hundred fragments and the only basis on which it can deal with them is principled opposition to all oppression.

Fourth, there is the issue of climate change, of which neither Lenin nor anyone else of that time had any inkling, which now threatens the very survival of society and perhaps of the species. Perhaps surprisingly Marxism, including the Marxism of Marx, turned out to be very well equipped to deal theoretically with the issue of climate change,[447] understanding it as a supreme example of human alienation from nature and from the products of our own labour diagnosed by Marx in the *Economic and Philosophical Manuscripts* of 1844 and a consequence of the "metabolic rift" between humans and nature produced by a society based on capital accumulation and production for profit.

But climate change is not a "thing" or single catastrophic event (like global nuclear war) that may or may not happen in the future. It is a process occurring now which is already impacting on many people's lives and will do so with increasing intensity in the years ahead, thus sharpening the class struggle and interacting with racism. It will therefore have to be part of the political armoury of revolutionary socialists to respond concretely to these interactions between climate change and the class struggle. I will say more on this shortly.

Obviously this list of post-Lenin issues can be greatly extended and it is certain that new ones will arise in the future. However, there is one major question that must be addressed in any study asserting the relevance of Lenin's politics to the present. This is the weakness of Leninism as an organised political force in the world today. The unfortunate fact is that organisations that pursue Lenin's goal, the goal of international proletarian revolution, are generally speaking marginal to society and to working class movements.

This marginalisation has deep historical roots. It is a product in the first instance of those two great catastrophes of the 20th century, Stalinism and fascism. Both fascism and Stalinism subjected socialist revolutionaries to the most brutal repression, but the Stalinist counter-revolution also drove genuine Leninists out of the labour movement in the name of Lenin and that proved very effective. For example, when Leon Trotsky launched the Fourth International in 1938, the founding meeting consisted of only 21 delegates from 11 countries meeting for a day in a house in France and of those 21 only one, the American Max Shachtman, represented a serious organisation.[448] And at that time no other anti-Stalinist revolutionary socialist tendency of any size existed anywhere.

This isolation, inflicted as part of the terrible defeats suffered by the working class and the socialist movement, was further compounded by the great post-war economic boom in which working class living standards rose and reformist tendencies flourished. Only with the faltering of the boom and the general radicalisation of the late 1960s did revolutionary Marxist politics start to come in from the cold with the International Socialists beginning to get a foothold in the rising industrial struggle of the period 1968-1974, with several Trotskyist groups (most notably the Ligue Communiste Revolutionaire or LCR) emerging out of May '68 in France and a large and very militant group of revolutionary "workerist" organisations appearing in Italy along with quite substantial Maoist splits emerging from the Communist Parties across Europe.

But the wave of struggle that swept Europe in the late 1960s and early 1970s and culminated in the Portuguese Revolution of 1974 ran into the sand and gave way in the second half of the 1970s to what Tony Cliff called the "downturn"; a decline in the level of strikes and other forms of working class militancy internationally. This change in balance of class forces either destroyed the new revolutionary organisations or blocked their further advance.[449] And since then revolutionary socialist organisations, despite being able on occasion to lead mass political campaigns,[450] have nowhere succeeded in establishing mass roots or membership in the working class.

In so far as new radical left political formations have emerged in response to the prolonged austerity following the 2008 crash, it has been, internationally, on a left reformist not a revolutionary basis (Syriza, Podemos, the Sanders campaign, Corbyn and his supporters in the Labour Party). The same was true, albeit wrapped in more revolutionary rhetoric, in Latin America with the movements supporting Hugo Chávez in Venezuela, Evo Morales in Bolivia and the Workers' Party in Brazil.

If the case made in this book for the contemporary relevance of Leninism is to mean anything, this state of affairs has to change. It is almost certainly not possible to build a genuinely mass revolutionary party which leads the majority of the working class outside of an actually existing revolutionary situation. However, in order to be able to grow into a truly mass party in such a situation, the revolutionary organisation needs already, at the onset of the revolution, to have reached a certain critical mass; it needs to appear to the masses as a potentially credible force and it has to have a voice in the national political debate.

Moreover, the achievement of this is now very urgent because the political polarisation that is occurring internationally creates a race for the future as to who will articulate the widespread anger of the masses— the revolutionary left or the racist and fascist right—and because the prospect of climate catastrophe sets an indefinite but nevertheless real time limit on the whole business. This raises the classic Leninist question: What is to be done?

What is to be done?

The roots of the isolation of revolutionaries are objective but long-term adaptation to objective circumstances can, and generally does, breed bad habits, habits not conducive to breaking out of those circumstances. Many of the small "Leninist" organisations, predominantly from the Trotskyist tradition, that are now scattered across the planet, have adjusted to their isolation by developing, often unconsciously, an institutionalised sectarianism. By sectarianism I mean not primarily an obsession with or hostility to other groups on the left (though there is plenty of that about) nor even a formal refusal to work in unions or participate in united fronts, but rather a method and style of working that, in practice, fails to engage with the working class where it actually is at.[451] The only way out of this is to make determined efforts to relate to and build bases in working class communities. The habits of sectarianism must be broken in practice.

Building roots in working class communities cannot be done, in the present circumstances, simply by means of propaganda; it requires agitation ie campaigning for very specific goals, both locally and nationally. What those goals are, and the nature of the campaigns, have to be determined on the basis of actually listening to what working class people want. My experience suggests this can be something of a foreign concept to some revolutionary socialists so I will spell it out. It does *not* mean that if local people want something reactionary (to blame the immigrants, exclude the refugees, prevent the location of a facility for the homeless, etc) revolutionaries should go along with this, not at all, but it does mean getting involved and championing their cause if they want to defend their swimming pool or keep some green space or resist an unfair tax or save a hospital or improve the community centre in their area.

Local campaigning is not here counter-posed to national campaigning; often one will feed into the other. But specific local campaigns are important for gaining footholds in local communities. A particular role here is played by environmental issues. The environmental movement as a whole tends, very understandably, to be focused on global issues (especially climate change) and to be predominantly middle class in composition, but at a local level environmental issues are often a crucial concern for working class people whose areas, after all, are most likely to be affected by pollution, unhealthy dumping of refuse, obnoxious development and the like. Something that needs to be understood here is that, generally speaking, working class people get involved in political campaigns when they think they can actually win and often people feel more able to win on local issues, than on big moral or global questions (end global poverty, stop climate change, etc). Of course, revolutionaries want to change this and broaden people's horizons but the way to achieve this is by starting where working people are actually at, not where we would like them to be.

In many countries, especially Britain, revolutionaries are more familiar with doing this sort of grassroots work in trade unions than in communities. Trade union work is, of course, vital and trade unions remain the most important mass organisations of the working class internationally. But it is also a fact that in recent years trade union struggles have in many countries been at a low level. The reasons for this can be debated but it remains a fact and in the face of this fact community campaigning can be an important road into the working class.

The Irish anti-water charges movement of 2014 onwards gives an example of this. In an ideal world the imposition of water charges would have been prevented by the employees of Irish Water refusing to install water meters or administer the charges. In reality, however, this was not going to happen. In reality the movement against water charges began in local working class communities with people blocking meter installation outside their front doors. It would have been folly—sectarian folly—to counterpose trade union action, which was unlikely, to community action which was real and which led on to mass demonstrations and mass refusal to pay.[452] Community struggle is also often a better basis than trade union work for electoral campaigning, which, as Lenin insisted, has to be part of revolutionary work.

Hand in hand with local campaigning, though it applies also to national propaganda, goes learning to put over revolutionary ideas in popular language, the language of the working people revolutionaries are addressing and hoping to influence. As a result of their isolation many revolutionaries and revolutionary organisations have developed a jargon and habits of speech ("as socialists we have to say") which are the product of getting used to speaking primarily to ourselves. How actually to do this is an art that has to be learned in the practice of interacting with people and, again, listening to people.

A book like this cannot set out guidelines, which in any case would vary from country to country, but a good example, from which I learnt a lot, were the statements issued on a regular basis by the Egyptian Revolutionary Socialists during the Egyptian Revolution. These statements expressed Marxist and revolutionary socialist ideas in the language of that revolution.[453] Another element in speaking to and with the people is that revolutionary Leninist organisations and individuals must master the effective use of social media which has now become an indispensable tool of radical propaganda and agitation[454] and permits the extensive use of video and alternative TV broadcasting in a way that was not formerly possible.

Obviously undertaking this kind of work will bring with it all sorts of reformist, localist and electoralist pressures which will be real and will have to be counteracted. But refusing the kind of work needed to relate to working class communities for fear of "contamination" is not a serious option. Revolutionaries have to learn how to work with non-revolutionaries in a popular and mass way, without being unprincipled or "opportunist" as Lenin would have called it.

A strategic issue that arises here is that as the mass of working people move from passive reformist voting or support for the so-called centre and mainstream to some degree of activism and radicalism, they have not moved, and do not deem likely to move, directly to revolutionary socialism. To meet and involve such people on their journey leftwards, Leninists are going to need to create, where possible, transitional organisations which are somewhere between traditional reformist parties and outright revolutionary parties. They should be a political space where revolutionaries and left reformists or, much more accurately, people who have not yet thought the issue of reform or revolution through can co-exist and work together.

Such spaces have indeed emerged in recent years but sometimes under the political and organisational grip of thoroughly pro-capitalist parties (as with the Sanders campaign inside the US Democrats and the Corbynistas within British Labour). This is entirely understandable because changing these already existing mass parties with an immediate shot at winning elections seems to people whose consciousness remains reformist a much more "realistic" method of achieving social change than trying to build a new party. And where this happens, revolutionaries have no option but to relate to the mass movement where it is at.

However, such "confinement" within this establishment terrain has major disadvantages, not only because socialist transformation of society is impossible through reformist means, but also because the bureaucracies and structures of these parties will actively demobilise the radical campaigners at their base, as has happened with both the Sanders' campaign (after Sanders endorsed Hilary Clinton) and is currently occurring with Corbyn supporters in Momentum and the Labour Party. It is this point, not doctrinal or "purist" refusal to engage in united front work with people who have even right wing reformist views, that is decisive here. To stay permanently within the Labour Party or similar traditional parliamentary social democratic parties, not to mention the thoroughly capitalist US Democratic Party, is to condemn the radical left to absorption in endless internal bureaucratic struggles with people who cannot be won over or even appeased—this is a recipe for demoralisation.

The experience of the left in Ireland is relevant here. A decade or so ago the Irish far left was undoubtedly weak but there were two small, but serious, parties from the Leninist and Trotskyist tradition, the Socialist Workers Party and the Socialist Party. The parties have both engaged in extensive grassroots campaigning over issues such as the "Bin Tax", "Household Charges" and, most successfully, Water Charges as well as non-economic questions such as a woman's right to choose. In the course of these campaigns both organisations built parties, People Before Profit (PBP) and the Anti-Austerity Alliance (AAA) respectively,[455] which constituted the kind of transitional space embracing militant grassroots activists and more thought-through revolutionaries and both have met with a certain amount of electoral success.

At the last general election in February 2016, the AAA and PBP formed an alliance and each party succeeded in getting three TDs (MPs) elected, making six in total (in comparison to the Labour Party's seven and Sinn Fein's 23). People Before Profit also won two seats in elections to the Northern Ireland Assembly in Stormont.[456] Most importantly, People Before Profit has been able to recruit substantially North and South and has a membership of over 1,250. In a country of only 6.4 million (Republic of Ireland, 4.6 million; Northern Ireland, 1.8 million) this is still very inadequate, but is real progress. In mathematical terms it is the equivalent of roughly 12,000 in France or Britain and 60,000 in the United States.[457]

In citing this experience there is no suggestion that People Before Profit constitutes some kind of model or template to be copied elsewhere. This would be absurd given the very different political landscapes that prevail in different countries; for example the situation with Podemos in the Spanish State or the difficult legacy of the NPA (New Anti-Capitalist Party) in France or the social weight of the Labour Party in Britain. Nevertheless it is an experience which can be learned from.

Consider, for example, the current situation in the United States. For decades many on the left have written off the United States as more or less a wasteland. But now it is clear, for anyone who can see beyond the headlines about Trump, that a substantial new left has emerged and is now a fact of US political life. This has been in evidence on the streets and in rallies in a series of mobilisations starting with Occupy in autumn 2011 and running through Black Lives Matter, the Sanders' campaign, the support for Standing Rock and the huge marches, nationwide, against Trump: 750,000 in Los Angeles is a significant figure by any standard. But so far no large or nationwide radical left or revolutionary organisation has been able to develop out of this ferment.

Serious Leninist groups do exist,[458] but it seems unlikely at present that they can directly attract large numbers, as opposed to recruiting in ones and twos or maybe handfuls. If, however, they were able to combine with others, such as the Democratic Socialists of America (DSA), which has several thousand members, to launch a credible national radical alternative to the Democrats, this might well be able to grow very substantially and constitute an arena in which people could be won to socialist and revolutionary politics. Similar opportunities are likely to arise in many countries.

My argument is that Leninists today should be actively looking to create them and be ready to seize them when the come. Clearly no such initiatives are guaranteed to succeed, on the contrary various mistakes and failures seem virtually inevitable, but that does not make taking initiatives a mistake. The global situation, the world of Trump, Le Pen and climate change, makes business as usual not an option.

Can it be done?

Revolutionaries understand that to change the world we also have to change ourselves but no amount of voluntaristic efforts of the kind urged above, necessary as they are, will avail if objective reality remains more or less as it is. As Marx put it, "It is not enough that thought should seek to realize itself; reality must also strive towards thought".[459] But objective reality is not going to remain the same. That is precisely what makes the efforts necessary.

Leave aside for the moment the political polarisation already taking place around the world and the possibility of another recession in the next couple of years, with all the incalculable political and ideological effects that will have. Leave all these things aside and we still face the scientific fact of rapidly intensifying climate change coming down the tracks. Once this reaches beyond a certain point and is grasped as an immediate reality rather than abstract speculation by millions of people, *as will happen*, this will tear up existing political allegiances as the great recession has done, only on a far greater scale.

At present there are a number of extremely simple one-line rebuttals of socialism and revolution (you can't change human nature, nothing ever really changes, revolutions always end in tyranny and the like) which continue to function as "common sense" in Gramsci's use of the term and which block mass support for revolutionary socialism, despite their intellectual poverty and despite our best efforts to counter them. The reality of climate change will change the terms of the debate. Whether we are talking about taking emergency action to prevent it reaching some runaway tipping point or trying to survive its onset with some measure of human decency, the abandonment of an economic system founded on production for profit will become an absolute necessity. Dealing with the immediate effects of climate change—its storms, floods, fires and desertification—will also push people towards collective action and collective solutions.

And there is a fundamental difference between climate change and economic crisis as an expression of the contradictions of capitalism. Provided the working class can be made to pay the required price, economic crises contain within themselves the mechanism for their own resolution. This is not the case with climate change. No amount of wage or benefit cutting will stop fossil fuel production or reverse the greenhouse effect; only planned and socialised production will do that.

Of course there will be an "alternative", at least for a period, and we can already see what that alternative will be: the Trumpian and, ultimately, Hitlerian "solution" of walls and barbed wire and concentration camps and letting climate refugees starve and drown on a scale that dwarfs the carnage we have recently seen in the Mediterranean, while the rich insulate themselves in their gated communities in the uplands.

This does not mean that climate change can or should be the main focus for immediate mass campaigning. At the moment the threat it poses remains too abstract for that to work. Nevertheless it must form a backdrop to all current propaganda and agitation and a reminder that our time is limited.

To avert the barbaric response to climate change it will be necessary, as Lenin understood with unmatched clarity, to build revolutionary workers' parties, defeat imperialism, smash the state and establish workers' power. That in turn means finding ways to relate these ideas to working class people where they are at now.

Postscript

In this book I have deliberately avoided focusing on Lenin's personality, except to rebut the Cold War travesty of it, or his peculiar and exceptional abilities because in arguing for the relevance of Leninist principles I did not want to suggest that socialists today should, or could, attempt to be new Lenins rather than working for basic Leninist politics. Nevertheless writing the book has necessarily involved a fairly sustained "relationship" with the man and it is more or less impossible not to be "captured" by him. Lenin exhibited what must be a nearly unique combination of deep intellect (especially in the areas of philosophy and economics) and immense concentration of will. He is not the equal of Marx as a thinker, who is? But he far excels his master as a political leader.

For me there are four outstanding moments in Lenin's life which really epitomise his character. The first is in the immediate run-up to the October Insurrection. Lenin has decided that the time for the rising is right but he has still to persuade a reluctant Bolshevik Central Committee. The letters and texts he writes at this time are the most intense and concentrated effort I have ever seen of one human being to win over another group of human beings to his point of view and get them to act, all grounded at the same time in a profound Marxist analysis.

The second is Lenin at the worst moments of the Civil War [I have quoted from Lenin's writing and speeches at this time in Chapter 6.] The ability to look an appalling reality in the face, without euphemism or evasion, and at the same time resist it, is, in my opinion, extraordinary and inspiring.

The third is Lenin at the very end of his life, his health failing and struggling desperately to think, work and write at all, and becoming aware of the growing threat of the bureaucracy and of Stalin. This is the only time when Lenin really doesn't seem master of himself or the situation and it is extremely sad just to read about it. And yet he fights on and there is the moving moment when he says "I suppose I have been very remiss with respect to the workers of Russia".

The fourth is in August 1914. Lenin is in Austria and the news of the outbreak of the War is accompanied shortly afterwards with the news of the Second International's capitulation. The latter is more shocking for revolutionaries than the former; war was expected, as Lenin, Trotsky and Bukharin all testify. Rosa Luxemburg was temporarily seized by despair and near to suicide. For all of them it is as though their political universe has suddenly collapsed.

Yet Lenin responds with extraordinary rapidity and vigour. Within a few days he had formulated his basic political response and fundamental slogans: total opposition to the war as imperialist, revolutionary defeatism on both sides, a break with the Second International and the call to "Turn the Imperialist war into a Civil War!" Consider for a moment that last slogan, which Lenin called "the only correct proletarian slogan", its sheer audacity and apparent harshness. To most on the left, even to many of his own comrades, faced with the terrible calamity of the war and the huge tide of patriotic war fever, this must have seemed like madness. And yet in three years he was proved right! The imperialist war was turned into civil war. Once again we see this unparalleled synthesis of the objective and subjective factors, of scientific analysis of the objective circumstances and iron determination to change them.

An imperialist nuclear war, which remains possible if not immediately probable, cannot, alas, be turned into a civil war but climate change, which will claim more lives than the First World War, can. Perhaps "Turn climate change into system change!" may serve well do service as a slogan in the years to come.

Notes

1   See John Molyneux "Lih's Lenin" online at http://johnmolyneux. blogspot.ie/2006/11/lihs-lenin-review-of-lars-t-lih-lenin.html.

2   G Lukács, *Lenin: A Study on the Unity of his Thought* (London, 1970), p89.

3   Lukács (1970), p101.

4   Slavoj Žižek, "A Leninist Gesture Today: Against the Populist Temptation" in S Budgen, S Kouvalakis, S Žižek (ed), *Lenin Reloaded: Toward a Politics of Truth* (Durham and London, 2007). This is broadly the spirit of a number of articles in this collection.

5   See the harrowing accounts and devastating analysis in Mike Davis, *Late Victorian Holocausts: El Nino Famines and the Making of the Third World* (London, 2001).

6   Danny Dorling, *Inequality and the 1%* (Verso, 2014), p2-3.

7   An increase in unemployment almost always produces an increase in suicide rates.

8   As Lenin repeatedly pointed out, nationalism can be either reactionary or progressive depending on whether it is the nationalism of the oppressor (eg British nationalism) or of the oppressed (eg Irish nationalism in the past or Palestinian nationalism today).

9   According to figures from the Stockholm International Peace Research Institute US military expenditure in 2014 exceeded that of the next seven countries (China, Russia, Saudi Arabia, France, UK, India, Germany) combined. http:// books.sipri.org/product_info?c_ product_id=496.

10   https://www.quandl.com/collections/ economics/gdp-as-share-of-world-gdp-at-ppp-by-country

11   Angus Maddison, *The World Economy:Historical Statistics* (OECD, 2003), p261.

12   For a powerful analysis of this development see Ha-young Kim, "Imperialism and instability in East Asia today", *International Socialism* 138. http://isj.org.uk/imperialism-and-instability-in-east-asia-today/

13   See Maddison (2003), p261, and Quandle https://www.quandl.com/ collections/economics/gdp-as-share-of-world-gdp-at-ppp-by-country

14   Global Strategic Trends out to 2045, gov.uk, 15 July 2014. https://en. wikipedia.org/wiki/List_of_countries_ by_military_expenditures#cite_note-MoD-5

15   See Ian Rappel, "Capitalism and species extinction", *International Socialism* 147. http://isj.org.uk/ capitalism-and-species-extinction/

16   Two local communities seriously affected by pollution near where I live in Dublin.

17   Figures taken from Maddison (2003), p259. He also estimates the growth in world *per capita* GDP at GK$436 in 1000 AD to GK$6049 in 2001 (and GK$ 27,948 for the US), p262.

18   L Trotsky, "For a Workers' United Front Against Fascism", https://www. marxists.org/archive/trotsky/ germany/1931/311208.htm

19   This clever quip is usually attributed to Fredric Jameson but he himself

attributed it to an unnamed "someone".
See http://newleftreview.org/II/21/
fredric-jameson-future-city.

20 The classic study confirming these
arguments empirically, at least as far as
the British state is concerned, was
Ralph Miliband, *The State in Capitalist
Society*, (London, 1969).

21 For a study of this see Roger Graef,
*Talking Blues: The Police in Their Own
Words*, (London, 1989).

22 See for example Ferdinand Zweig, *The
Worker in an Affluent Society* (London,
1961).

23 John H Goldthorpe, David Lockwood,
et al, *The Affluent Worker in the Class
Structure* (Cambridge, 1969).

24 For analysis of these tendencies see
John Molyneux, *What is the Real
Marxist Tradition?* (London, 1985).

25 Michael Hardt and Antonio Negri,
Multitude (London, 2004).

26 Guy Standing, *The Precariat: The New
Dangerous Class* (London, 2011).

27 Figures from Paul Bairoch and Gary
Goertz, "Factors of Urbanisation in the
Nineteenth Century Developed
Countries: A Descriptive and
Econometric Analysis," *Urban Studies*,
(1986) 23, pp285-305.

28 It is a general feature of the *Communist
Manifesto* that Marx and Engels used
the present tense to refer to tendencies
of development that they deemed to be
immanent within the capitalist system.
It is testimony to their astonishing
insight into the dynamics of the system
that statements about the world that
were plainly "false" or extravagant
generalisations at the time have become
more and more true with the passage of
time.

29 Minqi Li was a pro-free market,
neoliberal student who was arrested
after the Tiananmen Square revolt in
China who converted to Marxism as a
result of reading Marx and Mao while
in prison. He is now a Marxist
economics professor at the University
of Utah.

30 http://monthlyreview.
org/2011/06/01/the-rise-of-the-
working-class-and-the-future-of-the-
chinese-revolution

31 http://data.worldbank.org/indicator/
SP.URB.TOTL.IN.ZS

32 http://data.worldbank.org/indicator/
SP.URB.TOTL.IN.ZS

33 http://www.worldatlas.com/citypops.
htm

34 For a vivid description see
Leslie T Chang, *Factory Girls: From
Village to City in a Changing China*
(2008).

35 Hsiao-Hung Pai, "Factory of the
World: Scenes from Guangdong".
https://placesjournal.org/article/
factory-of-the-world-scenes-from-guan
gdong/?gclid=CjwKEAjwi4yuBRDX_
vq07YyF7l8SJAAhmorpS_
Q8iewicCnJSqeVgHzf54GjIjd7nQsV2

36 Hardt and Negri (2004), pp.xiv-xv.

37 For a powerful critique of this concept
see Kieran Allen, "Precariat: New Class
or Bogus Concept?", *Irish Marxist
Review* 9, 2014. http://www.
irishmarxistreview.net/index.php/imr/
article/view/111

38 See Slavoj Žižek, "The Revolt of the
Salaried Bourgeoisie", *London Review
of Books*, 26 January, 2012.

39 It should also be noted that relatively
highly paid (Western) workers may
possibly be *more exploited* than low
paid workers in the South in the sense
that more surplus value/profit is
extracted from their labour. See the
detailed discussion of this in M Kidron,
"Black Reformism: the Theory of
Unequal Exchange" in *Capitalism and
Theory* (London, 1974).

40 See the debate in *International
Socialism*: Simon Joyce, "Why are there
so few strikes?" *International Socialism*
145, http://isj.org.uk/why-are-there-
so-few-strikes/ and replies by Martin
Upchurch "The end of the "safe space"
for unions? A response to Simon Joyce"
and Donny Gluckstein "The question
of confidence: A reply to Simon Joyce"
in *International Socialism* 146. http://
isj.org.uk/issue-146-2/

41 "It is not a question of what this or that
proletarian, or even the whole

proletariat, at the moment *regards* as its aim. It is a question of *what the proletariat is*, and what, in accordance with this *being*, it will historically be compelled to do." Karl Marx, *The Holy Family*. https://www.marxists.org/archive/marx/works/1845/holy-family/ch04.htm.

42 K Marx and F Engels, *The German Ideology,* https://www.marxists.org/archive/marx/works/1845/german-ideology/ch01b.htm#b3

43 Okhrana report from R P Browder and A F Kerensky, *The Russian Provisional Government 1917—Documents* (Stanford, 1961), vol 1, p34, cited in T Cliff, *Lenin*, vol 2 (London, 1985) p78.

44 N N Sukhanov, *The Russian Revolution 1917—A Personal Record* (Princeton, 1984) p5.

45 A Gramsci, *Selections from the Prison Notebooks* (London, 1971), pp196-197.

46 L Trotsky, *The History of the Russian Revolution* (London, 1977), p171.

47 Within a week the Soviet had "1200 delegates meeting in daily session", Donny Gluckstein, *The Western Soviets* (London, 1985), p20.

48 See Gluckstein (1985), p21.

49 R P Browder and A F Kerensky, *The Russian Provisional Government 1917—Documents*, as above, vol 2, p848.

50 See L Trotsky *The History of the Russian Revolution*, as above, p421 and p981.

51 For a detailed account of this see T Cliff, *Lenin*, vol 2, pp98-102.

52 See the account in L Trotsky, *My Life* (New York, 1970), pp295-296.

53 Support for the Socialist Revolutionaries (SRs) held up, however, and they received 370 seats plus 40 for the Left SRs, but the SRs support was based in the peasantry not the working class.

54 In Petrograd, that is. In Moscow it took eight more days and a good deal of bloodshed, with about 700 casualties.

55 The Menshevik Sukhanov testifies specifically on this point. See Sukhanov (1984), pp505-507.

56 See John Reed, *Ten Days that Shook the World.*

57 Cited in Tony Cliff, *Trotsky: Towards October 1979-1917* (London, 1989), p274.

58 L Trotsky, *Lessons of October*, https://www.marxists.org/archive/trotsky/1924/lessons/ch7.htm

59 D Lane, *The Roots of Russian Communism* (Assen, 1969), p26.

60 See Lenin, "The Working Class and its Press" (1914), *Collected Works*, vol 20, p369.

61 See T Cliff, *Lenin: All Power to the Soviets*, as above, p160.

62 Sukhanov (1984), p323.

63 L Trotsky, *History of the Russian Revolution*, as above, p808.

64 Leonard Schapiro, *The Communist Party of the Soviet Union* (London, 1970), p75fn.

65 As happened to the German Communist Party (KPD) when, in March 1921, it attempted to "force" the revolution without having won over a majority of the working class. As a consequence of the March Action the KPD lost 200,000 members in a few weeks. See C Harman, *The Lost Revolution* (London, 1982), p198-202.

66 Sukhanov (1984), p648.

67 Martov to Axelrod, 19 November 1917, cited in I Getzler, *Martov* (Cambridge 1967), p172. Sukhanov and Martov were able to acknowledge these palpable facts and still *oppose* the insurrection because as Mensheviks they considered any seizure of power by the proletariat as historically premature and doomed to failure.

68 This would, almost certainly, be the background interpretation framing any TV documentary or newspaper feature on Lenin or the Russian Revolution.

69 There is a deep irony in this use of the term Machiavellian (now deeply entrenched in our culture) to signify cynical, calculating, manipulative and power-hungry, in that as Gramsci argued, the real Machiavelli was not Machiavellian but rather a proto-national democrat revolutionary. See A Gramsci, *The Prison Notebooks*

(London, 1982).

70 Robert V Daniels, *The Conscience of the Revolution* (New York, 1969), p11.

71 For my rebuttal see J Molyneux, *The Point is to Change it: An Introduction to Marxist Philosophy* (London, 2011), Ch 8 and J Molyneux, *Is Human Nature a Barrier to Socialism?* (London, 1993).

72 Marc Ferro, *The Bolshevik Revolution: A Social History of the Russian Revolution*, (London, 1985) p227.

73 Ferro (1985), p211.

74 For a detailed account of how US (and thus international) Sovietology was shaped by the needs of the Cold War, the US State Department, the CIA, the Ford Foundation and so on see Stephen Cohen, *Rethinking the Soviet Experience* (Oxford, 1985), ch 1.

75 Figures taken from T Cliff, *Lenin: Building the Party* (London 1986), p240.

76 Lenin refers explicitly to this phenomenon: "Take one of the very characteristic...external expressions of the Party crisis. I mean the flight of the intellectuals from the Party", V I Lenin, "On to the Straight Road" (1908) *Collected Works*, vol 15, p18.

77 Revolutionary defeatism was the view that it was the duty of revolutionary socialists to work for the defeat of their "own" ruling class in the war.

78 Lenin expressed this view in a speech to young Swiss socialists. See Robert Service, *Lenin*, p235.

79 V I Lenin, *What is to be Done?* (Moscow, 1969), pp31-32. https://www.marxists.org/archive/lenin/works/1901/witbd/ii.htm

80 Adam Ulam, *The Unfinished Revolution: An Essay on the Sources of Influence of Marxism and Communism* (New York, 1960), p170-171.

81 L Trotsky, *Stalin* (London, 1968), p58

82 For my views on the relationship of the formulation of Marxism to the working class see John Molyneux, *What is the Real Marxist Tradition?* as above. See also James O'Toole, "Marx and Self-Emancipation", *Irish Marxist Review 2*, 2012. http://www.irishmarxistreview.

net/index.php/imr/article/view/17/17

83 This has been noted by a number of writers but is particularly emphasized in Raya Dunayevskaya, *Marxism and Freedom* (Lexington, 2003).

84 V I Lenin, "Preface to *Twelve Years*", *Collected Works*, vol 13, p108. https://www.marxists.org/archive/lenin/works/1907/sep/pref1907.htm

85 Lenin, *Collected Works*, vol 9, p17. https://www.marxists.org/archive/lenin/works/1905/tactics/preface.htm

86 Lenin, "The Reorganisation of the Party"(1905), as above, vol 9, p155.

87 As above, vol 9, p32. https://www.marxists.org/archive/lenin/works/1905/reorg/i.htm#v1opp65-029

88 Lenin, "Good demonstrations of proletarians and poor arguments of certain intellectuals' (1905), *Collected Works*, vol 8, p31. https://www.marxists.org/archive/lenin/works/1905/jan/04b.htm

89 Lenin, "Draft and explanation of a Programme for the Social Democratic Party", (1896) *Collected Works*, vol 2, p93-94. https://www.marxists.org/archive/lenin/works/1895/misc/x01.htm

90 Lenin reiterates this position on countless occasions but probably the most comprehensive statement of it was in his 1905 book, *Two-Tactics of Social Democracy in the Democratic Revolution, Collected Works*, vol 9, pp15-140. https://www.marxists.org/archive/lenin/works/1905/tactics/. In the long run Trotsky's position that the Russian Revolution would begin as a bourgeois democratic revolution but, with the conquest of power by the proletariat, would grow over into a socialist revolution, his theory of permanent revolution, was to prove most accurate assessment of the dynamic of the Revolution, but he did not fight to embody this perspective in an organisation in the way that Lenin did.

91 Lenin, "On the 25th Anniversary of the Revolutionary Activity of G V Pleknanov" (1901) *Collected*

Works, vol 5, p321. https://www.
marxists.org/archive/lenin/
works/1901/dec/15.htm

92 Lenin, "Good demonstrations of
proletarians and poor arguments of
certain intellectuals" (1905), *Collected
Works*, vol 8, p31. https://www.
marxists.org/archive/lenin/
works/1905/jan/04b.htm

93 Lenin, "The Revolutionary Upswing"
(1912), *Collected Works*, vol 18,
pp102-109. https://www.marxists.org/
archive/lenin/works/1912/jun/17.htm

94 Lenin, "Classes and Parties in Russia"
(1915), *Collected Works*, Vol. 21, p318.
https://www.marxists.org/archive/
lenin/works/1915/s+w/ch02.
htm#v21fl70h-317-GUESS

95 See Lenin, *Collected Works*, vol 2.
https://www.marxists.org/archive/
lenin/works/1895/finesfactory/
finesfactory.htm

96 N Krupskaya, *Memories of Lenin*
(London, 1970), p62. https://www.
marxists.org/archive/krupskaya/
works/rol/rol01.htm

97 L Trotsky, *My Life*, (New York, 1970),
ch VII and ch XXIV.

98 Antonio Gramsci, cited in John
Merrington, "Theory and practice in
Gramsci's Marxism", *Socialist Register*
(1968), p165.

99 L Trotsky, *Stalin* (London, 1968),
p64-65.

100 Lenin, "Our Tasks and the Soviet of
Workers Deputies" (1905), *Collected
Works*, vol 10, p10. https://www.
marxists.org/archive/lenin/
works/1905/nov/04b.htm

101 L Trotsky, *Stalin*, as above, p65.

102 Lenin, "Can the Bolsheviks Retain
State Power?" (1917), (Moscow, 1967),
p34. *Collected Works*, vol 26. https://
www.marxists.org/archive/lenin/
works/1917/oct/01.htm

103 Lenin, "The Crisis Has Matured"
(1917), *Collected Works*, vol 26, p84.

104 L Trotsky, *History of the Russian
Revolution*, as above, p987.

105 L Trotsky, *History of the Russian
Revolution*, as above, p989.

106 Lenin, *Left Wing Communism—an
Infantile Disorder* (Moscow, 1981), p64.

107 Willie Gallacher stood for election in
1922 and several other occasions and
eventually became an MP in West Fife
in 1935.

108 Lenin, "The Question of Nationalities
or "Autonomisation" (1922), *Collected
Works*, vol 36, p600. https://www.
marxists.org/archive/lenin/
works/1922/dec/testamnt/autonomy.
htm

109 Lukács (1970), p26.

110 The Mensheviks, headed by Plekhanov,
believed it would be a bourgeois
democratic revolution led by the
bourgeoisie. Lenin believed it would be
a bourgeois democratic revolution led
by the proletariat. Trotsky agreed with
Lenin regarding the proletarian
leadership of the bourgeois democratic
revolution but thought that because of
this leadership it would grow over into
a socialist revolution as the first step
towards international revolution. This
was Trotsky's celebrated theory of
"permanent revolution". For a
discussion of these issues see John
Molyneux, *Leon Trotsky's Theory of
Revolution* (Brighton, 1981), ch 1 and
Joseph Choonara, "The Relevance of
Permanent Revolution: A Reply to
Neil Davidson", *International Socialism*
131.

111 Lenin, "The War and Russian Social
Democracy" (1914), *Collected Works*,
vol 21, p34.

112 Lenin, "The War and Russian Social
Democracy", as above, pp40-41.

113 Regrettably it is not possible to discuss
this here but this philosophical
renewal, the record of which is to be
found in his *Philosophical Notebooks* in
volume 38 of the *Collected Works*, was
extremely important in his intellectual
and political development. Evidence of
Lenin's new and deepened
understanding of the dialectic can be
seen in virtually everything he writes
post-1914.

114 Lenin, Preface to the French and
German Editions (1920) *Imperialism,
the Highest Stage of Capitalism* (Peking,

1975), p4.

115 Lenin, *Imperialism*, as above, p1.

116 Lenin, "Lecture on the 1905 Revolution" (1917), *Collected Works*, (Moscow,1964), vol 23, p253.

117 The term "imperialism" was then often used retrospectively to refer to earlier empire building, including by Lenin. "Colonial policy and imperialism existed before this latest stage of capitalism" but he also insists that "the capitalist colonial policy of previous stages of capitalism is essentially different". Lenin, *Imperialism,* as above, pp97-98.

118 One major reason for this immense influence was the cult status accorded to Lenin by international Communism (Stalinism); another was the way in which a distorted version of Lenin's theory was employed by Third World nationalism. For an analysis of the relation between Marxism and third world nationalism, see John Molyneux, *What is the Real Marxist Tradition?* (London, 1985).

119 Lenin, *Imperialism*, as above, p18.

120 Lenin, *Imperialism*, as above, p31.

121 R Hilferding, *Finance Capital*, cited in Lenin, *Imperialism*, as above, p52.

122 Lenin, *Imperialism*, as above, p69.

123 Lenin, *Imperialism*, as above, p72.

124 Lenin, *Imperialism*, as above pp73-74. It is interesting that while Lenin references Marx's demonstration of the inevitable transformation of competition into monopoly, he does not refer to the law of the tendency of the rate of profit to decline developed by Marx in *Capital*, vol 3. For some reason the question of the declining rate of profit was generally ignored by all the Marxist theorists of this period (Kautsky, Luxemburg, Bukharin, Preobrazhensky, etc). But it is clear that Lenin's theory of the export of capital, and of imperialism as a whole, could be related to the declining rate of profit and seen as a "counteracting tendency" to it by reducing the organic composition of capital in the imperialist countries. This would be a more satisfactory explanation of imperialism than Luxemburg's flawed notion that it is impossible to realize surplus value in a "pure" capitalist economy.

125 Lenin, *Imperialism,* as above, p76.

126 Lenin, *Imperialism,* as above, p79.

127 See Lenin, *Imperialism,* as above, p79-84.

128 Lenin, *Imperialism,* as above, p92-93.

129 Lenin, *Imperialism,* as above, p98.

130 Lenin, *Imperialism,* as above, p118.

131 Kautsky did not himself actually support the war but neither would he clearly break with those who did support it. Instead he systematically blurred and confused the issue.

132 Karl Kautsky, "Ultra-imperialism", *Die Neue Zeit* (September 1914). https://www.marxists.org/archive/kautsky/1914/09/ultra-imp.htm

133 Lenin, *Imperialism,* as above, p143-144.

134 Chris Harman, "Analysing Imperialism", *International Socialism* 99, p23. It should be said that this major article is an invaluable guide to charting the development of imperialism throughout the 20th century.

135 Lenin, "Imperialism and the Split in Socialism", *Collected Works*, vol 23, p109.

136 Lenin, *Imperialism,* as above, p112.

137 See, among numerous articles on the question, "The Right of Nations to Self Determination", *Collected Works*, vol 20, pp393-454.

138 Lenin was particularly concerned to combat the idea of "national-cultural autonomy" as a solution to the national question which was advanced by the Austrian Marxist, Otto Bauer and which he regarded as a concession to nationalism.

139 Though the fact that he was already *beginning* to think along these lines is shown by articles he wrote for *Pravda* on "The Awakening of Asia" and "Backward Europe and Advanced Asia" (1913) in *Collected Works*, vol 19. These were clearly influenced by the Chinese Revolution of 1911 which ended 2,000

years of imperial rule.

140 Lenin, "The Report of the Commission on the National and Colonial Questions", (1920) *Collected Works*, vol 31.

141 Lenin, *Collected Works*, vol 31, as above, pp144-151.

142 Lenin, *Collected Works*, vol 31, as above, pp144-151.

143 For the entire proceedings of this event see *To See the Dawn; Baku 1920: First Congress of the Peoples of the East* (ed), John Ridell (New York, 2012). This gives an excellent idea of this strategy in practice.

144 http://www.bbc.com/news/magazine-26048324

145 http://www.nytimes.com/books/first/k/keegan-first.html

146 Niall Ferguson, *The Pity of War* (Penguin, 1998), p462.

147 Ferguson (1998), p460.

148 C Clark, *The Sleepwalkers: How Europe Went to War in 1914* (Penguin, 2013), pp560-561.

149 "Congresses of Social Democracy", http://www.marxists.org/glossary/events/c/congress-si.htm#1912

150 In *International Socialism* 99 (2003).

151 Alex Callinicos, *Imperialism and Global Political Economy* (London, 2009).

152 For clarity I should stress that I am not saying here that either finance capital or the export of capital continue to play the same role that they did in Lenin's day or that he claimed for them. These are very complex questions, beyond the scope of this study. The export of capital, for example, has fallen and risen again since Lenin. Of interest here is Mike Kidron, "Imperialism, Highest Stage But One" in *Capitalism and Theory* (London, 1974), which criticizes the concept of finance capital as too much based on Germany and notes major changes in the patterns of capital exports, along with the afore mentioned studies by Harman and Callinicos.

153 Lenin, "Imperialism and the Split in Socialism", *Collected Works*, vol 23, p109.

154 Even where the dominant party was Communist not Social Democratic, as in Italy and France (for a period), these parties pursued reformist not revolutionary strategies.

155 Tony Cliff, "The Economic Roots of Reformism", in T Cliff, *Neither Washington nor Moscow* (London, 1982), pp115-116.

156 See for example T Cliff and D Gluckstein, *Marxism and the Trade Union Struggle: the General Strike of 1926* (London, 1986).

157 John Molyneux, "Understanding Left Reformism", *Irish Marxist Review* 6.

158 Lenin, "Imperialism and the Split in Socialism" (1916), *Collected Works*, vol 23, p120.

159 Lenin, *Imperialism,* as above, p76.

160 Lenin, *Imperialism,* as above, p117.

161 Chris Harman, "Analysing Imperialism" *International Socialism* 99, p20.

162 *Monthly Review* was then probably the world's leading journal of Marxist economics and the most important books associated with it were Paul Baran, *The Political Economy of Growth* and P Baran and P Sweezy, *Monopoly Capital*. It remains an important journal today.

163 P Baran, *The Political Economy of Growth* (Harmondsworth, 1973), p416.

164 A Gunder Frank, *Capitalism and Underdevelopment in Latin America* (Harmondsworth, 1971), pp35-36.

165 See the discussion of this process in John Molyneux, *What is the Real Marxist Tradition?* (London, 1985).

166 Despite the imperialist nature of the Soviet Union's relations with Eastern Europe and with the many oppressed nationalities within its borders and later with China, the real reason for the Sino-Soviet split.

167 Chris Harman, "Analysing imperialism", *International Socialism* 99, p32.

168 Lukács (1970), p91.

169 M Hardt and T Negri, *Empire* (Cambridge, MA, 2000), p31.

170 Hardt and Negri (2000), pp.xii-xiii.

171 One of the ways to "capture the zeitgeist" for sections of the intellectual left is to take the language and themes that are currently in vogue in the mainstream media and present them with a radical twist. If the bourgeois media is hyping the internet you write a book saying the next revolution will be an internet revolution. If globalisation and hybridity are all the rage you embrace radical globalisation and subversive hybridity. This has the appeal of looking "new" and up-to-the-minute but it seldom produces good theory (or practice) and is not at all to be confused with engaging with the current moment or real contemporary challenges.

172 Interview in *The New Statesman*, cited in Alex Callinicos, "Toni Negri in Perspective", *International Socialism*, 92, p53.

173 Kautsky had only raised "the possibility" of capitalism overcoming its tendency to inter-imperialist war and been condemned for it by Lenin. Negri declares it "impossible".

174 Joseph Choonara, "Empire built on shifting sand", *International Socialism* 109, (2006), p143.

175 Hardt and Negri (2000), p190.

176 According to figures from the International Institute of Strategic Studies, US military spending in 2015 stood at US$597.5 billion, compared to a total of US$522.0 billion for the next eight powers (China, Saudi Arabia, Russia, UK, India, France, Japan, Germany). https://en.wikipedia.org/wiki/List_of_countries_by_military_expenditures#cite_note-4

177 Perry Anderson "Jottings on the Conjuncture", *New Left Review* 48, Nov-Dec 2007. https://newleftreview.org/II/48/perry-anderson-jottings-on-the-conjuncture

178 Leo Panitch and Sam Gindin, "Global Capitalism and American Empire", in Panitch and Colin Leys (eds), *The New Imperial Challenge; Socialist Register 2004*, (London, 2003); Alex Callinicos, "Imperialism and Global Political Economy", *International Socialism* 108; Leo Panitch and Sam Gindin, "Imperialism and Global Political Economy—A Reply to Alex Callinicos', *International Socialism* 109; Alex Callinicos, "Making Sense of Imperialism: a Reply to Leo Panitch and Sam Gindin", *International Socialism* 110.

179 Leo Panitch and Sam Gindin, "Imperialism and Global Political Economy—A Reply to Alex Callinicos', as above, p195.

180 Alex Callinicos, "Making sense of Imperialism: a reply to Leo Panitch and Sam Gindin", *International Socialism* 110, p201.

181 For example, for an analysis of the complex conflict in the Ukraine based on Leninist principles see the excellent article by Rob Ferguson, "Ukraine: imperialism, war and the left", *International Socialism* 144.

182 Obviously this was only possible because he had already done the preparatory work in 1916 and early 1917. See V I Lenin, *Marxism on the State* (Moscow, 1976).

183 Lenin, "Note to L B Kamenev", *Collected Works*, vol 36, p454. https://www.marxists.org/archive/lenin/works/1917/jul/07d.htm

184 "Under the banner of Workers' Soviets, under the banner of revolutionary struggle for power and the dictatorship of the proletariat, under the banner of the Third International—*Workers of the World Unite!*" Closing words of Leon Trotsky, *"Manifesto of the First Congress of the Communist International,"* https://www.marxists.org/archive/trotsky/1924/ffyci-1/ch01.htm

185 With the adoption of the Popular Front strategy in 1934 and the parliamentary road to socialism in western Europe in 1951.

186 L Colletti, "Lenin's *State and Revolution,*" in *From Rousseau to Lenin* (New York, 1972). R Miliband, "Lenin's *The State and Revolution*" (1970) in *Class Power and State Power* (London,

1983).

187 F Engels, *The Origin of the Family, Private Property and the State*, cited in Lenin, *The State and Revolution* (Moscow, 1977), p10.

188 Lenin, *The State and Revolution*, as above, p10.

189 Lenin, *The State and Revolution*, as above, p11.

190 Lenin, *The State and Revolution*, as above, p13.

191 Lenin, *The State and Revolution*, as above, p17.

192 Lenin, *The State and Revolution*, as above, p46.

193 Lenin, *The State and Revolution*, as above, p17.

194 Lenin, *The State and Revolution*, as above p36.

195 Lenin, *The State and Revolution*, as above, p12.

196 Lenin, *The State and Revolution*, as above, p38.

197 Lenin, *The State and Revolution*, as above, p38.

198 Lenin, *The State and Revolution*, as above, pp30 and 38.

199 Lenin, *The State and Revolution*, as above, p41.

200 Lenin, *The State and Revolution*, as above, p42.

201 Lenin, *The State and Revolution*, as above, p42.

202 Lenin, *The State and Revolution*, as above, p42-43.

203 Lenin, *The State and Revolution*, as above, p43.

204 Lenin, *The State and Revolution*, as above, p48.

205 Lenin, *The State and Revolution*, as above, p79.

206 Lenin, *The State and Revolution*, as above, p114.

207 Lenin, *The State and Revolution*, as above, p93.

208 Lenin, *The State and Revolution*, as above, p112.

209 Lenin, *The Proletarian Revolution and the Renegade Kautsky*, https://www.marxists.org/archive/lenin/works/1918/prrk/democracy.htm

210 Lenin, *Left-Wing Communism—An Infantile Disorder,* as above. https://www.marxists.org/archive/lenin/works/1920/lwc/ch09.htm

211 This compresses into one paragraph the analysis presented in John Molyneux, *Will the Revolution Be Televised? A Marxist Analysis of the Media* (London, 2011).

212 Marx and Engels, *The German Ideology*, (1845). https://www.marxists.org/archive/marx/works/1845/german-ideology/ch01b.htm

213 http://www.theguardian.com/news/datablog/2010/may/31/senior-civil-servants-salaries-data

214 http://www.theguardian.com/society/2014/aug/28/british-society-elitism-privileged-owen-jones

215 http://www.independent.co.uk/news/uk/politics/british-army-could-stage-mutiny-under-corbyn-says-senior-serving-general-10509742.html

216 Lenin, *The State and Revolution,* as above, p17.

217 R A Dahl, et al, *Social Science Research on Business: Product and Potential,* 1959, p36, cited in Ralph Miliband, *The State in Capitalist Society* (London, 1973), pp4-5.

218 There was, naturally, a "theory" of "totalitarianism" (covering fascist and Communist states) to complement the theory of pluralism. See for example Carl Friedrich and Zbigniew Brzezinski, *Totalitarian Dictatorship and Autocracy* (Cambridge, 1956).

219 The classic Marxist critique of pluralist theory is to found in Ralph Miliband, *The State in Capitalist Society*, as above. Miliband's book contained much very useful material but, as has often been noted, suffered from methodological deficiencies which tended to lead to left reformist conclusions.

220 The class difference of trade unions can be "heard" by simply comparing the tone of voice and line of questioning of any TV presenter when interviewing a trade union official whose members are on strike and when interviewing other "elite" spokespersons.

221 F Nietzsche, *The Will to Power* s.636

p121. https://archive.org/stream/comp leteworksthe15nietuoft#page/120/mode/2up

222 F Nietzsche, *Beyond Good and Evil*, s.259. https://www.marxists.org/reference/archive/nietzsche/1886/beyond-good-evil/ch09.htm

223 M Foucault, "The Subject and Power" in H Dreyfuson and P Rabinow (eds), *Michel Foucault: Beyond Structuralism and Hermeneutics* (Chicago, 1983), p211.

224 M Foucault, as above, p212.

225 Lenin, *The State and Revolution*, as above, pp7-8.

226 M Bakunin, *The Programme of the International Brotherhood* (1869). http://www.marxists.org/reference/archive/bakunin/works/1869/program.htm

227 M Bakunin, "Letter to La Liberté" (1872). https://www.marxists.org/reference/archive/bakunin/works/1872/la-liberte.htm

228 Alexander Berkman, *What is Communist Anarchism?* (New York, 1972), pp290-291.

229 Berkman (1972), p233

230 Berkman (1972), p291.

231 *Organisational Platform of the Libertarian Communists* written in 1926 by Nestor Makhno, Piotr Arshinov and other Russian anarchists of the *Dielo Trouda* (Workers' Cause). http://www.nestormakhno.info/english/platform/general.htm

232 J Holloway, *Change the World Without Taking Power* (2002). http://web.archive.org/web/20110701110507/http://libcom.org/library/chapter-11-revolution

233 A Gramsci, *Selections from the Prison Notebooks* (London, 1982), p238.

234 A Gramsci, *Selections from the Prison Notebooks,* as above, pp238-239.

235 A Gramsci, *Selections from the Prison Notebooks,* as above, p235.

236 A Gramsci, *Selections from the Prison Notebooks,* as above, p240.

237 A Gramsci, "The Southern Question" in *The Modern Prince and Other Writings* (New York, 1972), pp30-31.

238 A Gramsci, *Selections from the Prison Notebooks*, as above, p238.

239 The term was widely used by Lenin and by the Bolsheviks in the context of struggling for working class hegemony in the democratic revolution and also had long standing ordinary bourgeois usage as in "Napoleon established his hegemony over much of Europe".

240 See for example Stuart Hall, "Gramsci and Us", *Marxism Today* (June 1987). http://www.hegemonics.co.uk/docs/Gramsci-and-us.pdf

241 See Santiago Carillo, *Eurocommunism and the State* (London, 1977).

242 Ernesto Laclau and Chantal Mouffe, "Post-Marxism without Apologies", *New Left Review* I/166, November-December 1987.

243 See Chris Harman, "Gramsci versus Eurocommunism", parts 1 and 2, in *International Socialism* 98 (May 1977) and 99 (June 1977). Ernest Mandel, *From Stalinism to Eurocommunism* (London, 1978), especially pp201-220. Peter Thomas, *The Gramscian Moment* (Haymarket, 2010).

244 A Gramsci, *Selections from Political Writings, 1921-26* (London, 1978), p340.

245 A Gramsci, *Selections from Political Writings, 1921-26,* as above, p343.

246 A Gramsci, *Selections from Political Writings, 1921-26,* as above, p357

247 A Gramsci, *Selections from Political Writings, 1921-26,* as above, p369.

248 A Gramsci, *Selections from the Prison Notebooks*, as above, p57.

249 A Gramsci, *Selections from the Prison Notebooks,* as above, pp180-183.

250 A Gramsci, *Selections from the Prison Notebooks,* as above, p183.

251 A Gramsci, *Selections from the Prison Notebooks,* as above, pp169-170.

252 Unfortunately this developed as an academic orthodoxy via lecturers who taught and students who received Marxism via Althusser and Gramsci (and commentaries on same); particularly in the 1980s it was common to meet both students and lecturers who had read Althusser and

(some) Gramsci, but not the Marxist classics.

253 A Gramsci, *Selections from the Prison Notebooks,* as above, p357.

254 A Gramsci, *Further Selections from the Prison Notebooks* (London, 1995), p507. "The majority of commentators, anxious to stress the decisive contribution made by Gramsci, or more subtly, to oppose Gramsci to Lenin, end up by underestimating the place of hegemony in Lenin's work and remaining almost completely silent on the Third International." (C Buci-Glucksmann, *Gramsci and The State* [London, 1980], p174).

255 S Carrillo, *Eurocommunism and the State* (London, 1977), p10.

256 Carrillo (1977), p12-13.

257 See https://www.marxists.org/reference/archive/althusser/1970/ideology.htm

258 Carrillo, (1977), p22-23.

259 Carrillo, (1977), p34.

260 Althusser quoted by Carrillo (1977), p49.

261 Althusser quoted by Carrillo (1977), p68.

262 Nicos Poulantzas, *State, Power, Socialism* (London, 2000), p20. Poulantzas, Althusser and their like are fond of such dismissive statements ("There is no Marxist theory of... ideology, politics, religion, etc, etc"). What it means is less clear. Does it mean there is no specific book on the subject? Well there is Engels's *Origin of the Family, Private Property and the State.* Or does it mean that there is no general theory embedded in Marx and Engels's writings as a whole? But Lenin's *The State and Revolution* would seem to demonstrate precisely that there is such a theory. Maybe it is just a fancy way of saying he doesn't agree with the theory that exists.

263 Poulantzas (2000), pp12 and 15.

264 Poulantzas (2000), p130.

265 Poulantzas (2000), p129.

266 Poulantzas (2000), pp132-133. Italics in original.

267 Poulantzas (2000), p136.

268 Poulantzas (2000), p141.

269 Poulantzas (2000), p254.

270 Poulantzas (2000), p258.

271 Poulantzas (2000), p258. It is worth noting that here Poulantzas explicitly distances himself from Gramsci writing, "It is not therefore a question of a straight choice between frontal war of movement and war of position, because, in Gramsci's use of the term, the latter always comprises encirclement of a fortress state". (p258).

272 The likes of Murdoch's News International, Time Warner, Disney, and so on.

273 See John Molyneux, *Will the Revolution be Televised?* (London, 2011).

274 Carrillo, (1977), p105.

275 Poulantzas (2000), p261.

276 Poulantzas (2000), p252.

277 "The question whether objective truth can be attributed to human thinking is not a question of theory but is a practical question. Man must prove the truth—ie the reality and power, the this-sidedness of his thinking in practice. The dispute over the reality or non-reality of thinking that is isolated from practice is a purely *scholastic* question."

278 This question was the subject of much debate at the time and it is quite useful to revisit what was said in those days. The author took part in a debate with Syriza supporter, Professor Helena Sheehan, in Dublin on "Syriza and Socialist Strategy" in March 2015. It can be seen here https://www.youtube.com/watch?v=v6xMwkKF6WA

279 For a good account of the genesis and peculiarities of the Greek state see Kevin Ovenden, *Syriza: Inside the Labyrinth* (London, 2015), ch 6, "Face to face with the Deep State".

280 For the political record and character of these Ministers see Ovenden (2015), pp118-130.

281 *Financial Times* (5 April, 2015), cited in Ovenden (2015), p130.

282 Syriza: The Thessaloniki Programme, http://www.syriza.gr/article/SYRIZA-

--THE-THESSALONIKI-
PROGRAMME.html#.
V9vRWVUrLIU

283 Syriza: The Thessaloniki Programme.

284 https://www.thenation.com/article/
made-usa/

285 N Bukharin and E Preobrazhensky, *The
ABC of Communism* (London, 1969),
p180. Trotsky in *The Revolution
Betrayed* records how the Soviet
Union's attitude to the League of
Nations changed under Stalin. See
L Trotsky, *The Revolution Betrayed*
(London, 1967), pp193-204.

286 http://www.newstatesman.com/
world-affairs/2015/07/yanis-
varoufakis-full-transcript-our-battle-
save-greece

287 http://www.independent.co.uk/news/
uk/politics/british-army-could-stage-
mutiny-under-corbyn-says-senior-
serving-general-10509742.html. It was
also reported that this "unnamed"
general had served in Northern Ireland
during "the Troubles" and was
disgusted at Corbyn's refusal to
condemn the IRA. Those who know
something of Irish history will
recognise in the general's statement a
threat to repeat the tactic used by the
British army in the Curragh Mutiny of
1914 which prepared the way for the
partition of Ireland.

288 Those who treat *What is to be Done?* as
such a book are seriously mistaken. It is
far from a rounded exposition on the
role of the party. Rather it is polemical
document in a faction fight in very
particular circumstances, as Lenin
himself made clear.

289 L Trotsky, *The Revolution Betrayed*
(1936). https://www.marxists.org/
archive/trotsky/1936/revbet/ch05.htm

290 L Trotsky, *History of the Russian
Revolution*, as above, p445.

291 Key texts include Tony Cliff, *Lenin*,
vols 1-4 (London, 1975-1979), especially
vol 1 *Building the Party*; Paul Le Blanc,
Lenin and the Revolutionary Party
(Chicago, 1993); Tamás Krausz,
Reconstructing Lenin (New York, 2015);
and Lars T Lih, *Lenin Rediscovered:*

What Is to Be Done? In Context
(Leiden, 2006). There is also my own
small contribution, John Molyneux,
Marxism and the Party (London, 1978).

292 At that time Social Democratic meant,
and was understood by everyone to
mean, revolutionary Marxist.

293 V I Lenin, "The Tasks of the Russian
Social-Democrats" (1897), vol 2,
pp323-352. https://www.marxists.org/
archive/lenin/works/1897/dec/31b.
htm

294 Lenin, "A Protest by Russian Social-
Democrats" (1899), *Collected Works*,
vol 4, p167. https://www.marxists.org/
archive/lenin/works/1899/sep/protest.
htm

295 Lenin, *What Is To Be Done?* (Peking,
1975), p153. https://www.marxists.org/
archive/lenin/works/1901/witbd/iv.
htm

296 Lenin, "A reply to the St Petersburg
Committee" (1901), *Collected Works*
vol 5. https://www.marxists.org/
archive/lenin/works/1901/oct/15.htm

297 Lenin, "A reply to the St Petersburg
Committee", as above. https://www.
marxists.org/archive/lenin/
works/1901/dec/06.htm

298 For much fuller accounts of the 1903
Congress and the Bolshevik-Menshevik
split see Tony Cliff, *Lenin*, vol 1, as
above, ch 5, and Molyneux, *Marxism
and the Party*, (1978), ch 2.

299 For a detailed analysis of this episode
see Tony Cliff, *Lenin*, vol 1 chs 15-17.

300 Lenin, "What Next?" *Collected Works*,
vol 21, p111. https://www.marxists.org/
archive/lenin/works/1915/jan/09.htm

301 The term "centrist" derived from the
Kautskyite "centre" in German Social
Democracy which stood between the
outright reformism of Bernstein, Noske
and Scheideman and the revolutionary
wing of Rosa Luxemburg and Karl
Liebknecht. It referred to tendencies
which vacillated between reform and
revolution or accepted "revolution" in
the abstract while repudiating in deeds.

302 Lenin, "Terms of Admission into the
Communist International" (1920),
Collected Works, vol 31, p207. https://

www.marxists.org/archive/lenin/works/1920/jul/x01.htm

303 Lenin, "The Tasks of the Russian Social-Democrats", *Collected Works*, vol 2, pp323-352. https://www.marxists.org/archive/lenin/works/1897/dec/31b.htm

304 Lenin, *What Is To Be Done?*, as above, p153. https://www.marxists.org/archive/lenin/works/1901/witbd/iv.htm

305 Lenin, *One Step Forward, Two Steps Back* (Moscow, 1969), p58.

306 Lenin, "The Tasks of the Russian Social-Democrats", *Collected Works*, vol 2, pp323-352. https://www.marxists.org/archive/lenin/works/1897/dec/31b.htm

307 Lenin, *What Is To Be Done?*, as above, p100. https://www.marxists.org/archive/lenin/works/1901/witbd/iv.htm

308 Lenin, *Left Wing Communism—an Infantile Disorder*, as above, pp37-38. https://www.marxists.org/archive/lenin/works/1920/lwc/ch06.htm

309 Lenin, *Left Wing Communism—an Infantile Disorder*, as above, p43.

310 Lenin, *Left Wing Communism—an Infantile Disorder*, as above, p44.

311 Lenin, "Speech in Defence of the Tactics of the Communist International" (1921). https://www.marxists.org/archive/lenin/works/1921/jun/12.htm

312 *Theses, Resolutions, and Manifestos of the First Four Congresses of the Third International* (London, 1980), p277.

313 Lenin, *Left Wing Communism-an Infantile Disorder*, as above, p28.85

314 K Marx and F Engels, *The German Ideology* (1845). https://www.marxists.org/archive/marx/works/1845/german-ideology/ch01b.htm

315 This point was also emphasised by Gramsci (as well as by Lenin and Cliff) but is not well remembered by academic Gramscians. See Antonio Gramsci, *The Modern Prince and Other Writings* (New York, 1970), p15.

316 Lenin, "The Reorganisation of the Party" (1905), *Collected Works*, vol 10,

p32. https://www.marxists.org/archive/lenin/works/1905/reorg/i.htm#v10pp65-029

317 A Gramsci, *Selections from the Prison Notebooks* (London, 1982), p335.

318 A Gramsci, *Selections from the Prison Notebooks*, as above, p340.

319 For an account see, Andy Durgan and Joel Sans, "'No one represents us': the 15 May movement in the Spanish state", *International Socialism* 132. http://isj.org.uk/no-one-represents-us-the-15-may-movement-in-the-spanish-state/

320 "Organised revolutionaries thus have to find the way to intervene in a constructive way in a movement which appears hostile to them. This means being open about our ideas while not becoming fixated on the visual presence of a set of initials". Durgan and Sans, as above, p34.

321 See John Molyneux, *Anarchism: A Marxist Criticism* (London, 2011).

322 Íñigo Errejón and Chantal Mouffe, *Podemos—In the Name of the People* (London, 2016), pp72-73.

323 Susan Watkins, "New Oppositions", *New Left Review* 98, p15.

324 Errejón and Mouffe (2016), p73.

325 Pablo Iglesias, "Understanding Podemos", *New Left Review* 93 (May-June 2015), p11.

326 John Molyneux, "Towards a Revolutionary Party in Ireland", *Irish Marxist Review* 16.

327 This had the unfortunate consequence of allowing Boris Johnson, Nigel Farage and the racist right to completely dominate the Leave campaign.

328 https://www.theguardian.com/uk-news/2016/nov/19/mcdonnell-backs-buckingham-palace-revamp-as-petition-grows

329 "We will take decisive action to end the undercutting of workers' pay and conditions, reinstate the migrant impact fund to support public services and back fair rules on migration". Cited in *Socialist Worker*, 22 November 2016. https://socialistworker.co.uk/art/43724/Labour+needs+clarity,+not'slippage,+in+defence+of+migrant+

workers

330 Leon Trotsky, "Lessons of October", in *The Challenge of the Left Opposition (1923-25)*, (New York, 1975), p252.

331 Eric Hobsbawm, *On History* (London, 2004), p326-327.

332 Similar conclusions are drawn in Tony Cliff, *Lenin*, vol 4, and in Duncan Hallas, *The Comintern* (London, 1985).

333 I have included here only examples where there was mass working class action and not guerrilla army revolution such as the Chinese Revolution of 1949 or Cuba in 1959.

334 See in particular Colin Barker (ed), *Revolutionary Rehearsals* (London, 1987).

335 See, for example, the accounts recorded in Ronald Fraser, *1968: A Student Generation in Revolt* (London, 1988) and John Molyneux "Reviewing 1968" *International Socialism* 38. I was lucky enough to be present in Paris for a few days in mid-May and the experience has lived with me for the rest of my life.

336 Groups such as Vive La Revolution, JCR (Jeune communiste revolutionaire), Voix Ouvriere and the OCI (Organisation communiste internationiste).

337 PCF leader, George Marchais, in *L'Humanité* (3 May), cited in Tony Cliff and Ian Birchall, *France: The Struggle Goes On* (London, 1968), p9.

338 For the best of many accounts of May '68 see Chris Harman, *The Fire Last Time*, (London, 1988). On a personal note it was this experience that convinced me of the need to build a revolutionary party and led to my joining a revolutionary organisation, the International Socialists in July 1968 and to my first book, *Marxism and the Party*.

339 The Battle of the Camel was seen on television screens round the world but was, in fact only one of many such confrontations across the country. (I owe this point to Sameh Naguib).

340 According to Human Rights Watch, which called it "one of the world's largest killings of demonstrators in a single day in recent history", a minimum of 817 people were killed in Rab'aa Square alone and the Muslim Brotherhood claimed about 2,600. http://en.wikipedia.org/wiki/August_2013_Rabaa_massacre

341 For an expanded version of the argument presented here see John Molyneux, "Lessons from the Egyptian Revolution", *Irish Marxist Review* 13, 2015. See also Philip Marfleet, *Egypt [Contested Revolution]*, (London, 2016).

342 Lenin, *What is to be Done?* as above, pp70-71.

343 Lenin, *What is to be Done?* as above, p72.

344 Lenin, *What is to be Done?* as above, p86.

345 Lenin, *What is to be Done?* as above, p97.

346 "In the United States of North America, every independent movement of the workers was paralysed so long as slavery disfigured a part of the Republic. Labour cannot emancipate itself in the white skin when in the black it is branded". (Karl Marx, *Capital*, vol 1, p284). For further discussion of Marx and the Marxist tradition's responses to issues of (extra-working class) oppression, see John Molyneux, *The Point is to Change It!* (London, 2012), ch 9, and Kevin B Anderson, *Marx at the Margins* (Chicago, 2016).

347 See Lenin's statement, "*What is to be Done?* is a controversial correction of 'economist' distortion and it would be wrong to regard the pamphlet in any other light". "Preface to the Collection *Twelve Years*", (1907), *Collected Works*, vol 13, pp107-108.

348 Lenin, "Lecture on the 1905 Revolution" (1917), *Collected Works*, vol 23, pp236-253.

349 Lenin, "The National Equality Bill" (1914), as above, vol 20, p172-173.

350 For a lengthy and interesting discussion of Lenin and anti-Semitism see the section on "Lenin and the Pogroms" in Tamás Krausz, *Reconstructing Lenin*

(New York, 2015), pp255-280.

351 See John Molyneux, "More than Opium: Marxism and Religion", *International Socialism* 119.

352 Dave Crouch, "The Bolsheviks and Islam", *International Socialism* 110, p43.

353 Cited in Crouch, "The Bolsheviks and Islam", as above, p45.

354 Crouch, "The Bolsheviks and Islam", as above, p45.

355 The other issues were the state monopoly of foreign trade, bureaucracy in the state and party, splits in the Politbureau and Stalin's power hunger and rudeness (including to Krupskaya). For full accounts of this battle see Moshe Lewin, *Lenin's Last Struggle* (New York, 1970), and Tony Cliff, *Lenin*, vol 4, pp188-236.

356 Lenin, "Memo Combatting Dominant Nation Chauvinism" (1922), *Collected Works*, vol 33, p372.

357 Lenin "The Question of Nationalities or "Autonomisation", (1922), *Collected Works*, vol 36, p600.

358 Lenin, *What is to be Done?*, as above, p86.

359 For the history of the Bund see Sai Englert, "The Rise and Fall of the Jewish Labour Bund", *International Socialism* 135. For Lenin's position see, "Does the Jewish Proletariat need an "Independent Political Party?" *Collected Works*, vol 6, pp330-336.

360 Lenin, "On International Women's Day (1920), *Collected Works*, vol 30, pp408-409.

361 Trade unions as mass organisations are always prone to reflect to some extent prejudices that exist in the wider society or have a currency with their particular base; examples include the National Union of Miners in Britain that began the Miners Strike in 1984 with a pin-up in its magazine (it had gone by the end of the strike) and the "British Jobs for British Workers' episode in 2012. But the significant thing is that these backward positions were overcome.

362 Lenin, "Fourth Anniversary of the October Revolution", *Collected Works*,

vol 33, p54.

363 It is important to note that Trump did not win the popular vote (he lost by 3 million) but was handed the Presidency by the undemocratic Electoral College system, which is a hangover from the days of slavery.

364 Both of these outrageous phenomena are currently contested by vigorous campaigns.

365 Karl Marx, "Letter to S Meyer and A Vogt" (9 April 1870), Karl Marx and Friedrich Engels, *Selected Correspondence* (Moscow, 1975), p221.

366 Shulamith Firestone, *The Dialectic of Sex* (New York, 1970) was a classic of this genre.

367 The passivity of the US labour movement with regards to racism was part of a wider passivity (and often corruption) with regard to fighting for workers' rights in general.

368 When the Commune was defeated the bourgeois "ladies" of Versailles were vicious in their revenge against the Communards, especially the women of the Commune. See Lissagaray, *The History of the Paris Commune of 1871* (London, 1976), p305 and p316.

369 See M. Weber, "Class, status, party", in C Wright Mills (ed), *From Max Weber*, (London, 1970), pp180-195.

370 See Jean-Francois Lyotard, *The Postmodern Condition: A Report on Knowledge* (Manchester, 1984).

371 This was true, in microcosm, in Dublin as it was in the United States.

372 For Marx, history is the history of class struggle not of identity struggle.

373 Here it is worth noting that in academic discourse in social theory and cultural studies there has been a tendency, by using the term "privilege" to conflate *social privilege* with analytical *priority*, as in "Marxism 'privileges' production over consumption or economics over ideology" or, of course, the working class. This causes confusion and can be misleading. For example if Marx regarded production as analytically prior to consumption in the analysis of

capitalism, the whole point of Marxism and socialism is to make production serve consumption (ie meet human needs).

374 G E M de Ste. Croix, *The Class Struggle in the Ancient Greek World* (London, 1983), p43.

375 Russia in 1920 was the first country in the world to legalise abortion.

376 See Mary Smith, "Women in the Irish Revolution", *Irish Marxist Review* 14.

377 See Lenin, "Fourth Anniversary of the October Revolution" (1921) *Collected Works*, vol 33, pp52-54.

378 See Lenin, "Letter to Inessa Armand" (17 January 1915), *Collected Works*, vol 35, pp180-185. The letters to Armand were private but political.

379 See Clara Zetkin, "My Recollections of Lenin", in Lenin, *On the Emancipation of Women* (Moscow, 1985), pp99-126

380 There are numerous conflicting estimates of the death tolls in these famines and the true figures will probably never be known but the figures I have cited here are at the bottom of the spectrum.

381 This argument was particularly appealing in the 1930s when Russia's economic dynamism could be contrasted with the Great Depression in the West. But it was also at this time that the Stalinist terror was at its height.

382 See the discussion of this "thrice shameful law" in Leon Trotsky, *The Revolution Betrayed* (London, 1967), pp149-151.

383 See Leon Trotsky, "Thermidor and Anti-Semitism", 1937. https://www.marxists.org/archive/trotsky/1937/02/therm.htm

384 Karl Marx, *Capital*, vol III (Moscow, 1966), p817.

385 For example: John Molyneux, *Is Human Nature a Barrier to Socialism?* (London, 1993); *The Point is To Change It: An Introduction to Marxist Philosophy* (London, 2012), especially ch 8; and "Do revolutions always fail?" *Socialist Review*, April 2014, http://socialistreview.org.uk/390/

do-revolutions-always-fail

386 Chris Harman, *A People's History of the World* (London, 1999), p545. See also Tony Cliff, "On the class nature of the people's democracies" in *Neither Washington nor Moscow* (London, 1982), pp86-100 and Chris Harman, *Class Struggles in Eastern Europe: 1945-83* (London, 1988), pp15-41.

387 For analysis of the Chinese and Cuban Revolutions and their class character see Tony Cliff, *Permanent Revolution*, *International Socialism* (1st series), 12, Spring 1963. John Molyneux, *What is the Real Marxist Tradition?* (London, 1985), pp41-65. Nigel Harris, *The Mandate of Heaven: Marx and Mao on Modern China* (London, 1978) and Mike Gonzalez, *Che Guevara and the Cuban Revolution* (London, 2004).

388 It is important to understand that there was an objective logic in this process which operated independently of the "correctness" or "sincerity" of Mao's or Castro's relation to Lenin.

389 Trotsky argued that if Lenin had not been present in Petrograd in 1917, the October Revolution would not have happened. Isaac Deutscher took him to task over this saying that Trotsky's claim violated the basic tenets of historical materialism and citing Plekhanov on the, very limited, role of the individual in history. See my discussion of the debate, where I side with Trotsky, in John Molyneux, "Is Marxism deterministic?" *International Socialism* 68, pp64-69.

390 See for example John Rees "In Defence of October", *International Socialism* 52, and the debate that followed: Robert Service, "Did Lenin lead to Stalin?"; Samuel Farber, "In defence of democratic revolutionary socialism"; Robin Blackburn, "Reply to John Rees", and John Rees "Dedicated followers of fashion" in *International Socialism* 55.

391 Witness the major debate within the Bolshevik Party over the Brest-Litovsk Treaty in which Lenin found himself, for some time, in a minority in his view that it was necessary to sign the Treaty

and in which it was only the unfolding of events that enabled him to gain the majority.

392 Victor Serge, *Year One of the Russian Revolution* (London, 1992), p76.

393 Serge, *Year One of the Russian Revolution*, as above.

394 See Tony Cliff, *Lenin,* vol 3 (London, 1978), p18.

395 Serge, *Year One of the Russian Revolution*, as above, p59.

396 Lenin, "To all Party Members and to all the Working classes of Russia" (1917), *Collected Works*, vol 26, p304. https://www.marxists.org/archive/lenin/works/1917/nov/06a.htm

397 Lenin, "Theses on the Constituent Assembly" (1917), *Collected Works*, vol 26, p381.

398 Serge, *Year One of the Russian Revolution*, as above, p75.

399 Rees, *International Socialism* 55, as above, p33.

400 Rees, *International Socialism* 55, as above, p36. This article provides detailed descriptions of the atrocities perpetrated by the Whites and gives a picture of the mindset and character of the White Guard generals and their armies.

401 Kaplan fired three shots at Lenin. One bullet lodged in his neck, one in his shoulder. The injuries permanently damaged his health and probably contributed to his early death. Kaplan was executed on 3 September 1918.

402 Rees, *International Socialism* 55, as above, p31.

403 Tony Cliff, *Lenin*, vol 3, as above, p90.

404 Lenin, "On the Famine; A Letter to the Workers of Petrograd" (1918), *Collected Works*, vol 27, pp391-398.

405 Lenin, "Everybody on Food and Transport Work" (1919) *Collected Works*, vol 28, p439.

406 Lenin, *Collected Works*, vol 28, as above, pp439-440.

407 Lenin, "Political Report of the Central Committee", *Collected Works*, vol 27, p88.

408 Lenin, "Resolution on War and Peace", *Collected Works*, vol 27, as above.

409 This is accepted even by the arch anti-Leninist, Leonard Shapiro. See L Shapiro, *The Russian Revolution of 1917* (New York, 1984), p184.

410 Tony Cliff, *Lenin*, vol 4, as above, p130.

411 Cited in Tony Cliff, *Lenin* vol 4, as above, p126.

412 Victor Serge, *Memoirs of a Revolutionary* (Oxford, 1980), pp80-81. For Mandel's assessment see E Mandel, "October 1917: Coup d'état or social revolution" in Paul Le Blanc, et al, *October 1917: Workers in Power* (London, 2016), pp78-79. Were Serge and Mandel correct on this point? Possibly, but the matter was complex, including the fact that the foundation of the Cheka was very much an initiative of the Left SRs and Lenin certainly did not have much control over it. Mandel recounts an "anecdote" that Lenin called in his old friend and adversary, Martov, gave him a false passport and told him "Leave the country immediately. If not the Cheka will arrest you in a few days and I would not be able to stop them". Tony Cliff, *Lenin*, vol 4, as above, p78.

413 See Lenin, *Collected Works*, vol 32, p173. See also the account of Trotsky, who opposed the attack, in L Trotsky, *My Life*, as above, pp457-460.

414 Particularly unfortunate in my view was the acceptance of this alleged "principle" of single party rule by Trotsky and the Left Opposition in the mid-1920s as if it were a doctrine of Marxist or Leninist theory when it was nothing of the kind and initially introduced only as a temporary emergency measure. Trotsky, later, corrected this in *The Revolution Betrayed*, as above, pp265-268.

415 Lenin, "On the Famine" (1918), *Collected Works*, vol 27, as above, pp391-398.

416 Serge, *Year One of the Russian Revolution*, as above, p129.

417 Serge, *Year One of the Russian Revolution*, as above, p128.

418 Lenin, "The NEP and the Tasks of the Political Education Departments"

(1921), *Collected Works,* vol 33, as above, p65.

419 Hence the emphasis on the principle of recallability from the Paris Commune through *The State and Revolution* to the Soviets.

420 See the extensive discussion of this in Tony Cliff, *Lenin,* vol 3, as above, ch 13.

421 Lenin, "Letter to Molotov" (22 March 1922), cited in Cliff, *Lenin,* vol 3, as above, p184.

422 For accounts of this period in Lenin's life and his conflict with Stalin see Moshe Levin, *Lenin's Last Struggle* (Ann Arbor, 2005), and Tony Cliff, *Lenin,* vol 4, as above, ch 11-12.

423 Quoted in E H Carr, *The Bolshevik Revolution 1917-23,* vol 3 (Harmondsworth, 1966), pp135-136.

424 See Isaac Deutscher, *The Prophet Unarmed* (Oxford, 1978), pp111-112.

425 See Harman (1982), ch 13.

426 In April 1924 in *The Foundations of Leninism* Stalin wrote: "The main task of socialism—the organisation of socialist production—still remains ahead. Can this task be accomplished, can the final victory of socialism in one country be attained without the joint efforts of the proletariat of several advanced countries? No, this is impossible." (Cited in L Trotsky, *The Third International After Lenin* [New York, 1970], p36). As I have noted elsewhere: "Stalin 'solved' this contradiction by rewriting this passage to read the opposite ('After consolidating its power and leading the peasantry in its wake the proletariat of the victorious country can and must build a socialist society') and having the first edition withdrawn from circulation. There was no new analysis, simply the assertion of a new orthodoxy which clearly reflected the earlier perspective. Only later were 'analyses' concocted to justify the new line." John Molyneux, *What is the Real Marxist Tradition?* (London, 1985), p44.

427 Nikolai Bukharin, who was allied to Stalin against Trotsky and then against Trotsky plus Zinoviev and Kamenev, was both the main "theorist" of socialism in one country and the representative within the Party leadership of the peasant interest. For this reason Trotsky and the Left Opposition saw Bukharin as constituting the right wing of the Party as opposed the Stalin in the centre.

428 Stalin, addressing a conference of business executives in 1931. Cited in Isaac Deutscher, *Stalin* (Harmondsworth, 1966), p328.

429 Isaac Deutscher, as above, p296

430 For example, Leonard Schapiro, *The Communist Party of the Soviet Union* (London, 1970), p282.

431 Alec Nove, *An Economic History of the USSR* (London, 1975), p207.

432 Michael Haynes and Rumy Husan, *A Century of State Murder? Death and Policy in Twentieth-Century Russia* (London. 2003), p64.

433 Tony Cliff, *State Capitalism in Russia* (London, 1974), p40.

434 Cliff, *State Capitalism in Russia*, as above, p35.

435 The likes of Zinoviev, Kamenev, Radek, Bukharin, Smirnov, Preobrazhensky, Serebriakov, Rykov, Tomsky, Rakovsky, Antonov-Ovseenko and, of course, Trotsky.

436 See Cliff, *State Capitalism in Russia*, as above, pp59-65. Victor Serge has left an absolutely devastating picture of daily life at the lower end of Russian society in the 1930s, especially as regards women and children. See V Serge, *Destiny of a Revolution* (London [nd]) pp26-40.

437 Samuel Farber, "In defence of democratic revolutionary socialism", *International Socialism* 55, p87.

438 Farber, *International Socialism* 55, p91.

439 Simon Pirani, "Socialism in the 21st Century and the Russian Revolution", *International Socialism* 128.

440 These issues have in fact been debated at great length in the pages of *International Socialism* (and elsewhere) beginning with John Rees, "In Defence of October", *International Socialism* 52,

followed by replies by Robert Service, Samuel Farber, David Finkel and Robin Blackburn and a further response by John Rees, all in *International Socialism* 55. The debate is resumed with Kevin Murphy and Simon Pirani in *International Socialism* 126 and 128 and John Rose and Sheila McGregor in *International Socialism* 129. Kevin Murphy, *Revolution and Counterrevolution: Class Struggle in a Moscow Metal Factory* (Chicago, 2005), is also a major contribution to this question.

441 Perhaps in an academic sense or in the sense of being an historical admirer as one might be of Spartacus or Gerard Winstanley.

442 "The nationalisation of the land, the means of industrial production, transport and exchange, together with the monopoly of foreign trade, constitute the basis of the Soviet social structure. Through these relations, established by the proletarian revolution, the nature of the Soviet Union as a proletarian state is for us basically defined". L Trotsky, *Revolution Betrayed*, as above, p248.

443 See for example, Ygael Gluckstein, *Mao's China* (London, 1957); Nigel Harris, *The Mandate of Heaven: Marx and Mao in Modern China* (London, 1978); Tony Cliff, "Permanent Revolution", *International Socialism* (first series) 12; John Molyneux, *What is the Real Marxist Tradition?* as above.

444 See Chris Harman, *Zombie Capitalism: Global Crisis and the Relevance of Marx* (London, 2009); and Michael Roberts, *The Long Depression* (Chicago, 2016).

445 The good work includes Alex Callinicos and Chris Harman, *The Changing Working Class* (London, 1987); Paul Mason, *Live Working or Die Fighting: How the Working Class went Global* (London, 2007) and Chris Harman, "The Workers of the World", *International Socialism* 96.

446 See John Molyneux, "Secularism, Islamophobia and the Politics of Religion", *Irish Marxist Review* 16.

447 See the work of John Bellamy Foster, especially his *Marx's Ecology* (New York, 2000) and Paul Burkett, *Marx and Nature: A Red and Green Perspective* (New York, 1999). Also Martin Empson, *Land and Labour: Marxism, Ecology and Human History* (London, 2014).

448 Shachtman represented the US Socialist Workers Party which had a claimed membership of 2,500. Most of the other delegates represented either tiny sects or more or less fictional organisations.

449 For an account of this process see Chris Harman, "Crisis of the European Revolutionary Left", *International Socialism* 4.

450 Examples would include the Anti-Nazi League/Rock Against Racism led by the British SWP in the late 1970s, the Anti-Poll Tax campaign led by the Militant Tendency in 1989-1990 and the anti-war movement of 2003, led by the Stop the War Coalition (in which the SWP was crucial) in Britain and often by other revolutionaries elsewhere.

451 Marx's comment on sectarianism is relevant here. "The sect sees the justification for its existence and its point of honour not in what it has in *common* with the class movement but in the *particular shibboleth* which *distinguishes* it from the movement"; Marx to Schweitzer, 13 October 1868. https://www.marxists.org/archive/marx/works/1868/letters/68_10_13-abs.htm

452 In fact some of the Irish trade unions came to play an important role in the Water Charges movement but through supporting the community struggle and calling the mass demonstrations not through organising industrial action.

453 I have learned a lot about how this can be done from my Irish comrades, particularly Brid Smith and Richard Boyd Barrett (both now TDs). For examples of my own efforts in this direction, see my pamphlets *People*

Power and Real Democracy http://
johnmolyneux.blogspot.ie/2015/01/
people-power-and-real-democracy.
html and *Profit versus the Environment*
http://johnmolyneux.blogspot.
ie/2017/03/profit-versus-environment.
html

454 Leaving aside the exaggerated nonsense
about the Egyptian Revolution or
other events of that time being
"internet revolutions" it is a matter of
fact that Facebook and twitter did play
a role in the struggle. Facebook was also
an important tool used by working
class communities in the anti-water
charges struggle in Ireland.

455 As I write the AAA have just
announced the change of their name to
Solidarity. I should also stress that in
both cases the SWP and the SP
continued to exist within the PBP and
AAA, respectively, as "Leninist"
revolutionary parties.

456 The seats were were in West Belfast and
Foyle (Derry) and the one in Foyle was
lost in the most recent election in
March 2017.

457 For more on the Irish experience see
Kieran Allen, *1916: Ireland's
Revolutionary Tradition* (London,
2016); Sean Mitchell and Kieran Allen,
"Ireland After the Elections", *Irish
Marxist Review* 15 and Kieran Allen,
"Socialist Strategy in Ireland", *Irish
Marxist Review* 17.

458 By serious groups I mean organisations
with a) a real grounding in the Marxist
theoretical tradition; b) more than a
fistful of members; and c) the political
maturity and anti-sectarian instincts to
enable them to work alongside both
other revolutionaries and people who
are not (yet) revolutionaries—in other
words groups like the ISO
(International Socialist Organisation)
and Socialist Alternative, but not, for
example, sects like the Spartacists.

459 K Marx, "Contribution to the Critique
of Hegel's Philosophy of Right,
Introduction", K Marx and F Engels,
On Religion (Moscow, 1955), p52.

Index